THE BLUEPRINT

THE
BLUEPRINT

LeBron James, Cleveland's Deliverance,
and the Making of the Modern NBA

JASON LLOYD

DUTTON

DUTTON

An imprint of Penguin Random House LLC
375 Hudson Street
New York, New York 10014

Library of Congress Cataloging-in-Publication Data
Names: Lloyd, Jason.
Title: The blueprint : LeBron James, Cleveland's deliverance, and the making of the modern NBA / Jason Lloyd.
Description: New York, New York : Dutton, 2017.
Identifiers: LCCN 2017022370 (print) | LCCN 2017039979 (ebook) | ISBN 9781524741914 (ebook) | ISBN 9781524741907 (hardback) |
Subjects: LCSH: Cleveland Cavaliers (Basketball team) | James, LeBron. | National Basketball Association—History. | BISAC: SPORTS & RECREATION / Basketball. | SPORTS & RECREATION / Coaching / Basketball. | BIOGRAPHY & AUTOBIOGRAPHY / Sports.
Classification: LCC GV885.52.C57 (ebook) | LCC GV885.52.C57 L56 2017 (print) | DDC 796.323/640977132—dc23
LC record available at https://lccn.loc.gov/2017022370

Printed in the United States of America
1   3   5   7   9   10   8   6   4   2

Set in Adobe Garamond Pro
Designed by Cassandra Garruzzo

For Alessia, Alexander, AJ, and Avamaria,
I love you.

For Mom and Dad,
Thank you for working so hard every day so I never had to.

CONTENTS

Contents

PREFACE

As a boy growing up in the west suburbs of Cleveland, I cried the day Michael Jordan eliminated the Cavs from the NBA playoffs on "the Shot." I sat in the hollow, decrepit Cleveland Municipal Stadium on countless summer nights and cheered for anonymous Indians teams filled with guys like Pat Tabler, Ken Schrom, Cory Snyder, Brett Butler, Tom Candiotti, and Ernie Camacho.

Celebrating championships was never a realistic expectation. Just being there had to suffice. Over time, I came to expect sports collapses and magnificent disasters, so it wasn't much of a surprise when the Indians blew Game 7 of the World Series in 1997 or when the Browns took losing to an all-new level and the city lost the franchise in 1995.

In Cleveland, devastation and heartbreak are just another food group. It's part of the terms of the deal when you root for these teams. I never had much interest in sticking around these parts after college, and while I had plenty of opportunities to move away, I never did. That's what made covering the 2015–16 Cavs season such an honor and privilege. From the time LeBron James returned to Cleveland in 2014, I have been by his side chronicling every step of the journey, first for the *Akron Beacon Journal* and now for *The Athletic*.

I was there the summer night a capacity crowd at Akron's InfoCision Stadium welcomed home their prodigal son. I was there the night he sat in the locker room, devastated, with a towel over his face for nearly an hour after the Cavs lost the NBA Finals to the Golden State Warriors in 2015. And most importantly, I was here for the four years he wasn't.

While James was off in Miami winning championships for the Heat, I was watching the Cavs painfully construct a daring plan to try to win him back. It involved a lot of losing, a lot of money, and a lot of luck. They made mistakes along the way, but ultimately 2016 will be remembered as Cleveland's greatest sports year in more than fifty years.

I'm the only one who has covered the Cavs every day, home and road, from the time James left until the day he returned. *The Blueprint* is a culmination of that four-year plan, a boy coming home to fulfill a promise and a city shedding its loser mentality to rise in glory. I hope you'll enjoy reading it as much as I enjoyed living it.

INTRODUCTION

There on the floor of his office, on a perfect summer morning, a grown man collapsed alone on his hands and knees in both joy and terror as the television hummed behind him.

The lights inside cavernous Cleveland Clinic Courts were mostly dim, the court was darkened, and the basketballs had been put away after an exhausting 2013–14 season, when the Cleveland Cavaliers were again among the worst teams in the NBA. All the years of planning, the meticulous preparation for the summer of 2014, and a team's future seemed to disintegrate in the fire of another crushing season. With most of his staff in Las Vegas and the temperature in Cleveland hovering in the low eighties, David Griffin, the Cavaliers' GM, milled around his office in jeans, a golf shirt, and flip-flops with the television on ESPN and the volume low.

It was July 11, 2014, and the rush of NBA free agency was essentially over. All of the marquee names had agreed to new contracts except one, the biggest one, the diamond jewel. Four years after leaving Cleveland in a rubble of smoke and ashes, LeBron James had the opportunity to go home. Unbeknownst to almost everyone—certainly to the fans— the Cavs had spent all of James's four years in Miami working tirelessly to bring him home, and to provide him with a fresh chance at ending Cleveland's long championship drought. But no one had any idea whether the plan would work.

The final preparations had begun two weeks earlier. It was Dan Gilbert's turn first. Four years ago, Gilbert had eviscerated James and his decision to play for Miami in a blistering letter, and the two men hadn't spoken face-to-face since. If James was going to come back, Gilbert knew he was going to have to apologize. Gilbert requested a meeting with James in the early days of free agency in July 2014, then secretly flew to Miami hoping to meet his former star one-on-one.

But when Gilbert arrived, James had the house full of his friends and business associates. He wasn't going to make this easy, not after all the names Gilbert had called him in that letter. Gilbert walked in clearly outnumbered. Still, he apologized for the blistering comments he'd written in the hours after *The Decision*, James's hour-long television show announcing his decision to leave Cleveland for Miami. James apologized, too, for the spectacle of the television show and the way he left town. The two men managed to glue back together some pieces of their long-fractured relationship, but Gilbert stepped back on his plane and flew home with no promises, no assurance that James was returning.

Griffin remained pessimistic throughout the free agency process. Would LeBron even want to come home? The Cavs had the worst cumulative record in the league the four years he was away and were coming off another miserable season of failed expectations, locker room dysfunction, and more turnover in the front office and coaching staff. They'd just hired a little-known coach from the other side of the world in David Blatt, who had no NBA experience. In Griffin's best-case scenario, James would return to Miami on a one-year contract—giving the Cavs a little more time to put their house in order—and if they met expectations in 2014–15, if they could contend for a playoff spot with a young roster and new coach, Griffin surmised that maybe they'd have a real chance at luring him home the following summer.

Griffin also knew he wasn't the only suitor. Three days after his secret meeting with Gilbert, James met with Heat president Pat Riley in Las Vegas. Riley had been the one who traveled to Cleveland in 2010 and convinced James to leave home and take less money to come to South Beach and win championships as part of a Big Three. Now he was chasing James into the desert, begging him to stay and see the plan through. But Riley left Vegas without a deal in place.

James wasn't going to another new city and starting over again. He was either staying in South Beach or going home. James's agent, Rich Paul, called Griffin during the early morning hours of July 11 to discuss personnel moves and the flexibility the Cavs had to add talent around James if he returned. Paul wanted a blueprint of how the Cavs could surround him with the pieces necessary to win, but he never hinted that James was actually coming. Griffin, still refusing to believe they were serious about returning, went back to work.

On that July morning, Griffin returned to milling around his office inside Cleveland Clinic Courts, the Cavs' $25 million practice facility, which was built in 2007 and spans fifty thousand square feet of offices; it includes a weight room, hot and cold tubs, and seventeen thousand feet of basketball courts in suburban Independence. The fact that it was constructed just off Interstate 77, a short drive from James's palace in nearby Bath Township, is no coincidence. Griffin sat in his office lining up a worst-case scenario in the likely event James was staying in Miami. The Cavs liked Gordon Hayward, but he was long gone. So were Chandler Parsons and Channing Frye. All of the free agents Griffin thought could fit this group had agreed to offers elsewhere. If James didn't come home, the Cavs would be left with a young team, a glut of cap space, and no one worthy of it. "There was no next step on the board," Griffin said.

Griffin had joined the Cavs' front office in 2010, only months after James left for Miami, but didn't receive the job as full-time general manager until May 2014. It was midmorning on his sixty-first day on the job when an exuberant Nate Forbes called him. Forbes was a minority owner of the Cavs and a friend of Gilbert's since college. Throughout the last four years, Forbes played a vital role in repairing the relationship between James and the Cavs.

"The king is coming home!" is all Forbes needed to say. Griffin was stunned. Within seconds, he turned to his TV and saw ESPN break into its programming with the same news. After winning two championships in four years in Miami, LeBron James was coming home to Cleveland. Griffin hung up so he could listen to the newscast, then dropped to his hands and knees in shock, exhaustion, and jubilation.

"It was at once the happiest I had been, and eleven seconds later just this overwhelming sense of, 'Oh my God, now we have to win a championship.' I had no transition," Griffin said. "It was literally sheer joy and then sheer panic all at one time."

James and Paul had executed their plan perfectly. They had it timed down to the minute. James had been in Las Vegas most of the week and met privately with *Sports Illustrated*'s Lee Jenkins Thursday morning to help him script a perfect essay that would be published under LeBron's name "as told to" Jenkins. LeBron picked over scrambled eggs and sipped on carrot juice while talking to Jenkins fifty-eight floors above the Las Vegas Strip. His hotel room at the Wynn overlooked the Spring Mountains. This, Griffin found out later, was where James voiced aloud that he was officially coming home.

Jenkins stitched everything together in the essay and sent it for approval to James, who made a few alterations during his long flight to Miami. By Friday morning, *Sports Illustrated* was ready to post the news that shook the NBA. First, James called Heat president Pat Riley and told him he wasn't coming back. Paul called Gilbert and then Forbes and told them the prodigal son was returning. Five minutes later, it was Griffin's turn. Now, as Griffin watched his television in stunned disbelief, so did James's own household, which was full of friends—and applause—when ESPN broke in with the news. An "Oh shit!" echoed off the walls of James's house as the plan was flawlessly executed. Both plans, actually—the Cavs' plan and James's plan. The Cavs' plan was just much longer in the making and required much more suffering.

When James had bolted Cleveland for Miami in 2010, fans had run into the streets burning his jerseys. That left James and everyone else wondering what the reaction would be in Miami. But this time, as word spread that James was leaving, all the television cameras parked in front of his house quietly packed up and left. In a tropical paradise where the weather is always sunny and bathing suits are appropriate attire, life went on as normal without a king. His departure was met with barely a twenty-four-hour whimper.

Griffin, meanwhile, went right to work. He was expected to meet the team in Vegas Friday afternoon for Summer League but missed the flight because his life had immediately changed. No longer were the Cavs scheming to get James back and planning for the future. Now it was time to win. Immediately. Griffin eventually made it to Las Vegas later Friday night, but he missed the team's celebratory dinner. His wife, Meredith, went in his place as the Cavs owners feasted and popped champagne. For David Griffin and the Cavs, it was time to get to work.

CHAPTER I

In the Beginning, King James Version

Cleveland sports is littered with tales of sadness, devastation, and heartbreak. But it wasn't always that way. Cleveland teams had a proud tradition of success in the mid-twentieth century up through the NFL's Cleveland Browns championship in 1964. The following fifty years, however, contained so many magnificent disasters that they were given their own legendary names, such as "the Shot," "the Drive," and "the Fumble."

LeBron James was supposed to change all of that. The phenom who grew up just down the road from Cleveland in Akron was regarded as basketball's best prospect by his junior year of high school. He was on the cover of *Sports Illustrated* for the first time as a junior at Akron's St. Vincent–St. Mary and was declared "the Chosen One" and the next great NBA superstar. James was ready to soar. And the Cleveland Cavaliers wanted to go with him.

During the 1998–99 basketball season, just as LeBron was getting media attention, the Cavs began losing more games than they were winning. They were sliding into NBA mediocrity, not good enough to compete for championships and not bad enough to draft elite talent. The teams with the worst records have the best chance at high draft picks, so in the NBA landscape, the absolute worst place to be is stuck in the middle. By the time James was entering his senior year of high school, it was clear he was the top talent available in an elite 2003 draft class that had scouts, coaches, and general managers swooning.

"Heading into that lottery and that draft, there was a lot of preparation that took place internally regarding the outcome of the lottery," Cavs senior vice president of communications Tad Carper said. "That draft was one of the strongest ever. History has proven that to be the case. We knew that going in. This was a loaded, powerful draft and we knew it was going to be a game-changing situation for us."

Carmelo Anthony was a freshman who guided Syracuse to a national championship. Chris Bosh was the ACC Rookie of the Year, leading Georgia Tech in scoring, rebounding, blocks, and field-goal percentage. Dwyane Wade was an explosive combo guard out of Marquette who kept rising on draft boards throughout the predraft process. Darko Miličić was a tantalizing European who dazzled during workouts. In all, the 2003 draft produced nine All-Stars and two NBA Finals MVPs. The jewel of the draft, however, was James. And the Cavs were determined to do everything possible to get him.

The Cavs had swung and missed badly at acquiring a superstar when they traded for Shawn Kemp in 1997 and signed him to the seven-year, $107 million deal his former team, the Seattle SuperSonics, refused to give him. As Kemp's weight ballooned north of three hundred pounds and his play deteriorated, the Cavs regretted giving him the deal almost immediately and spent at least two years trying to get out from under it. They finally did in 2000, dumping the last four years and $71 million on the Portland Trail Blazers. Removing the bloated Kemp erased the only star off the roster, and fan interest was waning. The Cavs faced the same problem the NBA in general battled at the time: a lack of star power.

Ratings had steadily declined following Michael Jordan's retirement in 1998. More than twenty-nine million people had tuned in that year to watch Jordan topple the Utah Jazz and win his sixth NBA championship. Ratings plummeted after that, and by the time James was a senior in high school in 2003, fewer than ten million watched the San Antonio Spurs beat the New Jersey Nets for the franchise's second championship. In Cleveland, attendance was down, and so were the gate receipts. The Cavs were losing more than $1 million a month. Cleveland, and the rest of the league, desperately hoped the 2003 draft would supply the needed star power to jolt fans back to the game.

"There was an acute awareness about LeBron and the path that he was headed down and how those roads were going to intersect eventually," Carper said. "There's that saying about how 'when the stars align.' It really was a situation where the stars aligned. Players and coaches go out to win every game. That was certainly the case with us. Everything that we did, I think, leading up to that was designed to allow us to be in that position to allow the stars to align."

The NBA instituted a draft lottery beginning in 1985 in an effort to dissuade teams from intentionally losing games—tanking—to get the number one pick. Now just being bad was no longer good enough.

Teams had to be bad and lucky. The team with the worst record entered the draft lottery with a 25 percent chance at landing the top pick in the draft, while the team with the best record of all the non-playoff teams had less than a 1 percent chance at the top pick.

As James entered his senior year of high school, the Cavs knew they had a future superstar in their own backyard. They won thirty-two games his freshman season, thirty his sophomore year, and twenty-nine his junior year. They were trending in the right direction, but not fast enough. The team with the worst record over the previous five full seasons had averaged about fifteen wins. The Cavs had the sixth pick in the 2002 draft, but if they were going to be in position to draft James the following summer, they had to get worse. Much worse. They needed to race to the bottom of the standings.

Prior to the start of the pivotal 2002–03 season, James's senior year at St. V, the Cavs traded away their top three leading scorers in Lamond Murray, Andre Miller, and Wes Person. All were decent veterans, but none of them were pillars of a championship organization. They got little back in return. Miller was arguably their best player and set a franchise record for assists in a season, but he was entering his contract year and wanted a max deal. The Cavs knew he wasn't worth max money, but he was good enough to keep them from losing enough to have a chance at James. They dealt him to the Los Angeles Clippers for Darius Miles, a prep-to-pro phenom who was high on potential but low on production. Miles could run and jump as well as anyone, but he couldn't guard a dead body and it quickly became clear he certainly couldn't play basketball in the NBA.

Cleveland began the season with the league's youngest roster.

Seven players had two years or less of experience, including guys like Smush Parker, Tierre Brown, and draft bust DeSagana Diop. Players and coaches compete to win every game, but the focus of ownership and the front office was simply to lose enough games to have a shot at James, or at worst, one of the other future stars in this talent-rich draft. Things seemed to be going according to plan, but at 8-34, coach John Lucas was fired around the midway point and replaced by interim coach Keith Smart. Lucas was never viewed as the long-term coach; he was always a stopgap measure to guide the Cavs through losing seasons. But Lucas's firing angered James because Lucas let him work out with the team. James had played with some Cavs, some other pros, and some college players at Gund Arena (now known as Quicken Loans Arena) the summer before his senior year of high school. James held his own against the veterans, even dunking on one. The workout, which was against league rules at the time because James was still in high school, was reported in the Cleveland *Plain Dealer*. Lucas was suspended two games and the Cavs were fined $150,000.

Despite that minor bump, everything else was going as planned until the Cavs closed the season by winning two of their last three games and three of their last seven. They needed a loss on the final day of the season to clinch the league's worst record and the best chance at landing James. Instead, Parker scored seventeen points, Brown scored sixteen points, and the Cavs beat the Raptors 96–86.

"It was really good that our fans got to see down the stretch that we did pull some games out at home," Smart said after the finale. "We had a tough season and it was good that the guys got a chance to win and get the feel of victory. They get to go home this summer glad they won their last game."

Not everyone shared Smart's joy. Dick Watson, the team's general counsel and a minority owner, was incensed as he stormed into the coach's office after the win. "You fucked it all up!" Watson screamed at Smart as he pounded on the desk. "We spent months on this and you fucked it up on the last day!"

Because of that win, the Cavs finished the season at 17-65 and entered the draft lottery tied with the Denver Nuggets for the league's worst record. That meant they also shared with the Nuggets the same 22.5 percent chance for winning the number one pick. No one knew at the time, but Tad Carper was already carrying a number 23 jersey in the Cavs' new colors with JAMES stitched across the back. Team owner Gordon Gund sat on the stage representing the Cavs at the lottery while general manager Jim Paxson stayed home to tend to his wife, who was undergoing chemotherapy for brain cancer. When NBA deputy commissioner Russ Granik revealed the Cavs had won the number one pick, the city of Cleveland erupted. Carper reached into his briefcase, grabbed the James jersey, and shot onto the stage as the television show cut to a commercial break. Carper handed the jersey to an elated Gund. It was the most important victory in franchise history.

"Nobody knew I had that [jersey]. Nobody," Carper said. "I went onstage and gave it to Gordon, and as I turned around—this is still during the commercial break—the members of the media that were there were looking at me with their eyes wide open and mouths dropped open saying, 'Oh my gosh! I can't believe you just did that! Did you know something going in? Isn't that arrogant or presumptuous?' I still remember standing there on the edge of the stage looking at them saying, 'Not presumptuous, just prepared.' That's what it was. The preparation, trying to prepare for success. It worked out. And if it hadn't, then the jersey would've stayed in my bag and no one would've known we had it. It was so obvious and so clear, we had no reservation about it. If we won the lottery, this was obviously going to happen and this was our pick. We had no hesitation in doing that. It was one of the rare moments in NBA draft history. Even if a team knows who they're going to take, there is leverage and reason to be gained by not talking about who you're going to take in advance. This was one of those very rare situations where there was no leverage to be gained, no benefit to be had. We were very clear about that."

LeBron Raymone James was born to a sixteen-year-old single mother on Hickory Street in one of Akron, Ohio's tougher neighborhoods— about forty miles south of Quicken Loans Arena. He was raised by his mother, Gloria, and grandmother, Freda, until his grandmother died of a heart attack on Christmas Day in 1987. James was a week away from turning three. Unable to keep up with the maintenance on their old house, which had been in the family for generations, Gloria and LeBron were eventually evicted and the house was razed. James spent his childhood bouncing between apartments, family, and friends. He moved twelve times in three years and missed nearly a hundred days of school in the fourth grade.

While James was struggling to survive, so were the Cavs, who didn't even exist until 1970 and wasted little time in capturing Cleveland's crown for sports stupidity. Ted Stepien purchased the team in 1980 and will go down, God rest his soul, as one of the worst scoundrels in NBA history. Stepien served in the air force during World War II and told people he once fell out of an airplane and lived to tell about it. The plane, he said, was about five hundred feet off the ground. Former *Akron Beacon Journal* sports writer Sheldon Ocker, who covered the Cavs when Stepien bought the team, approached him with the idea of spending a couple of hours together for a Sunday magazine piece. "Come over Sunday after church," Stepien told Ocker. "We'll sit out by the pool and watch porn."

The Stepien stories are endless. When Ocker went to his house that day, Stepien wasn't home. Instead, Ocker tracked him down at a nightclub on the east side, where he was judging the Cavs' first-ever cheerleader tryouts. Stepien and two of his associates were judging the pageant and taking notes. Stepien asked the girls questions such as "What's your favorite color? What's your sign? Would you ever attend a nude beach?" When one of the contestants replied that she'd go to a nude beach with her husband, Stepien grew flustered. "I didn't say anything about a husband," he snorted.

When the pageant was over, the judges and Ocker retreated to Stepien's house to tally the scores. Each judge wrote down a number between one and ten for each contestant on an index card and made comments about each. When Stepien got to a card he didn't like ("Shit, small tits!"), he'd throw it into the middle of the room. They finally narrowed the field of forty contestants down to twelve. There was only one problem: They were all white women. When it was pointed out to

Stepien he needed to have some minorities, Ocker said he started digging through the index cards on the floor he had previously discarded. "I think she was black," Stepien said about one. "She had nice tits and a nice ass. She's in." By the time they were finished, Stepien had added two African Americans. The dance team was complete.

On the court, Stepien never valued draft picks, discarding them like gum wrappers while chasing marginal talent. He traded Butch Lee and a future first-round pick to the Lakers in 1980 for the anonymous Don Ford and the Lakers' first-round pick that summer. The Cavs selected shooting guard Chad Kinch from UNC-Charlotte with the Lakers' pick. They traded him twenty-nine games into his rookie year and he was released by the Dallas Mavericks after the season, his NBA career over after one year. The pick traded to the Lakers became Hall of Famer James Worthy. Stepien, in fact, managed to trade away all of his first-round picks between 1982 and 1986 for little in return.

Stepien bungled the franchise badly enough that he nearly drove it out of the country—he was so despised in Cleveland that he wanted to move the team to Toronto. Attendance at the Richfield Coliseum bottomed out during the 1982–83 season, when the Cavs drew an average of 3,916 fans for games in an arena with more than twenty thousand seats.

"I just remember that building being hollow," said World B. Free, whose first year in Cleveland was Stepien's last. "One ball sounded like seventeen balls bouncing at one time because of the echo. There was about a thousand people in that gym and everybody was basically just sitting there. Nobody was excited about anything."

The Cavs made so many god-awful trades under Stepien that the league had to save him from himself by enacting a "Stepien rule" that prevents teams from making trades that leave them without a first-round pick in consecutive years. The rule is still enforced today.

When Stepien learned of the rule, he was enraged. Ocker called him to ask for his reaction and Stepien said now he wouldn't be able to trade for "Cream"—that's what he kept calling Hall of Famer Kareem Abdul-Jabbar. "If Cream wants to come here, now I won't have the picks to go get him," Stepien told Ocker. He was serious.

NBA commissioner David Stern desperately wanted to be rid of Stepien and all but begged the Gund brothers, George and Gordon, to buy the team. The Gunds owned the Richfield Coliseum, the arena in which the team played, but Stepien had so badly mangled the on-court product that the Gunds weren't interested. Stern was relentless and finally the two sides brokered a deal: The Gunds purchased the team for $20 million but had to pay Stepien only $2.5 million up front. They had ten years to pay off the rest. The deal included Stepien's Nationwide Advertising company, and the Gunds negotiated to buy four first-round picks from the league for $1 million to replace the picks Stepien had bungled away. The Gunds' purchase saved basketball in Cleveland.

When Gordon Gund installed Wayne Embry as general manager and Lenny Wilkens as head coach in the late 1980s, the Cavs began to rise to prominence. A nucleus of Mark Price, Brad Daugherty, Larry Nance, and John "Hot Rod" Williams won at least fifty games three times between 1988 and 1993. Each season ended in heartbreak, however, because they could never topple Michael Jordan and the Chicago Bulls. When James was four, the Cavs won fifty-seven games in 1988–89 but lost in the first round to Jordan's Bulls on the play that famously became known as "the Shot." When Jordan swept the Cavs out of the playoffs in the conference semifinals in 1993, it was the fifth time in seven years the Bulls had ended Cleveland's season.

Thirty years ago, Cleveland sports fans lived in a very different world. There was a time when success was expected. After the Browns, led by Hall of Fame running back Jim Brown, pounded the Baltimore Colts 27–0 to win the (pre–Super Bowl) NFL championship in 1964, no one even bothered to throw a parade. It was the Browns' fourth championship in fifteen years, so players and fans gathered at the Sheraton-Cleveland Hotel on Public Square hours after the game for a banquet. They ate dinner together. That was it. Then everyone went home. If anyone had known it was the last time Cleveland fans would have the chance to celebrate a championship for generations, maybe they would've put on some hats and gloves and reconsidered the parade.

As the years rolled into decades, Cleveland teams created spectacular ways to lose, from roster mismanagement to soul-crushing blunders on the field. Brown, arguably the greatest player in NFL history, became embroiled in a power play with owner Art Modell after the Browns lost the NFL championship to the Green Bay Packers in 1965. Brown was a budding Hollywood actor and filming for *The Dirty Dozen* ran long in 1966, which meant he was going to miss the start of practices. An angry Modell publicly challenged him, placing a deadline on when Brown had to report to the team or be fined. Brown didn't appreciate the threat and immediately retired. After playing for nine championships in sixteen years during the fifties and sixties, as of 2017 the franchise had yet to play for another one—but they invented new ways to cut the soul out of their fans while trying.

Brian Sipe's interception in the end zone during the final minute of an AFC playoff game will forever be known as "Red Right 88," the name of the play call that ended the 1980 season. They were in range for a game-winning field goal, but Sipe forced a pass to Ozzie Newsome that was intercepted by Raiders safety Mike Davis and the Browns lost, 14–12. But that was just the cocktail hour to the Browns' future feast of misery.

First, there was "the Drive." Bernie Kosar's forty-eight-yard touch-down pass to Brian Brennan gave the Browns a 20–13 lead over the Denver Broncos with 5:43 left in the 1986 AFC championship game. When Broncos rookie Gene Lang botched the ensuing kickoff return, the Cleveland Stadium crowd roared. The Broncos were on their own two-yard line and the Browns were less than six minutes from their first Super Bowl. Instead, John Elway drove the Broncos ninety-eight yards on fifteen plays to force overtime. His touchdown pass to Mark Jackson in the final minute of regulation stunned Browns fans. The thirty-three-yard field goal by barefoot kicker Rich Karlis in overtime brought them a little closer to death. Karlis hooked the kick enough that it barely slid inside the left upright—and some devout Browns fans will still argue he missed it. Typical Cleveland. A shot at the Super Bowl was snatched away by inches.

Then, "the Fumble." The Browns' shot at redemption came in the form of a rematch at Denver the following year but ended when Earnest Byner fumbled at the goal line in Mile High Stadium. They trailed

38–31 with a minute left in the AFC championship game and Byner had a clear path to the end zone, but the ball was stripped by Jeremiah Castille and the Broncos recovered. Byner, who totaled 187 yards and two touchdowns on the day while leading the Browns in both rushing and receiving, slumped to the ground alone in the end zone in disbelief. "What can I say except that I played my heart out," Byner said after the game. "I left everything I had out there on the field."

Including the ball. Typical Cleveland. A trip to the Super Bowl, yet again, was snatched away by inches. Byner was a terrific running back, but that fumble poisoned everything. The Browns gave him away to the Washington Redskins in 1989 for Mike Oliphant, who had more fumbles (three) than touchdowns (one) in two years in Cleveland. Oliphant's final season was 1991—the same year Byner won a Super Bowl with the Redskins. Typical Cleveland.

The Indians weren't faring any better. They traded away popular slugger Rocky Colavito days before the start of the 1960 season. Colavito had hit forty-one and forty-two homers the two previous years and was just entering the prime of his career, but Frank Lane was running the Indians at the time and didn't want to pay him. Lane was just another face in a long line of incompetent executives who have rolled through Cleveland. In his first three hundred sixty-five days on the job, Lane made ten trades involving thirty-two players. He gave away future single-season home run record holder Roger Maris and future Hall of Famer Early Wynn. But the trade that burned the worst was Colavito, a fan favorite who reciprocally loved Cleveland. Colavito tied for the American League lead in home runs in 1959, but Lane sent him to the Detroit Tigers for batting champion Harvey Kuenn. Lane kept Kuenn one year before trading him. The Indians won the World Series in 1948 and lost it in 1954. After trading Colavito, they finished as high as third once over the next thirty-three years. The Curse of Colavito was born.

That curse was nearly broken in 1997 when the Indians were three outs from a World Series victory over the Florida Marlins. Workers were busy wheeling champagne into Cleveland's locker room in Miami's Pro Player Stadium and hanging protective tarps across the stalls, but reliever José Mesa fumbled as badly as Byner. He couldn't hold the 2–1 lead, allowing a pair of singles to Moises Alou and Charles Johnson before Craig Counsell's sacrifice fly tied the game. The Marlins won it in the eleventh off Charles Nagy, who was supposed to start the game but instead entered as a reliever. Nagy took the loss, but Mesa was the target of fans' vitriol. He was the best reliever in baseball in 1995 and earned votes for both the Cy Young Award and Most Valuable Player. But like Byner's, his stay in Cleveland ended shortly after his disaster. He was traded the next season. "Game Seven of the World Series just stuck with people," former Indians general manager John Hart said. "We just didn't see it happening here for José."

James was an infant for the Drive and the Fumble, but he turned thirteen a couple of months after Mesa blew the World Series. After growing up in Akron, James now deeply understood the challenges of Northeast Ohio. This wasn't a city that people aspired to reach. No one grew up in New York or Chicago or Los Angeles hoping to one day make it to Cleveland, a city that had its best days in the 1940s and 1950s and began deteriorating in the 1960s, when folks left the city for the suburbs and racial tensions heightened. Pollution set the Cuyahoga River on fire multiple times, most notably in 1969, and the city's debt rose to $30 million in 1978, when it became the first city since the Great Depression to default on its loans.

Simply put, those who grow old there are usually born there. The talent drain is crushing, particularly when the talent is a six-foot-eight, two-hundred-fifty-pound cash register. James's entry into the library of Cleveland sports misery is the most debilitating: the Decision.

CHAPTER 2

"He's Gone"

Entering the 2009–10 playoffs, Anderson Varejao had attempted a total of twenty-five three-pointers in his first six years in the NBA. He made only one. The twenty-sixth was also the final shot of the season and served as the last shot taken with LeBron James in a Cavs uniform. A season with championship expectations instead died in the Garden in the second round. Boston stunned the Cavs in a perplexing series that included an incensed Dan Gilbert publicly chiding his team before they were eliminated.

"Our entire franchise has done everything in its power to put all of our players, and its coaching staff, in the best possible position to execute when it counts," Gilbert told the Cleveland *Plain Dealer*. "The last two home playoff losses, and the manner in which we lost these games, does not come close to being anywhere near the high expectations all of us have of our organization."

Gilbert said that after an embarrassing 120–88 loss to the Celtics in Game 5 at home when James was booed off his own floor in what was ultimately his final home game, although no one knew it at the time. But looking back now, it was clearly the beginning of the end. He scored fifteen points but shot just three of fourteen and seemed disengaged. In Game 6, James pulled off a triple-double—twenty-seven points, nineteen rebounds, and ten assists—but he also turned the ball over nine times and the Cavs stumbled quietly into the Boston night. Down nine in the final minute, with coach Mike Brown imploring someone to foul to stop the clock, no one did. The five on the floor resigned themselves to the fact the season was suddenly, stunningly over. The Cavs lost to the Celtics, 94–85, and James tore off his Cavs jersey before reaching the locker room for an ominous press conference.

Three times during a seven-minute postgame interview, James used the phrase "my team." Only he wasn't talking about his Cavs teammates or Gilbert or Danny Ferry or coach Mike Brown or anyone else within the organization. Now, for the first time, he was talking about his close friends and his agent, Leon Rose.

As James was transitioning into free agency, I was transitioning into the role of Cavs beat writer for the *Akron Beacon Journal*. My first night working for the *Beacon* was James's final home game against the Celtics, when he was booed off the floor. In other words, I showed up and all hell broke loose within the franchise.

This profession has taken me to thirty-one states, Canada, and South America. It has also forced me to cancel dinners, miss birthdays, and alter vacation plans. The schedule of an NBA beat writer is gruesome and unrelenting. Rarely are we in one city for more than a day or so and rarely are we home more than four days at a time. It's always home for two days, gone for three, home for four, gone for six. It's hard on marriages; it's particularly hard on children.

Not that I'm complaining. I've made two trips to the White House, tagged along for a round of golf with Byron Scott (while mocking his purple and gold Lakers driver), and stalked Dan Gilbert's private jet to the tarmac. I've driven through the night in a rental car from Cincinnati to Charlotte and nearly ran out of gas in the middle of Kentucky bluegrass just for the possibility Andrew Bynum might play in a preseason game the next night. He didn't. I've snuck into parking garages and unknowingly broken into a private airport. I've written millions of words on thousands of games. All part of the job, this beautiful, wretched, privileged, cursed job of flying around the country to watch grown men dribble. Only in America.

Back in the summer of 2006, James signed an extension with the Cavs that would allow him to become a free agent in the summer of 2010. He was entitled to sign for an additional five years but worked his contract so he could become a free agent after three seasons beyond his rookie deal. It was all part of his plan to enter free agency earlier, when he was entitled to a bigger slice of the salary cap.

In hindsight, the shorter contract placed a ticking clock on the franchise. Despite James's growing into the league's best player and winning two Most Valuable Player awards, one superstar isn't enough to win in the modern NBA. The Cavs' annual collection of trade-deadline deals and a couple of crucial misses on draft picks did not produce a winning formula.

Essentially, the Cavs scrambled for seven years to properly surround James with enough talent to win. Remember, they gutted the team his senior year of high school, trading their three leading scorers from the year before, just to be in position to draft him. Now that they had him, they had nothing to put around him. They missed the playoffs James's rookie year and then botched the contract of promising power forward Carlos Boozer, allowing him to leave through free agency when they still owned his rights. They used the tenth pick in the draft—their last lottery pick during the James era—on Oregon small forward Luke Jackson. The pick made sense; Jackson averaged 21.2 points his last year with the Ducks and shot 44 percent from the three-point line. But he had two herniated discs in his back during his rookie year, an omen of things to come. Jackson played just forty-six games for the Cavs and was gone after two years. He was out of the NBA after two more, injuries derailing a once-promising career.

Gilbert spent $375 million to buy the Cavs in 2005 during James's second season. They were 31-24 on March 1 but collapsed over the final six weeks and finished 42-40. They lost a tiebreaker for the final playoff spot, meaning James was 0 for 2 on making the playoffs. Gilbert fired coach Paul Silas before the ink was dry on his purchasing papers. General manager Jim Paxson was fired after the season. Gilbert replaced them with Danny Ferry as GM and Mike Brown as head coach.

In five years together, Gilbert, Ferry, and Brown guided a flawed roster to the top of the Eastern Conference. James dragged a supporting cast of Sasha Pavlović, Drew Gooden, Zydrunas Ilgauskas, and Larry Hughes to the NBA Finals, where they were swept by Tim Duncan and the Spurs. Always hearing that clock ticking above him, Ferry traded for aging stars like Shaquille O'Neal and Antawn Jamison in an effort to get James more help. And it sort of worked, at least during the regular season. The Cavs won sixty-six games during the 2008–09 season but were upset by the Orlando Magic in the conference finals. They won sixty-one games during the regular season in 2009–10, James's last season under contract, but that ended in bitter defeat to the Celtics. The Cavs were very clearly trending in the wrong direction in the playoffs, and now James was sitting at a podium inside the Garden talking about free agency.

"It's all about winning for me," James said after getting eliminated by the Celtics in 2010. "I think the Cavs are committed to doing that, but at the same time, I've given myself options to this point. Me and my team have a game plan we're going to execute and we'll see where we're going to be at."

The Cavs went into scramble mode. Gilbert never really wanted to fire Brown, but no one could get answers from James about what he wanted. Gilbert believed sacrificing Brown and his simplistic offensive schemes would appeal to James, who at times hinted he wanted to play in a more up-tempo style. On May 25, 2010, less than two weeks after a bitter end to the season, Gilbert fired the first full-time head coach he'd hired. Ferry disagreed with the decision to fire Brown, and his relationship with Gilbert had already become untenable. Ferry left the franchise when his contract expired a few days later.

The shocking announcement was made on June 4, 2010. I will always remember the day Ferry walked away because it was also the day my son AJ was born. My wife, Alessia, was in her hospital room awaiting her C-section when my phone buzzed. Ferry was leaving; conference call in an hour. I frantically texted and e-mailed my boss and Cavs people trying to coordinate who would handle the call for the *Beacon Journal,* my employer at the time. It certainly couldn't be me. My son was coming, and as the doctor and nurses wheeled my wife into the operating room, I trailed behind on my phone. "You're not really doing this, are you?" Alessia hollered with her head tilted back in my direction, although she couldn't turn it far enough to actually see me. "You're not really working on the day I'm giving you a child?!"

(Ferry returned to the San Antonio Spurs as an assistant after leaving Cleveland. I told him about the delivery debacle the next time I saw him, and he got a good laugh out of it. "Sorry," he said. "Did you name him Asshole for me?")

With his coach gone, a rookie GM in Chris Grant, and the fate of his superstar hanging in the balance, Gilbert needed a new head coach. Being a Michigan State graduate, he aggressively pursued the Spartans' Tom Izzo. The interest in the Cavs' coaching search was insatiable and the media scrutiny was at an all-time high. Everyone wanted to know when Izzo was coming to town and reporters did their best to find out—while the Cavs did their best to cover their tracks. On the day Izzo was scheduled to visit, they had planes scattered across Michigan and Ohio. Gilbert was on a plane landing at Burke Lakefront Airport.

Izzo was supposed to land there, too, but when the Cavs caught wind of all the media waiting for them at Burke, they rerouted Izzo's plane to little-used Cuyahoga County Airport.

I tracked the tail number of one of the planes Gilbert was using to Burke. I called my sister-in-law, Luciana, who was at my house visiting following the birth of AJ, and told her I was deputizing her to be a reporter for a day. She needed to grab her camera and get to Burke immediately if not sooner. I drove through an open gate and began looking for Gilbert's plane. There was a red button with a sign that read PRESS FOR ASSISTANCE. I certainly needed assistance, so I pressed the button and told the man on the intercom, "I'm looking for a plane that's supposed to be leaving in twenty minutes."

"Come on back," he said as the gate buzzed. "We'll help you find it."

Great! Just what I needed. After wandering around the tarmac for a few minutes, I found the plane tucked behind a building that served as sort of a boarding gate/waiting room for passengers. But there was another problem: Luciana struggled following my directions. The gate I had driven through was apparently designed to keep people like me out. While the rest of the media were where they were supposed to be, behind a fence, I had inadvertently trespassed and the gate was now closed. Luciana couldn't get back to me. But when another driver pulled up, the gate opened and she followed in behind. We sat inside the holding room for nearly an hour waiting for someone to arrive. Izzo? Gilbert? Grant? I thought it was Izzo's plane, but I couldn't be certain. My boss called during the ordeal and asked where I was. "Standing next to the plane," I said, and he howled.

After an hour of waiting, a black SUV with tinted windows drove right to the plane. Gilbert emerged from the back seat with his assistant and I told Luciana to start snapping pictures as quickly as she could. In a flash, Gilbert was out of the car and onto the plane. His driver spotted me and asked if I needed help. "No, I'm good," I told him, and he said I wasn't allowed to be back there. When airport personnel found out who I was—hey, they never asked—they told me I had to leave.

Disappointed that I had stalked the wrong plane and come up empty, I was sitting in rush-hour traffic on East Ninth Street in downtown Cleveland when my cell phone rang. It was a source from Michigan State. The school was holding a rally for Izzo on campus that evening if I could get there. No one was sure yet when Izzo was returning from Cleveland or if he would speak at the rally, but there was a chance. That was enough for me.

It takes at least three and a half hours to drive from downtown Cleveland to East Lansing even without heavy traffic. It was going to be tight. I called my wife and told her I wasn't coming home, that I had to drive to Michigan to try to catch Izzo. She had planned a family dinner for that evening with both sets of parents to celebrate the new baby, but I wasn't going to make it. I hung up and dictated part of a story to the desk while blazing a trail west on the Ohio Turnpike and north on I-75. I spoke to some students who were holding candles and had made signs pleading for Izzo to stay and soon realized East Lansing and Cleveland had a lot in common. The biggest stars of their cities, the icons who served as the sports lifeblood, were tempted to leave while the fans begged them to stay.

Izzo claimed to be intrigued by the NBA and Gilbert's pen never runs out of ink, so the size of the paycheck wasn't an issue. But Izzo was a god on campus. He wasn't going to throw away immortality just to be another face in the NBA, and he certainly wasn't going to Cleveland without assurance that James was coming back. Izzo, however, had about as much luck reaching James as the Cavs did. James wasn't talking to anyone. Izzo had to make the decision on his own, which ultimately made it an easy choice. Izzo stayed put.

Knowing how former players appealed to James, they pursued Brian Shaw and Byron Scott, eventually settling on Scott, the former Showtime Laker and three-time NBA champion. Scott believed he had a plan to reel in James, telling ownership they had to be firm with him. Scott had a long history of clashing with his former stars, including J. R. Smith and Baron Davis. The relationship with Davis grew so toxic during their time together in New Orleans that Scott banned Davis's personal trainer from the locker room. Davis eventually came around, however, apologizing to Scott years after they split for the way he behaved when they were together.

Now Scott was hoping for the chance to coach James, and was just cocky (crazy?) enough to take the job without a commitment that James was returning. The Cavs announced Scott's hiring in the early hours of July 2, right around the start of free agency. James's free agent meetings during the summer of 2010 created three of the most bizarre, surreal days in NBA history. One by one, some of the most powerful men in the NBA—and pop culture—filed into his LRMR offices (named after LeBron and his closest friends, Rich Paul, Maverick Carter, and Randy Mims) in the IMG building in downtown Cleveland to pitch him on why he should join their team. The New York Knicks decimated their roster and sat on cap space for two years on the off chance James felt like moving to Manhattan. The New Jersey Nets led off the meetings with billionaire owner Mikhail Prokhorov and Jay Z, and the Chicago Bulls closed them on day three. In between were the Miami Heat, the Los Angeles Clippers, and yes, the Cavs.

Gilbert and the Cavs staff went to great lengths to remind James this was his home. They rented billboards throughout Cleveland with HOME sprawled across them. Hundreds of fans formed a human tunnel down East Ninth Street, holding HOME signs and cheering wildly as James drove by. They tossed white powder into the air, mimicking James's old pregame ritual, and pleaded for their star to stay just as Michigan State fans had held a vigil for Izzo. Some of the meetings between James and prospective teams lasted more than two hours, and usually the executives met with the media after, and all said the same things: The meeting went well and they were optimistic they could land him. The Cavs' presentation was a bit shorter. It only lasted about ninety minutes, and afterward Grant had to address the media. Only one problem: No one could get the door open. As the gathered crowd of reporters chuckled outside, Grant and Carper waited for a building employee to arrive with a key card to get the door open. Grant eventually made it outside and addressed reporters for one minute without taking questions.

"Obviously we know LeBron well. I would characterize it as positive," Grant said of the meeting. "We think it's pretty incredible that LeBron chose to have these meetings here in Cleveland, at his home."

There's that word again. Home. Part of the Cavs' pitch was a playful cartoon featuring James and some of his teammates cracking inside jokes. More importantly, however, the Cavs had news for him. They had reached an agreement with the Toronto Raptors on a sign-and-trade for Chris Bosh. Then Raptors GM Bryan Colangelo knew Bosh wasn't returning and was willing to talk to just about any team in the league in an effort to recoup value for their departing star. Bosh was a five-time All-Star just entering his prime. He represented the type of player the Cavs had desperately pursued to pair with James but never could get. Even now, in their final days, they still couldn't close this kind of deal. The Cavs couldn't reach Bosh to gauge his interest in coming to Cleveland, so they appealed to James. If you can get Bosh to come here, they told him, the deal is already done. James sat back in his chair. "Man, I don't know him," he said.

On the day of *The Decision,* James attended his Nike camp at the University of Akron. The Cavs could feel him slipping away, so Scott went to the school hoping for one last opportunity to meet with him. But he couldn't get close. Scott just watched James scrimmage with a number of Cavs players for about an hour before leaving. "I'm always hopeful," Scott said on his way out of the gym.

James left the arena and went back to his high school, St. Vincent–St. Mary, to film scenes to use on his website. Then he spent a couple of hours driving around Akron to various spots from his youth, where he shot more footage for his website. It all felt like a going-away party, and soon we knew it was. James eventually left and flew to Connecticut, home of ESPN, for *The Decision.* At nine P.M. on July 8, James uttered the famous line about taking his talents to South Beach.

Bars in Cleveland packed with James's most loyal fans shrieked in disbelief. James's departure in 2010 hurt worse than anything Stepien had inflicted on the organization during his brief reign of terror. This once-booming steel town that had been crushed by the economy had its spirit crushed by one of its own.

It had been less of a surprise to the Cavs. In the days after their meeting with him in downtown Cleveland, Cavs executives could feel James slipping away. Communication from his side kept pulling back. His mother, Gloria, was the conduit between LeBron and the Cavs' ownership throughout the process.

But by the morning of the television show, Gloria James had stopped taking the Cavs' calls. The front office went through James's close friend Maverick Carter and his agent, Leon Rose. Responses from them had slowed to a trickle. As James was walking onto the set of *The Decision,* Grant's cell phone rang. It was Rich Paul, another of James's closest friends. "He's going. He's not staying," Paul said. Grant asked where he was going. "I have to let him announce that," Paul said. "But he's leaving."

No one was thinking about it in that moment, but in hindsight, the first step toward James's eventual return to Cleveland may have been that call from Paul to Grant. The two men maintained a mutual respect for each other in the midst of incredibly difficult and awkward times. Paul was working his way up the sports agency business, but he was also a Cleveland kid, born and raised. He supported his close friend, but he hurt for his city. Paul's personal connection to the Cavs, and to Grant, would be remembered, and nurtured, many times in the next few years.

But in 2010, at that moment, there was nothing but anger. Gilbert was attending a billionaires' conference in Sun Valley, Idaho—the same conference to which he'd taken James as his guest the previous summer—but the rest of the Cavs executives and coaches were positioned at Cleveland Clinic Courts to watch *The Decision.* All the important parties were on an open conference line to communicate with each other throughout the day. As James took his seat on the stage at the Boys & Girls Club in Greenwich, Connecticut, Grant broke the news to his owner and the rest of his staff. "He's gone," Grant told them. And Cleveland's heart didn't just break. It shattered.

Fans watching the television special in downtown bars ran into the streets devastated. News cameras captured fans burning James's jersey on the sidewalk outside Quicken Loans Arena. Police were called in to guard the ten-story LeBron banner that hung on an office building adjacent to the arena. It was pulled down the next day. Sitting in his director's chair back in Connecticut, James seemed disturbed watching live footage of his jerseys being burned by his hometown fans.

Less than ninety minutes after *The Decision* went off the air, Gilbert's infamous letter was posted on the Cavs' website and simultaneously reached media outlets across the country. How long Gilbert had been crafting the letter will never be known, but it was edited before it was released. The letter was sent from the e-mail account of Garin Narain, who worked in the Cavs' media relations office. But Narain couldn't hit the "send" button. He made his boss, Carper, hit it instead. The fallout was instant.

Gilbert called James's departure a "cowardly betrayal" and guaranteed the Cavs would win a championship before he did in Miami. He wrote that James had taken Cleveland's curse with him to South Beach. "This shocking act of disloyalty from our home grown 'chosen one' sends the exact opposite lesson of what we would want our children to learn," Gilbert wrote. "And 'who' we would want them to grow-up to become." The fact that Gilbert wrote a letter isn't at all surprising to those who know him best. Gilbert's screeching e-mails have become legendary within the organization. Gilbert was seething, but he wasn't done yet. When Associated Press reporter Tom Withers called him in Idaho, Gilbert kept dropping bombs, insisting James gave up during the series against the Celtics.

"He has gotten a free pass," Gilbert told Withers. "People have covered up for [James] for way too long. Tonight we saw who he really is. . . . He quit. Not just in Game 5, but in Games 2, 4, and 6. Watch the tape. The Boston series was unlike anything in the history of sports for a superstar."

The league fined Gilbert $100,000 for his comments, which inadvertently started a race war when Reverend Jesse Jackson accused Gilbert of viewing James as a runaway slave.

"These accusations endanger LeBron. His jersey is being burned in effigy, and he is being projected as a betrayer by the owner," Jackson wrote in a statement, calling Gilbert's words mean, arrogant, and presumptuous. "He speaks as an owner of LeBron and not the owner of the Cleveland Cavaliers. His feelings of betrayal personify a slave master mentality. He sees LeBron as a runaway slave. This is an owner-employee relationship—between business partners—and LeBron honored his contract. . . . LeBron is not a child, nor is he bound to play on Gilbert's plantation and be demeaned. He has been a model citizen and has inspired the children of Akron, Cleveland, the State of Ohio, and the United States."

The Cavs ultimately worked out a sign-and-trade with the Heat. LeBron technically signed a contract with the Cavs but was traded immediately to Miami in exchange for two future first-round picks. By constructing it that way, James was entitled to make more money under league rules. The Cavs, meanwhile, at least recouped a couple of future assets for the best player in the game. It wasn't much of a return, but it was something. The Cavs could've cost James millions by letting him walk away and forcing him to take a lesser deal from Miami, but Gilbert wisely chose what was best for his franchise. The picks eventually became more important than anyone could've imagined at the time.

A few weeks after James's departure, Gilbert's partner, Nate Forbes, was in South Florida on business. He happened to be lunching at the same spot as Heat owner Micky Arison and some of Arison's colleagues. Whne lunch was over, Forbes walked over to Arison and playfully slammed his check on the table.

"Here, Micky," Forbes said. "It's the least you can do!"

The days, weeks, and months after *The Decision* felt like a funeral. Part of the organization died the night James left. A team that had won 143 games the previous two years (including the playoffs) had completely unraveled in a matter of weeks. Ferry was gone. So were Brown and nearly all of his assistant coaches. Front-office executives Lance Blanks and Mike Winger left for other jobs. James's departure was an asteroid striking the organization and Gilbert's letter was a gas can that torched the remains. Grant was the only one left holding an ax and a hose.

Still numb from what he'd just endured, Grant began trying to rebuild immediately. He called the agent for Rockets point guard Kyle

Lowry from his car while driving home after *The Decision*. A few days later, the Cavs signed Lowry, a restricted free agent, to a four-year deal worth upwards of $24 million. Houston quickly matched the offer. Grant tried signing Matt Barnes to replace James, but Barnes took less money to play for championships with the Lakers.

If the Cavs had struggled to sign free agents with James, they certainly weren't going to get anyone to come to Cleveland now that he was gone. Hope left with him. The Cavaliers, and by extension the city, were devastated.

But there was a glimmer of hope—just a flicker, and one that Chris Grant and only a few others could admit to themselves. Do it right this time and maybe, just maybe, they could lure LeBron to come back home. He could be a free agent again in 2014, which gave the Cavs four years to build a nucleus of young talent that could appeal to James again someday. All it would take was several years, a lot of luck, and for a few bitter enemies to rebuild some dramatically burned bridges.

CHAPTER 3

Starting Over

The first season in Cleveland without James produced some of the darkest days in the history of the franchise. Byron Scott's positive attitude in the roughest of storms was a beacon for the entire organization and helped the Cavs with the first, tentative steps toward rebuilding.

Scott had championship cachet and L.A. cool after winning titles as a player with the Lakers. He was the head coach of rebuilds in both New Jersey and New Orleans. The Nets won just twenty-six games in his first year in charge. They won the East in his second and third years there. Similarly, the Hornets won only eighteen games in his first season. They steadily improved to thirty-eight, thirty-nine, and fifty-six wins each of the next three years, losing to the Spurs in seven games in the 2008 conference semifinals. Scott was fired eighteen months later, just nine games into the season. He sat on the team's charter flight on the runway in Phoenix following a loss to the Suns, with his team at 3-6, and told his wife at the time, Anita, he was going to get fired.

"They can't fire you," she laughed. "It's only been nine games."

The next morning, Scott was fired. He took time away from coaching and was working as an analyst for ESPN when the Cavs called in June 2010.

"Byron has already proven he can do the rebuild. He's not interested in another one," his agent, Brian McInerney, told me during the Cavs' coaching search. "Our next job has to be a place where he can win a championship."

The Cavs were embarrassed by Izzo's highly public withdrawal from their coaching search. They were paranoid Scott would back out also, particularly since rumors in Los Angeles swirled that Phil Jackson was going to retire. Scott, who was extremely tight with Lakers owner Jerry Buss, seemed a natural replacement. The Cavs, however, felt another public rejection at a time when they were still courting James would be viewed as a critical blow. Cavs personnel kept asking Scott if he was going to withdraw his name. "Withdraw from what?" a frustrated Scott told them at one point. "You haven't offered me anything yet."

Scott and Anita joined McInerney and his wife, Elizabeth, for a Father's Day gathering at Nate Forbes's home in Franklin, Michigan. The entire Cavs ownership team was there, along with Chris Grant. McInerney, lifelong friends with Scott, had purchased a home on Grosse Ile Island, coincidentally about forty miles from Franklin, that was constructed in 1874 near the former naval base airport. McInerney liked the location because he could get a Beechjet 400 (and larger planes) on and off the island in total privacy, which helps when one of your best friends is the shooting guard for the Showtime Lakers who likes to take annual summer trips to the island for walleye fishing. And it also helps when scheduling job interviews for that same man forty miles away.

The couples shared a casual, suit-and-tie-less Sunday with a focus more on Ping-Pong, pool, bowling, darts, dominoes, and cards than anything about the Cavs. The women spoke of their children and how to make their favorite recipes. The evening didn't end until well past midnight, when McInerney's wife was stopped for speeding through a construction zone, but the Michigan officer let her off with a warning. "The California plates with a Balboa Island frame holder, on a foreign car, get us stopped every time," McInerney joked. The whole evening was an enjoyable social gathering, hardly a job interview. Scott left without being offered the job.

The Cavs wanted to have a coach in place by the time James's free agency began on July 1, and as June ticked away, Scott and Lakers assistant Brian Shaw emerged as the top two candidates. Shaw, one of the hottest assistant coaches in the business at the time, was the last to interview. It was an awkward dance for all parties, given Scott's strong ties to the Lakers and Shaw's position as Phil Jackson's top assistant. Then there was the issue of Jackson and whether he'd retire or continue coaching, and if he did retire, whom the Lakers would prefer: Scott or Shaw? There were no easy answers, and with James's free agency looming, the Cavs could ill afford to make a mistake.

As Shaw and his agent, Jerome Stanley, were at Cleveland Clinic Courts for his interview, reports started trickling out that the Cavs and Shaw were working on a contract. The Cavs believed Stanley was leaking information to reporters while sitting at the team's headquarters, which set off a chaotic series of events. McInerney gave me a statement congratulating Shaw on getting the job, and reports about Shaw emerging as the front-runner began to surface. There was only one problem: The Cavs never even offered Shaw the job and certainly weren't negotiating a contract. The leaks infuriated Grant, who ended the interview and immediately dismissed Shaw as a candidate. The job was Scott's after all—as soon as someone could get ahold of him to tell him.

On July 1, the first day of free agency, Scott went off the grid. He was in his car driving south, and no one could reach him so he could sign off on the terms. After the Cavs spent all evening negotiating with his agent, Scott was finally reached around midnight. The team announced him as their new head coach in the early hours of Friday, July 2—about eleven hours before James held his free agent meeting in Cleveland with Pat Riley and the Miami Heat.

Scott came to Cleveland hoping to coach LeBron and instead got Samardo Samuels, Semih Erden, and Christian Eyenga. He inherited one of the worst teams since the Stepien era, but he never publicly complained about it once.

Nearly everyone who had helped the Cavs ascend to the top of the Eastern Conference either quit or was fired. As is standard protocol, Scott did not retain most of Brown's assistants. Ferry walked off the job when his contract expired, and when two other executives—Lance Blanks and Mike Winger—left for front-office jobs in other markets, Grant's front office was as depleted as his coaching staff. He needed another veteran front-office assistant, so he hired David Griffin, who had resigned from his hometown Phoenix Suns a few months earlier and passed on an offer as general manager of the Denver Nuggets.

Starting Over

As an outsider looking in, Griffin believed throughout the summer of 2010, before he started working for the Cavs, that James was leaving Cleveland. A couple of months later, he was sitting at dinner in a Cleveland restaurant with Grant and Scott. The next day he was sitting in Grant's office talking about moving ahead and how to proceed. The assistant's job was soon his and the path ahead was clear: Blow it up, blow it all up. Without James, the Cavs were left with a roster of complementary pieces and misfit parts. It was going to take years to rebuild and it would be painful, but there was no other choice. That rebuilding job Scott's agent said he didn't want, he now had.

"When I came here, it was like jumping into a burning building," Griffin said. "The emotions of this place were so raw."

James had taken so long to make his decision that all of the other top free agents had already agreed to new deals. With no picks in that summer's draft (they had previously traded the picks away in a frenetic attempt to get more talent around James), no marquee free agents, and no hope of a championship, the Cavs were caught in NBA purgatory. The big-name players were gone, soon to be replaced by fringe NBA youngsters and older veterans playing out the final days of their careers. Fans blamed James for not only leaving but wrecking the franchise.

"I know there's a lot of anger in the city, but I know Mr. LeBron James and I do not consider this personally," Cleveland mayor Frank Jackson said in a news conference at city hall the day after James left. "It was not personal against the city. His decision is not going to make or break Cleveland. The city is resilient and has a lot of assets that have sustained us in the past and will do so in the future."

Losing a superstar in the NBA is devastating. History indicates that it often takes a decade to return to contention. The Bulls missed the playoffs each of the first seven years after Michael Jordan retired and didn't win their first postseason series until nine years after he left. The Magic didn't win a playoff series for twelve years after losing Shaquille O'Neal in free agency, and the Celtics needed a decade to win a series after Larry Bird's retirement. If the Cavs couldn't win a championship and end the city's title drought with James, they weren't going to do it without him. And now history predicted a long road just to get back to respectability.

Grant had a belief that it was less risky to build through the draft than it was in free agency. If a team swings and misses on a free agent, they're locked into a hefty contract that potentially spans three or four years and that eats away a significant portion of the salary cap. But if a team misses on a draft pick, the financial consequences are far less severe, and in the extreme case where it's necessary, teams can get out of rookie contracts after just two years.

What were the tools? That was the first question Grant and the front office asked. Their sharpest tools were trades and the draft. The organization started to refine itself through that lens. Troubled Delonte West, with all of his baggage, was going to be released before his contract became guaranteed, but Grant instead dumped him on the Minnesota Timberwolves for Ryan Hollins and Ramon Sessions. A couple of years later, he would spin Sessions into a first-round pick. Those were the types of subtle but creative trades that highlighted the four seasons James spent in Miami.

Enough of those types of trades, enough high lottery picks and successful drafting, and who knows? Stay flexible under the salary cap, keep the books clean, hit on a couple of draft picks that play better than their rookie contracts, and suddenly anything is possible. Even luring LeBron back in 2014. After all, Phil Jackson and Kobe Bryant had reunited. Why couldn't Gilbert, the city of Cleveland, and LeBron James? As the Cavs tore the engine to their team apart and slowly put it back together one spark plug and crankshaft at a time, the thought loomed in the background: *If we do this right and things break a certain way, we have an opportunity to do something special.*

Hell, James said as much on his way out the door. Less than a week after *The Decision,* when the matches were still scorched on the sidewalks outside the Q and the sulfur from the burning jerseys was still wafting down East Ninth Street in downtown Cleveland, James told *GQ* writer J. R. Moehringer he was open to playing again in Cleveland someday.

"If there was an opportunity for me to return," James said in July 2010, "and those fans welcome me back, that'd be a great story."

So that's exactly where Grant aimed. In the weeks, months, and years following James's departure, Grant and the front office formulated a bold strategy: make their team appealing enough to bring him back at some point—perhaps as soon as 2014. His first seven years in Cleveland had been marred by a roster of quick fixes thrown together under the threat of his imminent departure. Now that he was gone, they could take their time on a rebuild. They had four years to get it right.

"From the time we were building it, we always talked about how there was a chance he would come back," Griffin said. "And Chris did a good job of maintaining the relationship with Rich Paul. I got to know

Rich pretty well during that time. It was always a thought. The guiding principle was get elite, high-valued assets, and that's what we did."

The roster was purged immediately. Zydrunas Ilgauskas followed James to Miami and Shaquille O'Neal left in free agency. O'Neal had been acquired prior to James's final season in Cleveland when the Cavs were preparing for another conference finals showdown with Dwight Howard and the Orlando Magic. Except they never even got there. They were eliminated by the Celtics one round shy of the Magic. Without James, there was no need for an aging, expensive, well-past-his-prime superstar like O'Neal. The only players they wanted to keep were Daniel Gibson and Anderson Varejao. Everyone else had a sticker price.

As the start of the first season without James approached, players did their best to keep a stiff upper lip when talking about him, but everyone understood the situation. Mo Williams, who believed he was one of James's closest friends on the Cavs, very publicly endured all five stages of grief in the days, weeks, and months after James left. In the hours after *The Decision,* Williams wrote on his Twitter account, "I still can't believe he's gone" (denial), "We all angry, mad" (anger), and "Let's pray he have a change of heart 2night" (bargaining). In the days before training camp began, Williams said, "This has been the worst time of my life. Dealing with family issues and everything with the team has been very hard" (depression). Finally, the day before training camp began, Williams did his best to move on from James without saying he was "over" James's leaving (acceptance).

"That's a big word, if that makes sense. I think at some point you've just gotta turn the corner," Williams said. "You're walking down this long hall. Everyone has been to high school before. You're in this classroom all the way down the hall and you gotta get all the way to the other side of the hall. It looks like this hall is so long, but once you turn the corner, you can't see that hall anymore. Right now today, we're turning that corner going to our next classroom. And we can't see nothing but forward now. There's no LeBron in this building. Whether we believe it or not, he's not coming back. This is who we've got. This is what we've got. I don't see the big TNT trailers, the ESPN trailers. I see you though. This is what we've got. This is the hand we're dealt and we have to play the best we can."

The city of Cleveland wasn't thinking about 2014 yet. They were focused on the present, and the one game that everyone in Cleveland badly, badly wanted the Cavs to win. From the time James flew to Miami covered by the darkness of night on July 8, 2010, the entire city of Cleveland prepared for his return on December 2, 2010, when the Heat would play the Cavs in Cleveland for the first time. James still recalls the date from memory because it was unlike any scene ever witnessed in NBA history.

"It was, uh, pretty hostile," James recalls now with a smile.

Williams arrived for work that morning wearing a Boston Red Sox jacket. He'd never worn that jacket on any other day that entire season, but he wore it on the day his former friend—a Yankees fan—was back in town.

Interest in the game reached historic levels for a random regular-season game in December. The media requests were on the level of an

Eastern Conference finals game, which created a logistical nightmare for the Cavs. For the playoffs, rows of seats are blocked off for media. But this was a regular-season game and those seats had been sold long ago. A number of media members were granted credentials but didn't have a seat in the arena bowl. They had to watch the game on televisions from the workroom or the dining room.

The Heat's plane struggled just getting into Cleveland. Miami hosted Detroit the night before James's big return, creating a lengthy flight prior to the back-to-back. The charter flight didn't land at Cleveland Hopkins airport until two thirty A.M. on December 2 and the flight crew reported a wing "flap issue" as the plane was on its approach. The crew alerted air traffic control, which dispatched two fire trucks to the runway—standard procedure for such events. But the plane landed without incident. It was a fitting start to a volatile twenty-four hours in Cleveland.

Cavs officials and owner Dan Gilbert begged fans to be on their best behavior when James returned. Booing was fine and so were some signs, but there was a fear within the organization that random fans might storm the court during the game. After all, the hatred for James—whom fans viewed as a traitor for deserting his homeland—had reached levels never before seen in sports.

The Heat held a walk-through the afternoon of the game at the Ritz-Carlton hotel that lasted a little more than an hour. Ilgauskas, the former fan favorite who had spent thirteen years in Cleveland and remains the franchise's all-time leader in games played (one of the few records James doesn't have), was the first player to emerge from the ballroom. Ilgauskas was close with James and followed him to Miami in hopes of winning a championship before he retired. He recognized some friendly faces and shook a few hands after exiting the ballroom. He eventually retreated to his room before James appeared outside the ballroom.

"Time for me to get some sleep," James said to no one in particular, but representatives from Nike and James's business partner Randy Mims were waiting on him for an impromptu meeting in the hotel lounge. The meeting lasted about an hour and James finally retreated to his room around three thirty P.M. The first bus departed the hotel for the arena at five fifteen. On his way out of the hotel lobby, James was asked by a former acquaintance if he'd be ready for the storm that awaited him inside his former home. "Yes, sir, I will be," James replied confidently. "I will be."

A few hours later, James entered the arena wearing sunglasses, a black leather jacket with TIME TO ROLL stitched across the back, and silver headphones over his black stocking cap. He gnawed on a stick of gum nervously as more than fifty media members stared at him in eerie silence while soothing Christmas music drifting out of the speakers in the background was ignored. James took seventy-three steps from security, down the hallway that once had been adorned with his pictures, and into the visiting locker room. The Cavs had waited until the morning of the first home game to pull down the life-sized images of James that decorated the hallways outside the locker room. The billboard-sized images had been replaced with a couple of tasteful square pictures of James that listed his accomplishments.

As James marched down the hallway that first night back, he slowed only to speak with sideline reporter Craig Sager, and then later to acknowledge a familiar face he recognized near the Cavs' locker room.

James pointed briefly, then disappeared into the visitor's locker room. When he emerged, he was dressed head to toe in the Heat's red and black colors.

The league provided extra security personnel to flank the tunnels leading to the court and surround James throughout the night. The visiting locker room at the Q is awkwardly shaped and includes an alcove at the far end, near the door to the trainer's room, that holds nine lockers. But for this night, the Heat cordoned off the entire alcove for James and planted security personnel in front of him so not even the reporters had access to him. As the Heat took the court for pregame warm-ups, it was clear the guards lining the court had been given zero-tolerance instructions. I was near the tunnel filming James's jog onto the court when a fan lunged over my shoulder just to point at James and yell obscenities at him. He was immediately spotted by the league's security team and ejected. He never touched James; he merely pointed and yelled in his direction. Gone.

Bud Hagy was one season ticket holder I spoke to in the days prior to the game. Hagy had two seats located four rows behind the visitor's bench. He was offered $10,000 for the seats. He declined. He had a message he wanted to deliver to James himself: "Kiss my ass!" That would hardly be the worst thing James heard that night.

The team's mascot, Moondog, was wearing a bulletproof vest when he took the floor for the national anthem and opening introductions. One by one, the Cavs marched out a pitiful list of the closest thing Cleveland had to celebrities. It was meant as a power play by Gilbert, who had painstakingly rounded up the names and planned their entrance, but it came off as sad and depressing as Browns players Josh

Cribbs and Shaun Rogers, Indians players Travis Hafner and Jensen Lewis, Browns legend Bernie Kosar, and comedian Drew Carey all marched to their courtside seats in a single-file line, each wearing his own personalized Cavs jersey as the sellout crowd roared. Gilbert saved his own appearance for last. The scoreboard camera filmed Gilbert, who was hailed as a hero by fans for the scathing letter he wrote the night James vanished, walking to his seat.

The explosion of the home crowd was so loud that it caught James's attention. When he looked up and saw Gilbert's face on the scoreboard, James simply nodded his head and tapped his feet. He marched down the line, barking instructions at his Miami teammates and pumping his fists in excitement as the cheers kept cascading down for Gilbert in waves. It was ultimately the fans' last chance to cheer.

James dominated his former team. He walked over to the home bench—the bench he'd sat on for seven years—and talked trash to his former teammates, who were helpless to stop him. James heard chants of "Ak-ron hates you!" every time he went to the free-throw line, but he smiled widely through his mouth guard and played on. There was some pushing and shoving at times in the stands—a few brave souls actually arrived wearing James Heat jerseys—at least one arrest was made, and the Heat bench was peppered at times with nine-volt batteries thrown from the stands. It was reminiscent of the Dawg Pound at the old Browns Stadium, when opposing players were hit with batteries and dog bones every time they were backed up deep near their own end zone.

The only assault inside the Q, however, was the performance James dropped on his old teammates. James came looking to give out an ass beating and he did, particularly in the third quarter, when he scored twenty-four of his thirty-eight points. James was spectacular in the face of hatred and the Heat crushed the Cavs, 118–90. After the game, James again refused to apologize for leaving or for his handling of the event in the form of *The Decision*.

"I never regret any decision I make," James said. "You just try to learn from some of the things in life. You try to handle situations the right way and you learn the next time. There's not a clock to turn back and do it all over again. My intentions were on point. Maybe the execution was just a little off."

That was the closest he came to an apology. The two teams departed in opposite directions that night. The experience galvanized the Heat, who won twelve straight and twenty-one of twenty-two before ultimately winning the East and advancing to the NBA Finals. The humiliating defeat, however, essentially ended the Cavs' season. They plunged into history, losing twenty-six consecutive games at one point and thirty-six of thirty-seven. The twenty-six-game losing streak tied the NFL's Tampa Bay Buccaneers for the longest in professional sports history. They went 0-15 in January, the first winless month in franchise history (minimum ten games). And yet, somehow, James and the Heat's dropping a prison beating on them wasn't the worst loss of the season.

Their humiliating 112–57 loss at the Lakers in January was the actual worst night of the season. The Cavs set franchise records for fewest points in a game and most lopsided loss. James and the Heat were in town to play the Los Angeles Clippers at Staples Center the next day and a giddy James tweeted, "Crazy. Karma is a b****. Gets you every time. It's not good to wish bad on anybody. God sees everything!"

(James, incidentally, sprained his ankle the next night against the Clippers and had to miss two games.) The Cavs' purge had finally reached rock bottom.

"In thirteen years, I can honestly say I ain't ever felt that embarrassed to be on the basketball court," said Antawn Jamison, one of the few remaining respectable veterans. "It can't get any worse than this. I don't know how much of this I can take. This, by far, is rock bottom."

Jamison was a two-time All-Star dealt to Cleveland from Washington at the trade deadline during James's final year with the Cavs. He had arrived expecting to play with LeBron and Shaquille O'Neal while competing for a championship. Instead, he spent the final year of his contract playing next to guys like Samardo Samuels, Semih Erden, Jawad Williams, and Joey Graham—none of whom played in the NBA again.

Samuels missed a road trip to Toronto because he lost his passport during the NBA lockout. Manny Harris won a roster spot during training camp of his rookie year, then sabotaged his own career when he wore wet socks into a cryotherapy chamber on Nike's campus and sustained severe freezer burn on his foot—despite warning signs not to wear wet clothing inside. He was ultimately released after one season. The Cavs' roster was a collection of misfits and defective parts.

When it was over, when the smoke and rubble were all that remained of a brutally painful 19-63 season, Scott walked out of his office the day after the season ended wearing a *CSI: Miami* T-shirt in honor of his favorite television show. It was a fitting end to a catastrophic season given the autopsy it deserved and the man in Miami responsible for the organization's demise. "I had a moment where I wanted to kill everybody on the team," Scott said, laughing.

The main mission of the season was to lose as many games as possible and aggregate the best odds of winning the draft lottery and the number one overall pick. To that extent, the Cavs even screwed that up. It was much like in 2003, when they won two of their last three games to pull into a tie with the Denver Nuggets for the league's worst mark. This time the Cavs won four of their last six games to pull ahead of the Minnesota Timberwolves. The burst allowed them to narrowly avoid becoming the first team in history to go from first to worst. No NBA team has ever plummeted to the worst record one year after enjoying the best, but the Cavs fell from a league-best sixty-one wins with James to nineteen without him. Their only saving grace was that the Timberwolves won just seventeen games. They entered the draft lottery with the second-best odds of winning the number one pick.

Unlike in 2003, however, this wasn't considered a devastating blunder, because there was no LeBron James in the 2011 draft. In fact, there was nothing but uncertainty. Although all seemed hopeless at the time, the wheels of fortune were finally beginning to turn in the Cavs' direction.

CHAPTER 4

Lottery, Luck, and Ping-Pong

The traditional way of building championship teams in the NBA is organically and through the draft, supplemented by trades and key free agent signings. The Lakers built a dynasty in the 1980s—with the help of former Cavs owner Ted Stepien—by selecting Magic Johnson in 1979, James Worthy in 1982 (thanks, Ted!), and A. C. Green in 1985. Add in key trades for an in-his-prime Kareem Abdul-Jabbar in 1975 and rookie Byron Scott in 1983, and the Lakers had enough firepower to rip off five championships in the 1980s. The same was true of the Celtics, who drafted Larry Bird, Kevin McHale, and Danny Ainge within a four-year span to form the nucleus that won three championships in the 1980s.

The league changed in 1995 with the addition of rookie scale contracts and again in 1999 when the league adopted max salaries. Suddenly words such as *mid-level exception* and *luxury tax* became as important to championships as pure talent. Teams began dumping contracts and giving away valuable assets, such as draft picks, just to create cap space or get under the luxury tax. The most famous example of that happened with the Suns. Griffin was an assistant in their front office when they were forced to give away two first-round picks just to entice the Seattle SuperSonics to take Kurt Thomas's contract. It was simply a cost-cutting move. Nothing more.

The Cavs, meanwhile, could never surround James with enough talent during his first reign in Cleveland to win a championship, in part because they missed on high draft picks the year before and after drafting him.

When James and Chris Bosh left for Pat Riley, Dwyane Wade, and the Miami Heat in 2010, they changed the way the league does business. Never before had two superstars, both in the prime of their careers, left their teams to join a third superstar in the prime of his. The 2011 lockout, which would loom over the 2011 draft, was in part a response to the Heat's machinations to clear the cap space necessary to pull off such a daring move. Owners, including Gilbert, wanted to incentivize stars to stay with their current teams in an effort to make sure three players couldn't join forces on one team ever again. Penalties were also stiffened for going over the cap and the league introduced a "repeat offender" status for owners who habitually pay luxury taxes.

But all of this was still months away when the Cavs' 2011 draft plan went into effect, the first significant step in the rebuilding process.

Shortly before seven P.M. on May 17, 2011, nearly a full year after James left for Miami, Dan Gilbert accompanied his vice chairman, Jeff Cohen, to an elevator inside the winding hallways of the NBA Entertainment campus in Secaucus, New Jersey. Before they parted ways, Gilbert left Cohen with one final instruction: "Don't come back with anything less than number one."

It was a long, painful path to get there. Gilbert dressed in a charcoal-gray suit, a crisp white shirt, and a navy tie littered with Cavs logos. He wore a Cavs pin on his left lapel. His hair was buzzed, cropped much shorter than it had been in the glory days when James was still around. An easy joke could be made that the nineteen-win season had caused the ultracompetitive owner to tear his hair out. In this new way of thinking, however, losing games and playing the draft lottery odds became more important than winning. Gilbert, Chris Grant, and the Cavs had endured all that pain of losing for this moment, for this day. Lottery day.

The two men, lifelong friends and business partners, said their good-byes. Cohen, much taller than Gilbert and completely bald, was dressed in a navy blue pinstripe suit and spotted blue tie with a Cavs lapel pin that matched Gilbert's. He traveled alone up the elevator and into Conference Room 3A.

As the Cavs surveyed the construction site, they knew simply losing games wasn't going to be enough. If they were going to expedite this re-building process and be in a position to lure James back in 2014, they needed additional draft picks—lottery picks. Those are the toughest to obtain and Grant was going to have to get creative. Luckily, he had an owner willing to spend. Gilbert wasn't afraid to write checks if it improved the club long-term—remember, the short-term didn't really matter.

No one was concerned with wins. Eventually, it was going to matter. But not now.

Grant, Griffin, and his assistants were instead searching for ways to create value where none existed. How is that possible? By acquiring bad contracts teams didn't want in exchange for high draft picks. Under the league's complicated salary cap system, teams either need enough space below the salary cap to absorb incoming players' deals or the contracts must come close to matching in order for the trade to be legal. There are some exceptions to this rule, but those are the basic parameters. And it's what made Delonte West's contract so appealing to the Minnesota Timberwolves in the weeks after James left for Miami.

West was battling mental health issues and facing weapons charges in Maryland when the Cavs traded his $4.6 million contract to the Timberwolves in exchange for Ramon Sessions and Ryan Hollins. The Timberwolves had no interest in West; they just wanted out from under Sessions's contract. West was the vehicle to make that happen. The full value of West's contract didn't guarantee for another week after the trade. Under league salary cap rules, the Timberwolves could acquire him before the guarantee date, release him, and only owe him $500,000.

Sessions had three years left on the four-year, $16 million deal he'd signed with the Timberwolves the year before, but he struggled picking up their offense. By making the deal with the Cavs, the Timberwolves rid themselves of the final three years and $13 million on Sessions's contract and it only cost them $500,000. Sessions, meanwhile, was a young, serviceable point guard for two years before the Cavs eventually flipped him to the Los Angeles Lakers in a wider deal that netted them a first-round draft pick.

Grant traded Jon Leuer to the Memphis Grizzlies in 2013 in exchange for Mo Speights, Wayne Ellington, Josh Selby, and, most importantly, a future first-round pick. The Cavs were far enough under the league's $58 million salary cap that they absorbed the $6 million total the three players were earning. From the Grizzlies' perspective, dumping that $6 million in unwanted salary allowed them to get under the luxury tax threshold and save millions in fines. The pick was most important to the Cavs because it was another future commodity that had tangible value.

And when the Cavs studied the financials on their opponents, they came across something curious with the Los Angeles Clippers: Baron Davis had a stretch clause in his contract before those were commonplace in the NBA. Essentially, if the Cavs could acquire Davis, they could eventually release him and stretch the remainder of his contract over the next several years to ease the financial burden.

Davis had a bloated contract—he was owed nearly $35 million over the next two and a half years—and a bad reputation as a locker room cancer. In other words, he was exactly what the Cavs needed. Davis played for an owner, Donald Sterling, who somehow managed to pass Ted Stepien on the scoundrel scale. Sterling was cheap, miserable, and eventually forced out of the league because of his racist views. At the time, however, the Cavs were most interested in his tight fist. Clippers general manager Neil Olshey was close friends with Griffin, so he and Grant negotiated for weeks to take Davis's contract off the Clippers' books—if Olshey and Sterling were willing to attach their first-round pick in the upcoming draft without protections.

It's common when teams are trading future draft picks to put a "top ten" or "top five" protection on the pick, meaning if the team trading the pick away (Team A) fails to make the playoffs during that season and is part of the draft lottery, they get to keep the pick if it falls anywhere within that protected top ten or top five range. If that occurs, the team acquiring the pick (Team B) must wait until the following year to acquire it. Depending on the terms of the trade, for example, Team A can make the pick "top ten protected" this season, "top five protected" next year, and "top three" protected in year three before the pick becomes unprotected in year four. Teams are free to negotiate the protections as they see fit, but it's rare to get an unprotected pick right away.

When the Detroit Pistons lucked into the second overall pick in 2003, for example, it was because of a trade they made 2,114 days earlier in 1997 with the Vancouver Grizzlies. The Grizzlies had enough protections on the pick that they didn't have to convey it from 1998 to 2002, but by 2003 the only protection on the pick was if it was number one overall. The Grizzlies were slotted to pick sixth entering the lottery but jumped up to number two. It was a worst-case scenario. They lost the pick, sending it to the Pistons to complete the trade made six years earlier. Such unexpected jumps in the lottery are why it's nearly impossible to acquire an unprotected pick from a surefire lottery team just four months before the draft without relinquishing a superstar.

Right about the same time the Cavs and Clippers were negotiating a trade, for example, the Utah Jazz traded away star guard Deron Williams to the New Jersey Nets for what became the third pick in the 2011 draft. Williams, though, was already a two-time All-Star entering his prime when the Nets acquired him. The Cavs were talking about sending spare parts to the Clippers for an unprotected pick.

Unlike the Pistons, the Cavs waited just eighty-three days to use the Clippers' pick and needed only Mo Williams and Jamario Moon—and a $21 million check (the difference in money owed between Williams and Davis)—to get it. Yes, Gilbert paid $21 million for a lottery ticket. Byron Scott was beginning his postgame press conference adjacent to the Cavs' locker room following a home loss to the Houston Rockets on February 23, 2011, when Williams emerged from the locker room, gave a pronounced wave to those watching him, and headed for the parking lot. Williams was nursing an ankle injury and wasn't even playing. Giving such an animated good-bye to everyone didn't make sense at the time, but it did about three hours later. Williams had just learned he'd been traded to Los Angeles. The Clippers had the eighth-worst record at the time of the trade, meaning they'd have the eighth-best odds of landing the number one overall pick. The trade all but assured the Cavs of having a pair of top ten picks to launch their rebuild.

Even more important, it provided the franchise with hope. The trade occurred less than two weeks after the Cavs ended that twenty-six-game losing streak. Morale was still down; the wounds from James were still raw. The Davis trade, despite his reputation, brought some energy, some life, some optimism that better days were ahead because of what the draft pick represented.

Olshey told reporters in Los Angeles it was important to clear the cap space to ensure they had enough room to re-sign guys like DeAndre Jordan and Eric Gordon rather than "speculating on another kid that's nineteen years old with one year of college experience," adding, "And I'm not that high on the draft to begin with this year."

He wasn't alone. The 2011 draft was dismissed as weak in the months leading up to it. It was going to be a draft heavy on overseas players, and the league's scouts and talent evaluators were down on its potential. The Cavs viewed it differently, however. Grant and his staff were bullish on the draft and thought there were some potential hidden gems. They were ecstatic to essentially purchase their own lottery ticket.

Three months later, on May 17, 2011, Cohen emerged from the elevator inside the NBA Entertainment studio, sealed his phone into a manila envelope (all communication devices were seized at the door), and took his seat at the front table inside Conference Room 3A. There was a nervous energy inside, with team officials anxious to see who would win. Security was stringent. The drawing is held about two hours before the results are aired on live television, so secrecy, particularly in the social media age, is of the utmost importance. A representative from each lottery team was invited to watch the drawing, as well as a select few media members. I was one of the few invited to watch.

Upon entering the room, each of us was given a booklet containing all 1,000 number combinations and which four-digit sequences were assigned to each team. The Cavs had two sets of numbers: 199 combinations tied to their own pick and an additional 28 combinations from the Clippers' pick. Add it up and they had a 22.7 percent chance at winning the lottery. The only team with better odds was the Timberwolves, who received 250 number combinations for ending the season with the league's worst record. That gave them a 25 percent chance to win the lottery.

The fourteen teams that fail to make the playoffs every season are included in the lottery. The worse a team is, the more chances they have to win. Fourteen Ping-Pong balls, numbered sequentially from one to fourteen, are dropped into a hopper and a four-digit number is pulled. The team with the winning numbers wins the first overall pick in the draft; then the balls are returned to the hopper and the process is repeated to determine the second and third picks. The rest of the teams are slotted based on the inverse order of their records. The lottery is designed to prevent teams from tanking, although plenty of them still do it—the Cavs were there because they were clearly tanking.

Cohen was studying the number assignments when I walked in. Since the Cavs had made the playoffs in each of the five full years under this ownership group, they were relative strangers to the lottery procedures. Cohen hoped he would be able to watch as the number combinations were assigned to each lottery team, but the NBA uses the same template every year.

By the time the actual drawing began, Cohen had realized that each of the 199 number combinations assigned to the Cavs' pick contained either a 1 or a 2. Yet Lou DiSabatino, the NBA executive presiding over the lottery machine, pulled the numbers 14-13-7-8 for the number one pick. Cohen panicked as he scanned the combinations because the first two numbers were so high. Jamin Dershowitz, the assistant general counsel to the NBA, quickly discovered the winning team. "The Cleveland Cavaliers," he announced. "From the Los Angeles Clippers' pick." Cohen raised both fists in victory as a soft, collective gasp filled the room. Gilbert's wish was granted ("Don't come back with anything less than number one") and his $21 million lottery ticket hit the jackpot.

The Clippers' pick had a 2.8 percent chance of coming up number one—roughly the same odds as walking into a casino and picking one number to win on the roulette wheel. Cohen walked out of Conference Room 3A with the first and fourth picks in the draft. After such a miserable first season without James, the Cavs' luck was finally changing. Cohen, however, couldn't tell anyone. Everyone who knew the lottery's outcome had to remain sequestered in the room for more than an hour until the live television show aired. Gilbert had brought along past and present Browns players such as Kosar, Josh Cribbs, and Joe Haden for good luck. When Deputy Commissioner Adam Silver finally revealed the Cavs as lottery winners, Cleveland's contingent in the studio erupted in cheers. Back in Cleveland, Grant and Scott screamed and embraced at the team's official watch party downtown. No one could believe the stroke of good fortune, but now came the hard part: Who to pick?

Kyrie Irving, the sensational freshman point guard from Duke, grew up a short drive from the NBA Entertainment studios and attended the lottery. He even posed for a picture before the drawing with Nick Gilbert, one of Dan's sons, who'd also made the trip. Irving was coming off a serious toe injury but remained a strong candidate to go number one overall just eight years after James went first overall to Cleveland. That marked the only other time the Cavs won the draft lottery, and immediately Irving was asked about the LeBron comparisons. The Cavs had lost their king; now they were getting a prince. Irving didn't appreciate all the questions about following James and quickly grew tired of them.

"I don't believe I'm following LeBron," Irving said in the moments after the Cavs won the lottery. "If I am blessed enough to go to the Cleveland Cavaliers, I just want to start a new legacy there."

A month later, Tristan Thompson exited the Times Square Westin and boarded a bus bound for Prudential Center in Newark, New Jersey, the site of the NBA draft. He was about to become a millionaire. Thompson was six foot nine with boyish good looks, a charming smile, and dimples. He had the type of carefree personality that made everyone like him. More importantly, he also had a motor that never stopped. Thompson left the University of Texas after his freshman year raw and unpolished. He could hardly shoot at all, but he was athletic and a tenacious rebounder. He was one of the first to board the bus headed to the NBA draft and he quickly grabbed a window seat. Irving climbed on a few minutes later, spotted the familiar face, and sat down next to him.

Irving was four when his mother, Elizabeth, died from sepsis. He was raised by his single father, Drederick, who was playing basketball professionally in Australia when Kyrie was born—giving Kyrie dual citizenship. Elizabeth was a classically trained pianist and the daughter of a Lutheran minister. She rocked Kyrie to sleep at night singing old church hymns. Kyrie inherited his mother's musical talents and his father's basketball skill. When he wasn't performing in high school musicals, he was playing one-on-one with Drederick, who taught him the angles of the backboard and how to use them to his advantage. At sixteen, Kyrie began to blossom as a player and beat his father in a game of one-on-one for the first time. He dropped all other sports and worked on the finer points of basketball: hanging in the air a little longer, making floaters with both hands, shooting off the dribble, learning a head fake, and even tinkering with moves in the post.

Thompson grew up near Toronto but moved to Newark prior to his sophomore year to attend St. Benedict's Prep and play basketball. During his junior year, Thompson's team was 19-0 when they faced Irving's St. Patrick High School in nearby Elizabeth, New Jersey. Irving's team smashed Thompson's team, 88–62, ending the perfect season. The bus ride from Times Square to Newark can take anywhere from thirty to seventy-five minutes depending on traffic. They spent the bus ride chatting about their past clashes on the court and the postdraft parties they were scheduled to attend later that night. They never considered they'd arrive at those parties as teammates.

Irving was viewed as the best of a flawed group of prospects—and even he came with enormous risk. Irving had dazzled at Duke with thirty-one points in a win against sixth-ranked Michigan State in early December. He vaulted up draft boards after becoming the fourth freshman in Duke history to score at least thirty points in a game, but his regular season ended prematurely after a toe injury forced him to miss nearly four months. He returned for the NCAA tournament and even scored twenty-eight points in the Blue Devils' final game of the season, a loss to sophomore Derrick Williams and Arizona in the Sweet Sixteen.

Irving wasn't the top recruit of his high school class. Harrison Barnes, Jared Sullinger, and Brandon Knight were all considered better players entering college. By the end of his freshman season, however, Irving had surpassed them all. His teasing freshman season—11 games, 303 minutes, and a wealth of potential—left the Cavs in an agonizing position. Their research revealed that no player had ever been drafted number one overall in any sport after playing so little the year before. With holes up and down the roster, there was a compelling thought to draft the explosive Williams first overall and take Knight with the fourth pick.

Williams's draft stock vaulted with a sensational NCAA tournament run, while Knight was one of the youngest players in the draft after a promising but inconsistent freshman season with the Wildcats. Grant did his best to direct smokescreens, insisting Williams was sensational during his private workout and that the Cavs weren't sure who they would take with the first pick. Since they held two high picks, Grant was trying to leverage the situation any way he could by being secretive. Inside the walls of Cleveland Clinic Courts, however, he was adamant: Irving was the choice. He told no one outside the organization—not even Irving or his agent. Irving learned he was the top pick when NBA commissioner David Stern announced it from the podium to begin the draft.

The fourth pick remained murky. They liked bruising Lithuanian center Jonas Valančiūnas, but he remained under contract to a European team and the Cavs wanted to be assured of the terms of his buyout. He was also represented by Leon Rose and Creative Artists Agency—the same agent and firm who represented James during the Decision. Animosity remained between the Cavs and Rose. Thompson was also affiliated with CAA, but he was more represented by Rich Paul, James's close friend and the one who called the Cavs to tell them that James was leaving for Miami.

After the Cavs selected Irving first, the Timberwolves took Williams second and the Utah Jazz selected center Enes Kanter third. The Cavs were back on the clock with a decision to make. Valančiūnas was a true center and considered the better prospect, but Thompson had been rising in the weeks prior to the draft and was widely considered a top ten pick. Grant loved Thompson, his makeup, his heart, his family, and his background. Grant believed Thompson was a winner.

In a surprise to the rest of the league, the Cavs chose Thompson with the fourth pick. Rivals in high school, he and Irving were NBA teammates drafted seventeen minutes apart. "We were sitting on the bus together," Thompson said. "It's almost like it was destined to happen."

The Cavs were ripped for passing on Valančiūnas, who went just after Thompson to the Toronto Raptors—Thompson's hometown team. "It's only a surprise if you didn't watch the workouts," Thompson said. "If you ask ownership and Coach Scott and CG [Chris Grant] and even Griff, if you watched the workouts, there's some other guys in that workout that probably shouldn't have went in the pick they went."

Even after the Thompson selection, Grant wasn't done. The Cavs were high on Washington State sharpshooter Klay Thompson (no relation to Tristan), so Grant continued working the phones on draft night, determined to add a third pick in the top ten. Byron Scott was familiar with the Thompson family because he played with Klay's father, Mychal, while with the Lakers. Klay set the school's single-season scoring record with 733 points and left after his junior year ranked third on WSU's all-time scoring list.

Cavs executives, particularly Griffin, loved Thompson and were dangling young power forward J. J. Hickson to try to move back into the top ten and get him. The Cavs were offering anything they could—except for future picks. They refused to trade future picks. Hickson had one year left on his rookie contract and showed promise, but everyone in the league knew the collective bargaining agreement was expiring and a nasty lockout was looming. The Cavs didn't want to pay Hickson the type of money he was seeking in his next contract, and they weren't sure how much of a season there would be in 2011–12, so they were motivated to move Hickson right away.

The Sacramento Kings made it clear the number seven pick was in play and the Cavs tried getting it. But the Kings instead traded the pick in a three-team deal, dropped down to number ten, and drafted Jimmer Fredette. Thompson went with the next pick to the Golden State Warriors and blossomed into one of the best shooting guards in the league, pairing with Steph Curry to form the Splash Brothers.

Although they missed out on Klay Thompson, the front office staff celebrated with beers and wine in Grant's office after the draft. The Cavs believed they had a future star in Irving, if he could stay healthy, and a nice complementary piece in Tristan Thompson. Grant knew Thompson wasn't going to be a superstar, but he also knew Thompson wasn't going to get fat and lazy and bust out of the league in four years, either. Grant believed in his character and work ethic.

It's unique for one team to hold two picks so high in a draft. Prior to 2011, the last time it had happened was in 1983, when the Houston Rockets took Ralph Sampson first overall and Rodney McCray third. The fourth pick in that draft was Byron Scott.

Hickson landed in Sacramento anyway. A week after the draft, the Cavs traded him to the Kings for Omri Casspi and a future first-round pick. Grant was more interested in the pick than in Casspi, but he was at least a small forward, something the Cavs had lacked since James left. Casspi was expected to be a placeholder for a few years. Hours after the trade was announced, owners locked out the players and a nasty labor battle ensued for the next 161 days while a new collective bargaining agreement was negotiated.

A number of owners—with Gilbert at the forefront—took it as an opportunity to ensure the superpower team assembled in Miami couldn't happen again through free agency. An emphasis was placed on giving small-market teams a chance to retain for the long term players they drafted and developed well. In the new NBA, the revenue pot was more evenly distributed between owners and players, but more important to the product on the court, stars would theoretically have a tougher time forcing their way out of markets. Teams were given steep financial advantages in an effort to retain their own free agents, but it came at a price. Twenty percent of the season was lost to the lockout. As part of the new CBA, teams were allowed to release one player under what became known as the amnesty clause. Those players still received all of their guaranteed money, but it didn't count against a team's cap.

The Cavs moved quickly to waive Davis under the amnesty clause for a couple of reasons. Although he had been a model citizen in Cleveland, they remained concerned he would become a problem in the locker room and negatively influence an impressionable player such as Irving. Beyond that, the stretch clause in Davis's contract made releasing him and paying him off easier. Most important, releasing him allowed the Cavs to turn the offense over to their promising rookie. With Davis out of the way, Irving started at point guard and played in fifty-one of the sixty-six games, averaging 18.5 points and 5.4 assists to win Rookie of the Year. However, he missed time with a sprained shoulder and a concussion, which did little to dispel the injury concerns that he carried into the league following his toe problems at Duke.

Thompson split his time as a starter and reserve, averaging 8.2 points and 6.5 rebounds as a rookie. His shooting numbers remained woeful, but he was athletic, durable, and stayed out of trouble. Grant knew the Cavs had something special in Irving, a precocious teenager with the handle, shot, and mind-set of a veteran.

As rookies, Thompson and Irving helped the Cavs to a 21-45 finish. Two pillars, and the overall first step, of the rebuild were in place. Cleveland finished tied with the New Orleans Pelicans for the fourth-worst record and returned to the lottery looking for more luck. They won a coin flip with the Pelicans in what turned out to be another franchise-altering outcome, but not in a good way. Instead, the Cavs fell to fourth again in the draft and began the process anew of whom to choose.

But Irving's emergence as a young superstar added fuel to the idea James might return. That first year he was gone, it was just a dream. But Grant and the rest of the front office knew Irving had the potential to be a superstar and an appealing piece of bait to lure James back. It was after Irving's first year in the league when the Cavs galvanized the plan to not spend in free agency, preserve cap space, and work hard to succeed in the draft while waiting for 2014 and the Summer of LeBron.

CHAPTER 5

Old Memories, New Hopes

The old, cramped practice court on the fourth floor of Quicken Loans Arena is a relic these days. The Cavs used it as their primary practice gym until 2007, when they unveiled Cleveland Clinic Courts, a state-of-the-art, fifty-thousand-square-foot practice facility and team headquarters in suburban Independence. It cost $25 million to construct and remains one of the league's finest facilities.

Opposing teams still occasionally use the abandoned court inside the Q for practices and morning shoot-arounds when they're in town to play the Cavs and the main floor isn't available. James stood near the corner of that old practice court wearing his Heat jersey on a chilly February morning in 2012 when he made two franchises and the entire NBA stop and look up.

"It would be fun to play in front of these fans again," James said. "I had a lot of fun times in my seven years here. You can't predict the future. I am here as a Miami Heat player and I am happy where I am now. But I don't rule that out in no sense. And if I decide to come back, hopefully the fans would accept me."

Counting the *GQ* article in the weeks after he first departed for Miami, this was the second time James volunteered he'd like to come home someday. When he said it to *GQ*, Cleveland was in too much shock and pain to really notice. Miami was so elated to have him that it didn't take it seriously. After all, who actually leaves Miami and moves to Cleveland? The comment to *GQ* was quickly dismissed and forgotten. Eighteen months later, when he said it again, *everyone* noticed. This wasn't nostalgia talking. Like everything else with James, this was calculated. When Associated Press reporter Tom Withers, who had a good relationship with James after covering him since he was in high school at St. V, asked if he would like to play in Cleveland again someday, James never hesitated. This was his warning shot to both the Cavs and the Heat. Eight miles away, inside his office at Cleveland Clinic Courts, Chris Grant was listening.

The Cavs had started rebuilding their team, and James was already talking about returning, even though he had two and a half years left in his contract. But there was still a long road ahead, and the public hatred toward James was going to take years to turn. So James got to work early. "The media is going to fuck this up," one of his closest allies told me that day. "It's at least two years from happening and it's still a fragile relationship on both sides. A lot has to happen first and now isn't the time. He's not coming back without a championship. He has to win one first."

Until that point, the thought of James returning had been more hope than reality, although it was a strong, well-nourished hope. Grant remained in close contact with Rich Paul, who left CAA in the fall of 2012 to start his own agency, Klutch Sports. Among his first clients? LeBron James and Tristan Thompson. James left the reputable and powerful Leon Rose/CAA and trusted his friend since high school with his future. Thompson went, too, which worked out conveniently for the Cavs. Grant and Paul were in constant contact because they shared an interest in Thompson. As for James, the conversation was always open-ended, in the vein of "You never know what can happen."

The Cavs—and James—knew early in Irving's rookie season they had a potential superstar. As they watched him blossom and flourish, coupled with James's own remarks, the idea of his returning suddenly began to feel real. Yes, the Cavs' record was a mess and there weren't many other pieces, but even a young Irving was more talented than any teammate James had during his seven years in Cleveland. He was also better than any point guard James had ever played alongside, and James knew it.

"This is transforming into a point guard league," James said during Irving's rookie season. He went on to name guys like Derrick Rose, Russell Westbrook, Chris Paul, John Wall, and, yes, Irving. "If you have a really, really good point guard, you have a chance to win. It's like having a really good quarterback in the NFL."

By All-Star Weekend in 2013, Irving's second year in the league, his star was shining bright. There was the "Uncle Drew" character he developed for Pepsi Max commercials that appealed to the younger crowd, but his on-court game was where he was going to make real money and earn respect throughout the league. Since the Cavs were atrocious and never on national television, Irving always viewed All-Star Weekends as his chance to shine.

He scored thirty-four points and made all eight of his three-point attempts to win the MVP award of the Rising Stars game during the 2012 All-Star Weekend. His eight threes were the second most in the history of the competition, behind only his Cavs teammate Daniel "Booby" Gibson. Suddenly, the tarp was getting pulled back and the rest of the league was beginning to see the type of potential bursting in Cleveland. Irving grinned widely as he was escorted into a makeshift photography studio for the required pictures with his MVP trophy. Irving lowered the crystal trophy a few inches. "Make sure you get the Cleveland," Irving said, referring to the block CAVALIERS lettering stitched across his home white jersey. It wasn't so long ago that James had shunned the city Irving was now propping up. The comparisons between them only intensified following his terrific All-Star Weekend.

"People are making a mistake if they're looking at him to be the next LeBron," Shaquille O'Neal told me prior to Irving's MVP performance. O'Neal, of course, was with James for his final year in Cleveland. "What LeBron did was fabulous and legendary. There will never be another LeBron with how he did it and how he came in and took over. Kyrie is also a leader. I'm not trying to take anything away from his game. But I would urge people not to put too much pressure on him."

Irving's star was red-hot, which only heightened the questions within the organization about James. He wasn't going to come home if there was no talent on the roster, but who better for him to come play alongside than a twenty-two-year-old point guard who was already an All-Star?

The Cavs, however, stuck to their plan of building through the draft, collecting lottery picks and future trade assets while preserving cap space. They steadfastly boycotted free agency. The most notable veteran free agent they signed after James left was C. J. Miles. It wasn't that Gilbert didn't want to spend; he did. Grant didn't want to get stuck with a bad contract—or worse, sign a veteran who would actually help them win games. Winning would come later.

The front office convened in Chicago again for the NBA combine in May of 2012, where the prospective draftees gather to be measured, weighed, and put through drills and five-on-five competitions for league executives to evaluate them. It was also the month Irving won the Rookie of the Year award with 117 of a possible 120 votes. The group of about ten team executives, led by Grant and Griffin, dined at Rosebud Steakhouse while they watched Game 6 of the Eastern Conference finals on the big-screen television in front of them. The Heat, who had lost to the Dallas Mavericks in the NBA finals in six games during James's first season in Miami, now were facing elimination again. They trailed the series 3–2 and were on the road at Boston, a place that haunted James throughout his career and ended his time in Cleveland. Now James was one more loss away from another embarrassing finish and another lost season without a championship.

Grant, David Griffin, and the rest of the front office chewed on some of Chicago's finest steaks while LeBron swallowed up the Celtics that night with forty-five points, fifteen rebounds, and five assists in one of the greatest performances of his storied career. Now, because of

James's decision to leave, the Cavs were at the draft lottery watching on television as the Heat staved off elimination with a 98–79 win. And, for more than one reason, that was exactly the result they all wanted. Miami also won Game 7 to eliminate the Celtics, then beat the Oklahoma City Thunder in five games in the NBA Finals. In his ninth season in the NBA, LeBron James finally had his first championship ring, clearing perhaps the highest hurdle for his return to Cleveland.

LeBron still was locked into his contract for two more years, however, and the Cavs were still a mess. They needed more elite young talent with bright futures. When New Orleans won the draft lottery, Grant made a long-shot pitch to GM Dell Demps, dangling the number four pick while offering to take every bad contract off the Hornets' hands in exchange for the number one pick and the draft rights to Anthony Davis, the consensus top player available in the draft. The contracts totaled more than $100 million. Demps wisely declined. He wanted Davis for New Orleans, which was under new ownership and looked at Davis as a future superstar around which they could build something. The Cavs stayed at number four.

Throughout the rebuild, the Cavs made several assumptions. One of them was that if James returned to Cleveland, their draft picks held significant value as either the pick or the player. Either the player they drafted would bloom into a talent they could use in Cleveland, or if whoever they drafted didn't, he could be dealt for someone who did fit with James. They were going to have to move some pieces around. Not all of them would fit with James, and he wasn't going to return to play with a bunch of kids. Some of the young players with high ceilings would have to be traded for veterans. Unless the player blossomed into

78

a superstar, such as Irving, Grant and the front office knew some of these pieces could be bundled and moved for more established, veteran pieces.

With Irving and Thompson in place, the Cavs entered the 2012 draft looking for another playmaker to take some of the pressure off the reigning Rookie of the Year. Davis was the clear choice to go number one, but after that the lens was blurry. Michael Kidd-Gilchrist—another Rich Paul client and a high school teammate of Irving's—went second to the Charlotte Bobcats and Bradley Beal went third to the Washington Wizards. The Cavs liked both players. They loved Kidd-Gilchrist's makeup and competitiveness, but they were scared off by his unorthodox jump shot and inability to make open shots. They really liked Beal but refused to trade future picks to move up one spot.

The obvious and safe bet at number four was Harrison Barnes, the freshman small forward out of North Carolina. Barnes was widely considered the top freshman entering college, and he shared Irving's agent in Jeff Wechsler. And he happened to play the same position as James, but that's not why the Cavs soured on him. They viewed Barnes as a spot-up shooter who didn't do much else well. They thought he'd struggle to get to the basket in the NBA and they didn't think he made players around him better. Barnes's poor performance against Ohio University in the NCAA tournament stuck in their heads. He'd managed just twelve points and shot three of sixteen against the Bobcats. If he struggled to get good looks against weaker college players, they reasoned, how was he going to do it in the NBA?

The guard they liked the most was senior Damian Lillard from little-known Weber State. When the Cavs were in Portland during a

West Coast trip during the 2011–12 season, Grant scouted Lillard's game against Portland State. Lillard made eight three-pointers and scored thirty-eight points in front of a plethora of NBA personnel. I met Grant for a drink after the Cavs-Blazers game the following night, and he was raving about Lillard. That's also the night I told him that the rumors about LeBron perhaps coming back to Cleveland were only growing louder. Grant gave an uncomfortable chuckle and sipped on a glass of wine. "Did you see that letter?" he asked, referencing Gilbert's now-famous scorched-earth response to James's leaving for Miami. Grant didn't want to spend much time talking about the possibility, but it was clear the Cavs had heard it and wondered themselves if they could actually pull it off.

As for Lillard, Grant was so enamored with him that he sent a representative to Lillard's private workout in Utah prior to the draft, even though the pick wouldn't have made sense, due to Irving—between the two, the Cavs were fearful the team would be too small to guard anyone and neither player would be happy sharing the ball with the other. "He'll be better than Knight," Grant told me during the combine, referring to Brandon Knight, the second point guard off the board behind Irving the year before.

With Beal gone and Lillard not deemed a viable option, the guard Grant and the Cavs kept coming back to was Syracuse sophomore Dion Waiters. He attended four high schools while growing up in a tough section of South Philadelphia—two of his cousins and his best friend were all shot to death within about a year. Yet Waiters remained a Philly street legend even though he never started a game in college.

Waiters had attitude problems. He sulked at times and clashed with Syracuse coach Jim Boeheim so badly as a freshman that Boeheim thought he might transfer. Waiters was good enough to start, but Boeheim was being loyal to the upperclassmen guards in front of him. He kept telling Waiters he would have to wait his turn. Starter or not, Grant and Byron Scott loved Waiters's playmaking ability. They thought he could attack the basket and still facilitate for others. Scott compared him to Heat superstar Dwyane Wade. There was only one problem: The Cavs never actually talked to Waiters.

Grant and Trent Redden, the team's director of college personnel, made countless trips to Syracuse to watch Waiters, to study how he interacted with teammates. Syracuse assistant Mike Hopkins was one of Grant's friends from high school. These are the ways the Cavs had to get their information because Waiters's agent, Rob Pelinka, pulled him out of the combine. Pelinka said he had a promise from a team to draft him, but that team wasn't Cleveland. Grant stressed throughout his first year as GM how important it was to sit down with these players and try to get to know them, but they never had that opportunity. They took him anyway. "We did an enormous amount of research," Grant said. "Maybe more than we've ever done."

Scott watched film of Waiters at Syracuse. Every time he watched another highlight, he grew a little more impressed. Waiters had the same stocky build as Wade, the same ability to get to the basket, and a knack to create for others. After watching about fifteen tapes of Waiters, Scott had his answer. Much like with Tristan Thompson the year before, the Cavs shocked everyone by taking Waiters fourth overall.

"He's a pit bull," Scott said. "This kid isn't afraid of anyone."

With their second pick in the first round, the Cavs traded up to take North Carolina center Tyler Zeller. Within two years, the Cavs had selected four players in the first round. They had addressed every position in the draft except small forward—LeBron's position. Now they had to put it all together, which proved much more difficult than they expected. Almost instantly, folks around Irving were upset the Cavs didn't take Barnes. Waiters's game never fit well alongside Irving, who was the superior player. They were two ball-dominant guards who kept getting in each other's way. On top of that, Waiters had the alpha dog mentality and was constantly nipping at Irving. He couldn't understand why Irving was the favored son. He accused Irving and Thompson of playing "buddy ball" during one heated confrontation in the locker room following a game in Minnesota and teammates eventually grew tired of him. Waiters was known for sulking, for always thinking he was a victim.

Within a few months of Waiters's rookie year, the Cavs realized the pairing wasn't going to work and they were probably going to have to eventually trade him. That was fine in their minds because Waiters, in trade value, represented a different type of veteran piece if James returned. They could move Waiters when the time was right and get what they actually needed to fit around LeBron. For now, they endured a toxic locker room that lacked veteran leadership.

The downfall to not signing any veteran free agents is that the locker room can turn into a preschool with the children constantly bickering. But Grant was concerned that bringing in a veteran who wasn't going to play would do more harm than good to the locker room. The veterans they had those first couple of years, such as Anthony Parker and

Antawn Jamison, weren't the type of vocal leaders who would keep young players in line. Parker was well respected by his teammates, but Jamison was caught in purgatory after James left and was looking for any door that would get him out. Jamison announced after the final game of the season he was leaving; there may still be skid marks on the pavement from how quickly he bolted Cleveland. He didn't even show up the next day for locker cleanout.

Waiters averaged 14.7 points as a rookie, second only to Irving's 22.5. James's free agency was now just a year away, and Gilbert wasn't seeing enough growth. He had gotten impatient with Scott, who always coached as if he had more time. Gilbert loves teams built around defense, yet the Cavs were abysmal defensively. They had the worst defensive field-goal percentage in the league and ranked near the bottom in most all defensive categories. The Nuggets traveled to Cleveland in February 2012 and shot 50 percent from the floor to end the Cavs' brief three-game winning streak. "We have made good progress recently," Gilbert wrote on his Twitter account after the game, "but when the Cleveland Cavaliers arrive back to the top tier of the NBA we will be a DEFENSIVE 1st team." Even before he sent that tweet, Gilbert had made up his mind. He was firing Scott at the end of the season. That was made apparent to me during All-Star Weekend in Houston, when a conversation with Gilbert prior to All-Star Saturday Night seemed to make it clear ownership was unhappy with the coach and Scott was in the hot seat.

Meanwhile, a reunion with James seemed to be inching closer. The Heat visited in late March riding a twenty-three-game winning streak and suddenly more James jerseys were resurfacing inside the Q. Police, however, still swept the arena before James's games with a bomb-sniffing dog.

"Is this standard for every game?" I asked one officer.

"Nope," he said. "Only for that asshole."

He was still booed, but each return brought fewer boos and more cheers. One James superfan bragged all day on social media that he was going to storm the court—and he did—while wearing a homemade white T-shirt with WE MISS YOU scribbled on the front in black Magic Marker and 2014 COME BACK written out across the back. James tapped him on the head as the fan was led off the floor by security. Sentiment toward James was clearly changing.

Gilbert tweeted before the game, "Cleveland Cavaliers young talent makes our future very bright. Clearly, LeBron's is as well. Time for everyone to focus on the road ahead." It was subtle and poignant, two characteristics not always attributed to an owner whose tachometer typically ran in the red. Forget about an olive branch; this felt like Gilbert digging up the entire olive tree and planting it in James's yard.

With every trip Miami made back to Cleveland, with every rumor surfacing that James could return in 2014, the cheers for James grew a little louder. Suddenly, 2014 was inching closer and closer, but the Cavs were still a disaster on the court. They actually led the Heat that night 67–40 and maintained a twenty-point lead with 3:28 left in the third quarter, but James and Shane Battier had the game tied within five minutes. The Heat ultimately won 98–95. A week later, while playing without both Irving and Waiters, the Cavs blew a fourteen-point lead to the Celtics in the game's final eight minutes. They ended the night missing eight of their last nine shots and committing three turnovers, while Scott took three time-outs home with him rather than calling one prior to the final possession.

Shaun Livingston ended the night with a miss from the elbow, just inside the lane where the free-throw line meets the lane line. It was a good look, but Livingston simply missed the shot. Scott said the next day that if Irving was in the game, he preferred to let him make a play before the defense could get set. But in that case, with Irving out nursing an injury, he should've called a time-out and drawn something up. "The biggest thing [with calling a time-out] is you give them a chance to set up on defense, and sometimes just having that spontaneity, just letting guys go, is sometimes the best thing to do," Scott said the next day. "But sometimes with the group we have now, it might not be the best thing to do. That's one of the things I probably learned. We get in that situation in any other game, maybe I'll just go ahead and burn that one and set up something especially for that person to try to get a better shot."

By that point, it was too late. Gilbert's mind was already made up. Aside from the time-out issues, he didn't like the way Scott was subbing Irving in and out of the game and he really didn't like the way the defense showed no progress. No one within the organization felt like Irving was being held accountable with his attitude. He was young and immature and acting like it, but he wasn't learning how to be a professional. When Scott grew irritated with his starters in a late-season loss at Philadelphia, he pulled all of them except Irving. That infuriated the upper levels of the organization, who felt like that sent the wrong message to Irving and the rest of the team. It became clear to me during All-Star Weekend that Gilbert was unhappy with Scott. It was all but confirmed for me during the final home game that he was getting fired.

The last game of the season was at Charlotte. I called Byron at his hotel that afternoon and asked if he had any idea what was coming the next day. He said no, that when he was fired at each of his two previous jobs he suspected it. This time, however, he had gotten no indication it was coming. I told him to be prepared, because he was going to be fired the next morning. The Cavs lost to the Bobcats that night to end the season 24-58, the third-worst record in the NBA. Scott indeed was fired the next morning. With James's free agency now only fourteen months away, it was time for the Cavs to start winning. Figuring out how to get Irving and Waiters, the team's two best players, to learn how to play together became someone else's problem.

CHAPTER 6

Old Faces, New Mistakes

The firing of Mike Brown in 2010 had been difficult on everyone in the organization, particularly Chris Grant. The two had been friends since their days together at the University of San Diego. They played together on the basketball team for one season and immediately became close friends. They attended each other's wedding and held each other's children as newborns. In college, however, they were a modern-day Felix and Oscar. Brown was the point guard and studious son of a military man, Grant the bruising six-foot-ten, fun-loving prankster who went out of his way to piss off head coach Hank Egan, the man who in later years became Brown's most trusted assistant coach in Cleveland.

"Chris was a good rebounder and a good defender, a smart player, but he was always a practical joker," said Egan. "He kept the team light and loose and tried to drive me crazy every chance he could. And he did a hell of a job with it."

Grant knew Egan liked to pick up stray pennies and place them in his shoe for good luck, so on road trips, Grant broke into his coach's hotel room and scattered hundreds of pennies across the floor. When Egan was ready to throw the ball up one day to begin practice, Grant (only a freshman at the time) wiped the sweat off his own face using his coach's shirt. He even went out of his way to lower his shoulder and run over Egan during practice. "Chris had no couth," Brown said, laughing. "He didn't care or think twice about it. He'd take his shoulder and run right into [Egan] and just kept playing like nothing happened. Coach Egan, to say the least, knew to get out of his way."

Since neither Grant nor Gilbert had really wanted Brown fired the first time, pursuing him again after Scott was fired didn't take much convincing on either side. Brown had been hired and fired by the Lakers while Scott was in Cleveland. Danny Ferry, meanwhile, was now the general manager in Atlanta and equally interested in reuniting with Brown. Knowing there was competition for him, Grant and Gilbert moved quickly. That was frustrating for Griffin, who was pushing for the team to look at Butler coach Brad Stevens—the rising star in the college ranks. Grant was leery of college coaches in general because few have ever made the transition to the NBA successfully, and Stevens was never really considered for the job. Three months later, Stevens was hired as the Celtics' head coach. Other names were considered—Grant sent Griffin and Redden on a scouting mission to Memphis late in the season to check out Grizzlies coach Lionel Hollins, who everyone knew was soon going to be fired.

Brown was always the primary target, though, and after the obligatory call to Phil Jackson to see if he wanted to coach again (he didn't), the team moved quickly to finish the deal with Brown. Less than a week after Scott was fired, Brown met with top Cavs officials near Gilbert's Michigan home. By the end of the night, the framework of the deal was in place. Brown was named the head coach again on April 24, 2013. He received a five-year deal worth more than $20 million, and at the introductory news conference, Gilbert admitted firing Brown the first time was a mistake.

"For sure it was a mistake," Gilbert said. "That summer . . . was a unique time for us as a franchise, there was a lot of uncertainty on all levels. We're very happy that we get to rectify any position we took back then by Mike being available right now. Maybe it's meant to be here. We're very excited about today and the future."

Gilbert's admitting to a mistake was important. It showed LeBron and his inner circle that he would accept accountability when he erred. At some point, if James was ever going to return to Cleveland, Gilbert needed to apologize for writing the Letter. Admitting a mistake with Brown was the first small step. And although their time together had seemed strained near the end, James spoke fondly of Brown after he went to Miami and credited his former coach with teaching him the importance of defense. Grant received assurances that James would have no problem playing for Brown again should he elect to return to Cleveland.

Brown, meanwhile, thought Grant was crazy when he first heard the idea of wooing James back to Cleveland.

"At first I didn't believe it. It was kind of far-fetched," Brown said. "As time went on and you see some of the dominos fall, you relize, 'You know what? Yeah, he has a plan and he's been working on this for years.

This could really happen.' So then there's more excitement than anything elese. That's exactly what the organization needed and what the city needed. It was the right time for him to leave and the right time for him to come back. I was excited for the plan."

But the pressure to improve the roster was mounting. James was in the business of winning championships, not steering rebuilding projects. If they were going to have any shot at getting him back in the summer of 2014, Gilbert believed the Cavs needed to start winning. That plan began with bringing back Brown, whose teams made the playoffs every year he was the head coach. That quickly became the expectation again, particularly after the Cavs managed to win the lottery for the second time in three years. They couldn't win games on the court, but they couldn't stop winning off it.

Nick Gilbert, Dan's son, represented the Cavs onstage each of the first three years the team was in the lottery. He snagged the number one pick in two of the three years. The television studio at NBA Entertainment erupted in cheers when the Cavs were victorious again. They jumped from number three to claim the top pick and they also held the number nineteen pick in the first round. With Brown back, a young nucleus, and another number one pick coming, Gilbert was certain the Cavs were postseason bound.

"We were hoping regardless of what pick we got that this would be our last lottery," Dan Gilbert said the night the Cavs won the top spot again. "We thought originally after everything had to be reset that it would be a three-year process. You never know, it could be four. We thought three years, but having number one and nineteen, we've got a pretty good chance of this being the last one for a while."

There was only one problem: There was no one worth choosing first overall. The critics who thought the 2011 draft headlined by Irving was bad ran out of the burning building screaming and crying at the choices in '13. One opposing front-office executive said the draft was full of, at best, guys who would generally go sixth or seventh overall in a typical draft year. Scouts called it the worst draft in at least a decade and likely one of the worst ever. "You have to be fortunate enough to have the first pick in the right pool. We went into that lottery hoping to God we didn't get number one," Griffin said. "We literally felt like we were choosing from the least of all bad options. It was the best of a bad option. And that's why we wanted to trade down."

Grant tried trading the pick but couldn't find any takers. It's rare for the top overall pick to be traded. The Magic dealt top pick Chris Webber to the Warriors in 1993 and received the third overall pick in that draft and three future first rounders just to move up two spots. The Cavs weren't going to command anywhere near that type of value in this draft because no one else liked it, either. The Magic, drafting second, offered only a second-round pick to move up one spot. Grant was trying to get the traditional trade value out of the top pick, only everyone knew this wasn't a normal year. There was no Chris Webber or Shaquille O'Neal or LeBron James or Anthony Davis or Kyrie Irving or John Wall. There didn't even seem to be a Kenyon Martin, who had gone number one overall in a similarly feeble 2000 draft class. Martin played fifteen seasons and made an All-Star team. It was debatable whether there was an All-Star to be found in this group.

That made the process of building their draft board excruciatingly stressful. There was no consensus number one pick. Nerlens Noel was widely considered the top prospect, but he was coming off a torn ACL and the Cavs had never been overly impressed. He was too skinny, too limited offensively, and going to miss most (or all) of what should have been his rookie season rehabbing. All those years of stockpiling draft picks were over. It was time to start winning. Noel was eliminated from the conversation early on.

The Cavs liked center Alex Len out of Maryland, but Len was dealing with a stress fracture in his left foot. During his visit to Cleveland, team doctors scanned the other foot just to be cautious and found the beginning of a stress fracture in his right ankle, too. It's not clear if the Cavs liked Len enough to take him number one overall, but finding the stress fracture in his "healthy" foot eliminated him from the conversation. No one knew if Len was aware he had problems in his other foot or not, but the Cavs sat him down and told him before his predraft workout with the team was over. Len went fifth to the Suns and had surgery to correct the problem prior to his rookie season.

Gilbert liked Indiana guard Victor Oladipo, a six-foot-four package of muscle and athleticism. But Grant was concerned there was no discernible NBA skill. He played hard and he was athletic, but what was his definable skill? The decision for him instead came down to two players: Ben McLemore or Anthony Bennett. McLemore was a quick, explosive guard who averaged 15.9 points and shot 42 percent at Kansas. But he came from a troubled background and NBA personnel were concerned about some of the people in his inner circle. The Cavs already had Irving and Waiters struggling to play together on and off the court. Adding a third top guard to the backcourt could also complicate matters, and since McLemore measured only six-four, it could've been difficult to play all three together.

Griffin spent a lot of time in Las Vegas and did all of the background work on Bennett, who was an undersized power forward at six-seven. Grant was low on Derrick Williams in the 2011 draft because of his size; Grant saw him as a role player because he was a "tweener"—too small to play power forward, too big and slow to play small forward. Bennett was sort of the same way. He wasn't a good scorer in the post with his back to the basket, but hardly anyone is these days in this NBA game of pace and space and stretch fours. To that end, Bennett drew comparisons to another athletic-but-undersized power forward out of UNLV: Larry Johnson.

Johnson was listed at only six-six, but he played ten years in the league and made two All-Star teams. He scored more than 11,000 points and grabbed more than 5,300 rebounds in his career, and the Cavs were hoping for similar numbers out of Bennett, who was explosive with great range for a big man. But he needed surgery after his freshman season to repair his rotator cuff. Teams knew he was going to miss all of the pre-draft workouts, the combine, and the Summer League, all of which complicated this draft. Three of the top prospects—Noel, Len, and Bennett—were rehabbing injuries and couldn't do much.

The pressure on Grant was immense. He knew Gilbert was expecting a winning team and the playoffs after three years of losing, and winning the top overall pick again only increased those expectations. But the front office knew it was debatable how much they were going to get out of the number one pick. Choosing between so many flawed prospects was keeping him up at night. He had to get this right. And much like with Williams two years earlier, Grant did not like Bennett. He wouldn't listen to any debate about Irving or Williams. He made up his mind early on he was taking Irving. This time, however, there was no other clear-cut contender. Grant was high on McLemore, but everyone knew he wasn't in Irving's league in terms of talent and ability. So when the Cavs front office sat down before the draft to cast their vote on who to take, the final tally was 9–1 in favor of Bennett. The one vote against taking him? Chris Grant.

I talked to Grant on his way into the office the morning of the draft. He wouldn't tell me who they were taking because he insisted he didn't know yet. He said it was down to two, but he wouldn't divulge which two because he hadn't spoken to their agents. Ultimately, Grant bowed to the rest of the staff. The talk leading up to the draft was that Bennett could tumble out of the top ten. Instead he was the stunning choice at number one.

Oladipo, Gilbert's favorite, went second to the Magic. Noel slid to the Sixers at number six, while McLemore went to Sacramento with the following pick. Grant wasn't giving up on McLemore. He was close to a deal with the Kings for the seventh pick and thought he had something done, but the Kings backed out when McLemore fell to them. They took him for themselves instead. Much like when they drafted Irving, the Cavs didn't even tell Bennett or his agent he was going number one. The pick stunned the rest of the league, including Bennett. "I'm just as surprised as everybody else," Bennett said.

I spoke to one team after the draft who said that at one point in their draft prep, they took Bennett's name completely off their board. Grant, meanwhile, hardly gushed over Bennett when he met with the media after the draft.

"As we did our evaluations throughout the entire year, we just kept coming back to his ability and his talent and how it fit with our guys," Grant said of Bennett. "A lot of times, like [2012 and Anthony Davis], it's just clear-cut. But for us, through the year, we always had him very high in our rankings and as we went back and reviewed the film and went on campus and visited everybody, we came away saying he's a great kid. He's willing to work and do the right things and he's got a bunch of talent."

Notice how the phrase *franchise player* was never used. There were never any comparisons to other All-Star-caliber players, which is customary with this sort of pick. Brown was high on Bennett because UNLV was recruiting his son Elijah. Brown watched the Rebels play on several occasions and walked away impressed, believing Bennett could evolve into a small forward in the NBA. The pick, however, was a disaster.

Bennett purchased a home in Independence, not far from the Cavs' facility so he would be close. But it didn't take long for team officials to begin questioning his work ethic, and it soon became clear Bennett couldn't play either forward position. He started out as a rookie behind Tristan Thompson, Anderson Varejao, and free agent pickup Andrew Bynum. He never passed any of them. He showed up to his first training camp overweight by at least fifteen pounds and out of shape. When he appeared in the team's intrasquad scrimmage on the campus of Baldwin Wallace University in early October, Bennett was gassed after only a couple of trips up and down the floor. The questions about his conditioning started early and never really went away.

He fell behind and never caught up. His best performance in a Cavs uniform was his second preseason game at Orlando when he showed off nifty post moves, a step-back jumper, and three-point range. He scored sixteen points, including fourteen in the fourth quarter.

Then the regular season started and Bennett missed the first sixteen shots of his career. He didn't score his first basket until the Cavs' fifth game. His only points prior to that were two from the free-throw line. He was booed by home fans within the first month and he ended his rookie year with meager averages of 4.2 points and three rebounds. He did not start any games and never even got off the bench in nearly half of them. Brown tried everything to get him acclimated. He tried him at small forward and power forward. He tried playing him during garbage time. He tried giving him a few days to clear his head. It didn't matter. What the Cavs steadfastly refused to do was send him to the Development League. He clearly needed to play and wasn't getting enough minutes, but the team feared sending him to the D-League would damage his already-fragile psyche. It was a wasted pick.

"The issue with Anthony was, and we had no way of knowing it at the time, the kid had no desire to overcome adversity whatsoever. As soon as it was hard, he was out," Griffin said. "His whole life, he rolled out of bed bigger, better, and more talented than everybody else. As soon as it was hard, it was over. And I was the one on campus at UNLV. I'm the one who got sold the bill of goods and I bought it hook, line, and sinker. You fuck up sometimes. But I feel bad Chris took it for that, because Chris was the one guy who wasn't sure."

Bennett played for four teams in four years. He began the 2016–17 season with the pitiful Brooklyn Nets and still couldn't get on the floor. Bennett was waived the following January after appearing in only twenty-three games and averaging five points. Unable to find another

NBA job, he ended the season playing in Turkey. He will go down as the worst number one overall pick in draft history, yet his failures in Cleveland were just a small microcosm of what went wrong during the all-important 2013–14 season. That draft was the kickoff to a summer and season of discontent. The Blueprint was suddenly in doubt.

CHAPTER 7

Grant's Tomb

I t was time. James's free agency was so tantalizingly close. But the Cavs had plenty of work to do with the roster and on the court. After three seasons of concentrating on the draft, and trying their best *not* to win, the Cavs wanted to show LeBron that they could be playoff contenders. The expectation, and the pressure, was on everyone, but especially Mike Brown.

Brown's first act as head coach upon returning to Cleveland occurred in Las Vegas during Summer League. We met that July in the lobby of the Four Seasons high atop Mandalay Bay in Las Vegas as he talked defense using cell phones, salt and pepper shakers, and napkins to diagram plays and defensive sets. He was in his element demonstrating the defensive side of the game. But plenty of coaches know X's and O's. The truth was, Brown struggled to connect with his young roster, and in fact turned some of them off immediately.

During the first day of Summer League practice, Brown lined up the players across the baseline and instructed for nearly three hours—unheard of during the usually casual summer sessions. Only a handful of the players, like Dion Waiters, Tyler Zeller, Carrick Felix, Matthew Dellavedova, and Kevin Jones, even had a realistic chance of making the actual team in the fall. Anthony Bennett was a rookie out with shoulder surgery, and the other rookie, drafted nineteenth, Sergey Karasev, was still playing overseas. Nevertheless, Brown pulled players off the baseline one at a time, instructed and drilled with them, then returned them to the baseline and pulled off another player. This went on all morning. "Damn, man, three hours," Waiters said afterward. "I ain't never seen nothing like that."

Brown's teams had reached the playoffs every season he had been a head coach, and fair or not, that was the expectation again for 2013–14. Gilbert made that clear the day he brought Brown back. James's free agency was coming fast now, and the Cavs' house wasn't in order. They had the league's worst cumulative record over the previous three seasons and a dramatic leap was necessary. The Cavs had won twenty-four games in Byron Scott's final season, but the average number of wins needed to secure the final playoff spot in the East was right around forty. Brown had his work cut out for him.

The Cavs had spent three years hoarding cap space and stockpiling trade assets in preparation for the summer of 2014 and what they hoped would be the return of James. Within the first couple of weeks of free agency in 2013, however, all of that changed. Gilbert was applying pressure to upgrade the roster by any means necessary and the Cavs dipped into free agency for the first time since James departed. All of that work to protect the cap space was undone in one month. It was the first time since the idea of LeBron's returning was really set in motion that the Cavs got away from the endgame. Once they committed to spending, they knew they'd have to dump money—and assets—the following summer if James truly wanted to return. At this point, however, Gilbert was concerned with simply making the team competitive.

It wasn't easy. Chris Grant arrived at Kyle Korver's door at 12:01 A.M. on July 1, the first moment teams could talk to free agents. Korver was thirty-two and one of the best shooters in the league, which is what the Cavs needed. They had two drive-and-kick guards in Irving and Waiters, but no one to consistently space the floor and knock down shots when defenses collapsed. Korver wasn't interested in Cleveland's rebuilding project, spurning the Cavs to take less money to remain with the Atlanta Hawks. Grant tried Mike Dunleavy next, but like Korver, Dunleavy took less money to go to Chicago. These were not elite-level free agents but quality veterans who could make a big impact in Cleveland. Still, the Cavs had had a hard time luring marquee free agents to Cleveland even when James played there. Trying to do it without him was next to impossible. Gilbert was relentless: Go find somebody. The Cavs knew they would have to overpay. The plan they had intricately followed for three years was gone. But was this the next step or a total change in direction that would threaten the entire idea? At this point, it was hard to tell.

"That was a very difficult summer. We sort of lost our way a little bit," Griffin said. "We had been really clear and direct about what our game plan was up to that point and that was the first time we sort of hit a fork in the road. Did we try to be better? Did we not try to be better? That was the first time we had real discord in that regard."

Gilbert had been patient during three awful years, abiding by the plan. In the time since James had left, Grant had acquired six additional first-round draft picks. Some of them had been used already, such as drafting Irving and Zeller, and some were tucked away in the war chest of trade assets to be used—in a best-case scenario—to build the team around James. But now suddenly Gilbert was pushing hard for the front office to spend and win.

"We probably have to show we're going to be a playoff team," Griffin said. "'Bron is not coming to a crappy team."

Grant had been hesitant to bring in veterans to police the locker room because the Cavs were committed to the youth movement. Now he was looking for veterans who could play. Jarrett Jack was a thirty-year-old reserve guard coming off a terrific season with the Golden State Warriors. He wasn't the best fit because the Cavs already had two ball-dominant guards in Irving and Waiters, but they were running out of options and felt pressured to make a move—something—to upgrade the roster. As expected, they had to overpay for Jack by giving him a four-year deal worth $25 million. The fourth year, at least, was a team option. Jack was expected to provide guidance and leadership to a locker room that lacked both. But the Cavs weren't done. Gilbert was pushing for more. Gilbert wanted Andrew Bynum.

Bynum was two years removed from an All-Star season. He won two championships with the Lakers and evolved into one of the best centers in the game before knee problems kept him out for the entire 2012–13 season. The Cavs were interested in trading for Bynum in 2012, but he was instead shipped from Los Angeles to Philadelphia in an enormous four-team deal that sent Dwight Howard to the Lakers. Bynum was hampered by knee problems throughout his one season in

Philadelphia and never played for the 76ers, instead opting to have arthroscopic surgery on both knees in March. The trade wrecked the Sixers and forced a dramatic rebuild and overhaul of the roster similar to what was happening in Cleveland. Four months after Bynum's knee surgery, the Cavs were the only team to offer him a contract.

The front office was cool on Bynum as a player from the start. As negotiations between the two sides were only beginning, one team executive texted me: "If he comes, great. If he doesn't, I'm already over it." And when the two sides reached an agreement, I called Grant to congratulate him. "We'll see," Grant said. "I don't know if we've won anything or not." Gilbert, however, was thrilled. He sent out a tweet praising Grant for landing Earl Clark and Jack in free agency. "What's next CG?" Gilbert tweeted.

Realistically, the Cavs weren't sure what Bynum had left or even if he wanted to play basketball anymore. He had two championship rings, $73 million in NBA checks, an All-Star appearance, and now two bad knees. What was left to prove? Grant wanted to protect himself in case the Bynum experiment blew up. He structured the contract so that only half of his $12 million salary was guaranteed up front. The other half was guaranteed in early January. In a worst-case scenario, if Bynum didn't work out, his contract created a pseudo trade deadline and left the Cavs as the only shoppers. They could theoretically deal his contract to another team that would promptly release him and shed salary if necessary.

The Cavs were cautious with Bynum and held him out the entire preseason because of his knees. He debuted in the season-opening win against the Brooklyn Nets. He played less than eight minutes, but he scored three points, grabbed a pair of rebounds, blocked a couple of shots, and passed for two assists while tying up Nets All-Star center Brook Lopez. It was an encouraging start, but there was no rhythm to the Cavs' system because he hadn't really been practicing or playing in preseason games.

It sounded strange, but Brown kept insisting that the games, at least early in the season, were going to have to serve as the team's practices because of Bynum. Bynum was highly intelligent and fairly quiet. He kept to himself. When the locker rooms were open to the media prior to games, Bynum generally sat at his locker with a cup of coffee, wearing headphones and an electronic muscle stimulator on his knees. When he did play, Bynum still had pain in his knees, which was discouraging. He admitted he wasn't having any fun and he'd considered retiring before eventually signing with the Cavs.

"It was a thought, it was a serious thought," he said one day in late November while sitting in Temple's gym in Philadelphia following practice. "At the moment, it's tough to enjoy the game because of how limited I am physically. I'm still sort of working through that. I'm a shell of myself on the court right now. I'm struggling mentally. I'm trying."

On the court, his insertion into the offense was just another obstacle in a season full of them. Waiters was wearing thin on his teammates and Brown was struggling to connect with Irving. No matter how many times he encouraged him, no matter how many times he praised him, Brown couldn't get any traction. Irving's agent, Jeff Wechsler, had represented Larry Hughes during Brown's first era in Cleveland. Brown and Hughes clashed badly, culminating in a heated meeting with the pair in Ferry's office when he was the general manager. Brown threatened to bench Hughes for the rest of the season and showed that he had ownership's backing, regardless of Hughes's hefty contract. Shortly after that meeting, Hughes was traded away—less than three years after he signed a five-year deal in Cleveland.

Plenty of people believe the experience with Hughes and Wechsler impacted the relationship between Brown and Irving, but to what extent will never be known. What's clear is a disconnect existed between Irving's advisers and the Cavs. There was tension between Grant and Wechsler and tension between Brown and Wechsler. The Cavs were aware that Irving's father, Drederick, constantly criticized Brown's decisions and his coaching style in the VIP lounge adjacent to the court during home games. Those within Irving's inner circle began hinting early during his third season that he might need to get out of Cleveland. Irving strongly refuted that idea whenever asked and grew frustrated that it became a recurring topic. It's still a sensitive issue for him even today.

"Y'all were some fuckers," Irving says now of the media.

He has always had a contentious relationship with reporters, likely because of what he endured entering the league. There were so many comparisons between him and James since both went to Cleveland as number one picks. Irving had the unfortunate timing of arriving before the ashes of James's departure even cooled, so he was left to answer plenty of questions he'd never expected about LeBron. Add in the rumors that he wanted out and it's easy to see the root of his frustration.

"It was all the attention of what was going to be Cleveland after [LeBron's leaving]," Irving said. "Everyone was jockeying for position. Who was going to have the first story? It started off with me, then we're seeing what goes on with Coach Scott. Everyone wanted to have the first story about who was going to get traded, what Kyrie was feeling today, who was going to do this, then who are we going to draft? Everyone was trying to be that Cleveland breakout story because after 'Bron left, everything else that came out of here was negative. Everyone was jockeying for position on who was going to release this story on this, and I was that guy that took most of those hits."

Irving's correct in that most of the stories were negative. Of course, there isn't much positive to write about a team that didn't spend money in free agency and compiled the worst cumulative record during the four years James was in Miami. Even though there was a long game in play, it was often difficult for most to see.

"It was something I had to get used to," Irving says now. "It's what has helped me grow in a lot of ways and helped me understand what goes on in this NBA world. It's ridiculously political, it comes with a lot of extra attention, sometimes unwarranted. But hey, you guys have a job, too, as well as we do. You've just got to leave it there and understand that if you believe in yourself as much as you say you do, then everyone else's opinion doesn't really matter. This life outside of basketball, what's supposed to matter to me in terms of what the media puts out, what's important and what I go home and think about, it's not realistic. It's not real. Everyone plays the guessing game, everyone has this particular person who's the source. Everyone has this story to put out and that's not my life. I don't live by those terms. I don't live by what goes in the newspaper. It's not real for me."

As for Brown, Irving later said he was trying to teach him, then just a kid, how to lead a franchise.

"Was I ready for that? Probably not," Irving says now. "There wasn't one time where Coach Brown wasn't trying to elevate me into being in that position. Mentally, I didn't know how. It was an overload. I was trying to play basketball, I still had individual goals, I still had things I wanted to do, and ultimately being the leader, you have to give a part of yourself up for the greater good of the team. That's all he was trying to get me to realize. Playing harder defensively, knowing everyone's plays, knowing where everyone is offensively, and understanding spots. Just understanding what's going on and everything that goes on with the team. I had to be in control of that."

Irving was excited for his third season. In the days before Scott was fired, he referenced players like Chris Paul, Kevin Durant, and, yes, LeBron—guys who took a leap their third season and whose teams exploded around them. James averaged 31.4 points during his third season, still his career high, and the Cavs won fifty games, reached the playoffs, and even won their first-round series. That also happened to be Brown's first year as coach. Similarly, Durant led the league in scoring during his third season (30.1 points per game), and the Thunder won fifty games and advanced to the playoffs for the first time. It was the same story with Paul, who led the league in assists (11.6 per game) and steals (2.7) per game while averaging 22.8 points and guiding the Hornets to fifty-six wins and the second round of the playoffs. Irving was expecting the same kind of leap: a career year in terms of numbers, a winning record for the first time, and a return trip to the playoffs. But it didn't work out that way. While he was elected a starter to the All-Star game for the first time, his scoring was down and his shooting percentage was worse.

More importantly, the Cavs weren't exploding; they were imploding. They struggled terribly to start the season, ending November just 5-12. They lost six straight to close December and slumped to 10-21 entering January. They were yet again outside the playoff picture trying to dig their way up, and by January they were doing so without Bynum. He and Brown had clashed at times during their days together with the Lakers, and some of those problems carried over to Cleveland. Brown kicked him out of practice one day in late December when Bynum kept shooting the ball whenever he touched it, regardless of where he was on the floor. It wasn't just that one incident; it just happened to be the final incident. By the end, the Cavs were convinced that the rumors were true and that Bynum didn't particularly enjoy playing basketball. He was just a monster of a man, he was a good player, and basketball had made him rich, so he played. But his heart wasn't in it. He was suspended for the incident in late December and told basically to stay away from the team. As the team previously feared going in, the experiment had failed.

"We've got fourteen guys in that locker room who are very focused and determined and ready to take on any challenge that's in front of them," Brown said the day Bynum was suspended. "They're great guys, they're focused guys, and they know how to play the game the right way, and that's what I'm focused on, just helping those guys win."

The Cavs began shopping Bynum immediately, eventually trading him ten days later, prior to the deadline when his full $12 million contract became guaranteed. The Cavs dealt him and the first-round pick they received from the Kings in the Hickson deal to Chicago for Luol Deng. The Bulls waived Bynum immediately, wanting only his unique contract to get them out of the luxury tax. The Cavs violated their own rule not to trade future picks, but the pick from the Kings had heavy protections on it, and it was unclear at the time if it would ever vest into the first-round pick they hoped it would be when they acquired it.

Deng was in the final year of his contract, but the Cavs were hopeful they'd found a piece who could stabilize the locker room, bring veteran leadership, and reinforce Brown's defense-first message. His agent was Herb Rudoy, who also represented Zydrunas Ilgauskas, one of Grant's close friends. Rudoy and Grant had a good relationship and Grant envisioned Deng as a piece that could play long-term in Cleveland next to James if they could persuade him to return. It would take some cap machinations, but it was all doable.

As for how it pertained to the 2013–14 season, it was a Hail Mary. The Cavs were 11-23 at the time in the pitiful Eastern Conference and three games out of the final playoff spot, but they needed to climb over five other teams to get there. More alarming, they were only three and a half games ahead of the league's worst record. Pressure was mounting on Grant. His job was on the line and the prospect of James's returning seemed to be fading away.

Ultimately, Deng wasn't enough to save anything. He came from a strict culture in Chicago under Tom Thibodeau and quickly realized how chaotic things were in Cleveland. The Cavs lost an embarrassing road game at Sacramento, 124–80, in his second game with the team and the season slowly circled the drain. Teammates complained about Waiters and Irving, the two young stars just trying to find their way. Video clips of Irving ignoring his teammates quickly went viral. Irving was constantly dribbling through three defenders to shoot while

Waiters stood on the perimeter waving his hands for the ball. "He'll give you the ball one time," one Cavs player said of Irving. "And if you miss, you won't see it again." Waiters, meanwhile, "doesn't think anything is his fault," another player said, while Irving was "acting like he doesn't care."

After a dismal home loss to New Orleans near the end of January dropped them to 16-29, Brown said the team's "competitive spirit [was] nonexistent." It was all enough to make Grant finally face the media—something he loathed doing. Grant typically only formally addressed reporters on media day, on draft day, and if they made a trade. But with the Dumpster officially on fire, Grant was forced to answer for a season that was falling woefully short of expectations. It was ultimately his last press conference.

"The lack of effort is just not acceptable," he said. "It's not who we are and who we want to be. It's got to be addressed head-on. There's no excuses for that, but we've seen our guys compete and execute consistently and that's really what we've got to do a better job of."

His speech had little impact. The Cavs were embarrassed and dismantled at Madison Square Garden on national television the next night, 117–86. After the game, Irving had to answer another round of questions about his future since ESPN draft guru Chad Ford had reported earlier in the day that Irving was privately telling people he wanted out of Cleveland.

"I'm still in my rookie contract and I'm happy to be here," Irving said after the loss to the Knicks, but he wouldn't say whether he'd accept the contract extension waiting for him after the season. "It's still too early to say. I'm still trying to get through this season. Everybody is trying to antagonize this team and put it on me. I'm here for my teammates, I'm here for Coach Brown and the coaching staff, and I'm going to play my heart out every single night for the Cleveland Cavaliers."

The timing of Ford's report was curious. People within the Cavs believed he waited until the team was in New York—the world's media capital—as payback for Grant not telling him who the Cavs were taking number one in the draft the year before. Ford maintained throughout each of his seven mock drafts the Cavs would take Noel, but they had actually eliminated him as a candidate for the top pick early on in their process. It was the first time Ford had ever missed on the number one pick in his final mock draft and people within the Cavs wondered if this was his way of getting even.

By the time the Lakers arrived in Cleveland on February 5, 2014, the pressure within the organization was enough to make the Q's roof rumble. The Lakers were struggling through their own hellish season and brought just eight healthy bodies to the game. Didn't matter. They were still embarrassing the Cavs by twenty-one at halftime and twenty-eight in the third quarter as a stunned home crowd booed the lethargy and ineptness. Then the Lakers' Nick Young hurt his knee and Chris Kaman fouled out.

When Jordan Farmar went to the bench with a calf injury and four minutes left, the Lakers were out of subs as the Cavs rallied to close within ten. But when Robert Sacre fouled out, he was allowed to stay in the game because, well, there was no one left. In a season of Cleveland absurdity, this vaulted to the top of the list. The Lakers beat the Cavs 119–108 with just four eligible players remaining. Gilbert had seen enough. The embarrassing display, highlighted by Kaman stretched out across five chairs on the Lakers' bench during the strangest game of the season, was Grant's final night as the Cavs' general manager. Gilbert summoned him to the Q and fired him the next morning. David Griffin was named interim general manager.

"We have what we need," Gilbert said right after firing the man who had given him what he needed. "A general manager and a front office does more than just make tactical decisions on draft picks and trades and free-agent signings. At this point after the amount of time the former general manager had, we just felt it was time. We needed a shift in certain cultural aspects and a different environment."

There is a general belief that drafting Bennett ultimately got Grant fired, which is ironic since Grant never wanted him. The free agent acquisitions of Jack, Bynum, and Clark were all disappointments. But that was as much ownership as the front office, losing patience and pushing to add veterans in an effort to make the playoffs. Mistakes were made along the way, but Chris Grant, the architect behind the plan to bring LeBron James back to Cleveland, was now gone, and with the Cavs tumbling further and further out of contention for the final playoff spot in the East, the whole thing seemed to be disintegrating anyway.

But in this theater of the absurd, Grant soon returned to the Q—for at least one memorable, ultimately hugely significant night.

CHAPTER 8

Z

Zydrunas Ilgauskas was a skinny twenty-one-year-old kid from Kaunas, Lithuania, when the Cavs selected him with the twentieth pick in the 1996 draft. Kaunas is located in south-central Lithuania and serves as the nation's second-largest city. Ilgauskas experienced the collapse of the Soviet Union as a teenager and watched Lithuania become the first republic to gain its independence from the crumbling USSR. He grew up loving soccer and volleyball until his massive frame grew to seven foot three and basketball became the obvious career choice. It's also Lithuania's most popular sport. He didn't know a syllable of English when he was suddenly dropped into the fast-paced culture of the NBA life.

He was quickly befriended by Danny Ferry upon arriving in Cleveland. Ferry played ten years in Cleveland before moving on to San Antonio. He eventually returned as the team's general manager when Gilbert purchased the Cavs. During his playing days, Ferry helped acclimate

Ilgauskas to American life and language. Ferry brought Grant to Cleveland as his assistant in 2005 and Grant struck up a friendship with Ilgauskas that remains today.

Ilgauskas missed all of his rookie season because of left foot surgery, and problems with that foot plagued him throughout the early years of his career. He scored sixteen points and grabbed sixteen rebounds in his NBA debut against Hakeem Olajuwon and the Houston Rockets and was ultimately named the MVP of the Rookie Game during All-Star Weekend, which Cleveland coincidentally hosted in 1997. But his foot problems persisted and Ilgauskas was limited to just twenty-nine games over the next three seasons. At only twenty-five years old, his career was in jeopardy. He endured five painful foot surgeries during his first six seasons, the final being a revolutionary procedure that inserted twelve screws into his foot and reshaped its arch. Ilgauskas was one of the first to have such a procedure, which left him with two different-sized shoes because his right foot was now a size bigger than his left.

To the surprise of most everyone, including Ilgauskas, the surgery worked. He enjoyed ten seasons without debilitating foot problems after he returned, eventually leaving Cleveland as the franchise leader in games played, rebounds, offensive rebounds, and blocked shots. He's second in scoring behind only James. Ilgauskas was beloved by Cleveland, be it for his perseverance in coming back from the foot problems, his humble beginnings in Lithuania, or just his generally likable demeanor. He was loyal, hilarious, and a wonderful teammate.

Ilgauskas was in Cleveland for all seven of James's years there. On the surface, the two appeared to be complete opposites with nothing in common, but James adored Z and the feeling was mutual. When the Cavs upset the Pistons to win the East and advance to the finals in 2007, one of the iconic images was James jumping into Ilgauskas's arms. When James left for Miami in 2010, he wanted Z to go with him, and he did. It was an adjustment for everyone.

"It was so hard for me emotionally," Ilgauskas said. "I remember sitting in Miami in the locker room looking at that Heat uniform. I couldn't put it on right away. It probably took me fifteen minutes just to put it on."

Ilgauskas never won that elusive championship. The Heat lost to the Mavericks in the finals during his lone season in Miami, and then he retired. But at the encouragement of Ferry, Ilgauskas remained in the game following retirement. Ferry told him he was going to get bored and encouraged him to try something new, so Ilgauskas rejoined the Cavs as a special assistant to Grant. He spent two years learning the business side and exploring whether he wanted to pursue a career as a front-office executive. In the end, he chose to return to civilian life. But he remained beloved, and two years later, during the 2013–14 season, the franchise decided to retire his number 11 jersey. The team asked Ilgauskas to provide them with a guest list so they could make the proper arrangements and get everyone to Cleveland. The most prominent name on that list? LeBron James.

Obviously, this was going to pose a bit of a problem. The boos had certainly eased since James's initial return game, and the cheers for James inside the Q seemed to swell a little bit every time the Heat returned. But the idea of James's walking back into Quicken Loans Arena as a fan and spectator all seemed a little too surreal. But James's presence that evening was important to Ilgauskas, who said he wasn't sure if his jersey ever would have been retired if James had never played in Cleveland.

"Without LeBron getting drafted here, there's a good chance my jersey's not hanging in those rafters. Who knows? I might get traded or leave myself, just being tired from the losing," Ilgauskas said. "Who knows how the story would've been written? It would've been a totally different chapter if he'd have been drafted by the Nuggets. He was part of the story of why my jersey was hanging there. That's why I wanted him there."

Trying to balance the personal schedules of so many on the guest list was difficult, particularly trying to get Ilgauskas's parents there from Lithuania. Finally, the Cavs and Ilgauskas reached a mutually agreeable date: March 8. To the benefit of everyone involved, the Heat were off that night and James was in Chicago, just a short flight away from Cleveland. Logistically speaking, it was possible to get him to Cleveland and back. The fact the Knicks were in town and the New York media would be there to capture it made the theater aspect all the better. James was delighted to get the invitation and quickly accepted. So three years, seven months, and twenty-seven days after James left town amid burning streets with the Decision, he returned to the Q to celebrate a piece of Cleveland history.

And what a party they threw. The ceremony was so lavish and included so many moving parts that they needed a midweek walk-through to ensure everyone knew their role and places. The Cavs rented a projection system to create a video tribute that stretched across the floor, turning the ninety-four-foot court into a 3-D movie screen. Wayne Embry, the general manager who drafted Ilgauskas, returned with a speech. Gilbert spoke. Ilgauskas's parents attended and his father, a retired bus driver, kissed the Cavs logo at center court after the ceremony.

Everyone affiliated with the night insists it was done that way because Ilgauskas deserved it after so many painful foot operations, so many hours of agonizing rehab, and a sparkling career that ended with 10,616 points and 5,904 rebounds in a Cavs jersey. The fact James was there to witness it and feel it . . . well, no one will dispute that was an enormous side benefit.

"Part of me was kind of hoping it would provide moments where I could reach LeBron," Ilgauskas said. "First and foremost though, I wanted him there as a former teammate and friend. I didn't care if he played another game in Cleveland. That didn't matter to me. It was more about the past than the future. But I did think him coming back, seeing how Cavs fans can be and how they are most of the time, how much passion they have for their players and their city. He was right there on the floor. From what I saw and heard, people had a good time. People were nice to him and he was able to reconnect with old coaches and players. I think that could do nothing but help with the decision to come back."

The Heat were not pleased with the whole idea and sent assistant coach Ron Rothstein to Cleveland with James. Rothstein had been an assistant in Cleveland early in Ilgauskas's career, so both sides were comfortable with Rothstein there to chaperone. James arrived to the game early in the first quarter and was given a private suite. He eventually made his way down to the court and had the opportunity to say hello to old friends and Cavs support staff members he probably hadn't seen in years. The Cavs.com crew even tried filming a spot with James, who was eager to do it, prior to the halftime ceremony. But Cavs media relations guru Tad Carper saw what was happening and shut the whole thing down because it just wasn't a good look given all of the history between the two sides.

Just one month after he was fired, Chris Grant was back inside the Q to enjoy the celebration he had helped create. Grant contemplated staying home, wondering if it would be awkward given all of the factors at play. Ultimately he chose to go support his friend. Ferry and Jim Paxson were there, too, also former general managers fired by Gilbert. They all congregated for a conversation and a laugh just outside the Cavs' locker room.

James's appearance on the court created an added buzz in the arena—particularly when James sat down on the Cavs' bench for the show. Whether it was fate or the devious work of a perfect lineup, James took his seat next to Grant, of all people. Grant had literally spent four years trying to get James back on that bench. For at least one night, he'd accomplished it. The night was an illustration of months—years—that Grant, Forbes, and the Cavs spent repairing a relationship that had been destroyed in a matter of hours one night in July 2010.

And this night, Ilgauskas's night, was a subtle reminder for James: This could all be yours again. The jersey in the rafters, the adulation of an adoring fan base. The immortal legacy. Sure, they cheered loudly for LeBron James in Miami. But Miami wasn't home. No one could ever love him like his home could love him, if only he'd give them that chance again.

James mingled with all of his former teammates both before and after the event. He posed for pictures with Daniel Gibson and Delonte West; he hugged old friends and relived a few cherished memories. The celebration was heartfelt and touching. And when it was over, James climbed onto his charter flight and flew back to meet his team in Chicago, to return to the life he'd chosen for himself nearly four years earlier.

CHAPTER 9

Outside the Box, Other Side of the World

The Cavs had steadfastly prepared for that moment—LeBron sitting back on their bench with fans cheering, thinking, they hoped, about coming back to sit on their bench again. They were about to find out if all the preparation was worth it. The next step in the plan, though, would be under new leadership. Chris Grant had returned to his home in suburban Cleveland, out of work following a season where it all unraveled. David Griffin was now running the Cavs at least temporarily for the rest of the season while Gilbert searched for a permanent replacement.

Griffin is a ginger, short in stature with a little less hair on top than he had when he joined the Cavs as Grant's top assistant two months after LeBron's departure. Like James, Griffin left his hometown team to work elsewhere. He spent seventeen years with the Phoenix Suns after growing up in a lower-middle-class neighborhood in West

Phoenix. He left the organization after a contentious falling-out with Suns owner Robert Sarver and moved to Cleveland, which was still sweeping up the debris from James's ugly exit.

Griffin was a hard worker who loved basketball but never planned on making a career out of it. He majored in international finance at Arizona State and minored in Chinese. He wanted to be part of the westernization of China until he took a job as an intern in the Suns' media relations department two years before graduation. Before advanced stats computer software churned out data like it does today, Griffin was producing the type of stats that made the Suns' front office take notice. He was an advanced stats computer unto himself. A few years after he was hired as an intern, Griffin crossed to the basketball operations side and started over from the bottom cutting up film. It involved watching hours of game tape and cutting up the plays the coaches wanted to see and splicing them together onto one tape. He worked his way into the number two chair in Phoenix before leaving.

Griffin passed on general manager jobs in Memphis and Denver, waiting for the right opportunity. He thought he had found it in Cleveland following Grant's dismissal. "This thing is teed up," he told me the night the Cavs' season ended with a home win against the Nets. Irving was eligible to sign a max extension over the summer, and while the Cavs had internal debates over whether to trade him, ultimately Griffin knew they would offer him the extension. But no one in the organization knew whether Irving would accept it. The relationship was frayed, and if Irving balked at signing the full extension, the Cavs were prepared to begin shopping him.

If negotiations with Irving went smoothly, then they could start swinging big. Yes, James was the number one target if he opted out of his contract in Miami and became a free agent, but there was a stretch when Griffin didn't believe James was actually coming. At least not during the summer of 2014. The Cavs were a mess. They weren't winning enough to remain in playoff contention and Griffin didn't believe James would return to a team that wasn't ready to win.

Even if they swung and missed on James, he still believed there was enough free agent talent to drastically improve the Cavs. He was particularly high on Gordon Hayward, although other free agent options such as Chandler Parsons, Trevor Ariza, and Channing Frye were also available. The mistakes from the previous summer limited their cap space, but there was still optimism. The Cavs were finally ready to get something done in free agency. How much and how high they'd swing depended on James's future, but Griffin wasn't even sure he'd be the one to put it all together.

Griffin met with Brown during that uncomfortable period when he was only the interim GM and Brown's own future was again in doubt.

"If it's you or me, it's going to be you," Griffin said. "You've already made your money. Now I'm going to make mine."

Gilbert took three months after the season to search for Grant's permanent replacement, ultimately settling on the person who was in his own building the whole time. But that wasn't the only change he made. The day Griffin had the "interim" tag removed, Brown was fired as the head coach after just one year. Gilbert may have admitted once already that firing Brown was a mistake, but that didn't stop him from doing it again 384 days later. Gilbert never held a press conference, instead issuing a release with both decisions included.

"This is a very tough business. It pains all of us here that we needed to make the difficult decision of releasing Mike Brown," Gilbert said in a statement. "Mike worked hard over this last season to move our team in the right direction. Although there was some progress from our finish over the few prior seasons, we believe we need to head in a different direction. We wish Mike and his family nothing but the best."

Gilbert offered to meet with Brown after firing him to explain his reasons, but Brown declined. He had been brought to Cleveland to provide structure, improve the defense, and win more games. He'd done that. The Cavs had won nine more games than they had the previous season, they'd improved their defensive field goal percentage from dead last in the NBA to twelfth, and their defensive rating (which measures how many points teams allow per hundred possessions) had jumped from twenty-seventh to seventeenth in Brown's one season in charge. But it wasn't enough to save him.

Griffin began an exhaustive coaching search. Grant and Gilbert had rushed to hire Brown within a week of firing Scott, but this time the Cavs wanted to prove they were taking their time to find the right candidate. In the meantime, Griffin's first duty as full-time general manager was representing the team at the NBA's draft lottery, a job reserved for Dan's son, Nick Gilbert, the last three years. Teams can send anyone they want to represent them during the lottery. Sometimes it's an owner or player or head coach or GM. The Cavs had won the top pick two of the three years that Nick was on the podium. Now it was Griffin's turn.

The Cavs finished the season 33-49—yes, a nine-game improvement over the previous season, but far short of the playoff expectations

Gilbert had placed on the franchise. They missed the eighth seed in the playoffs by a disappointing five games, but the season essentially ended with a bad road loss at Atlanta in early April. The Cavs began the night just two games behind the Hawks and Knicks for the eighth seed but put forth a lousy effort in a lopsided 117–98 beatdown. It dropped them three games behind with five games left and essentially extinguished what flickering playoff hopes they had left.

The loss irritated Luol Deng, the one veteran who understood how to win. Irving and Waiters never grasped how to play together and how to share the ball, two things that aggravated a veteran trying to teach youngsters the right way to play.

"Sometimes you don't want to say stuff like this, but at the same time we have to be honest with each other and know when we're at our best, it doesn't have to be go out and score thirty," said Deng, whose comments were clearly aimed directly at Irving and Waiters. "If it's the flow of the offense, I'm playing well and making shots, I'll go with it. But if I recognize how the game is going, how guys are playing and how they're playing defensively, just move the ball. Move the ball to move the ball."

Deng was in the final year of his contract when Grant acquired him in January 2014. He was a two-time All-Star and the closest thing the Cavs had on the roster to a veteran leader. He had been brought to Cleveland with the understanding he could stay long-term with an extension, but when Grant was fired, that feeling changed on both sides. He departed for good after the season ended, ultimately signing— of all places—with the Miami Heat.

Griffin met with Timberwolves president Flip Saunders two days before the draft lottery. Saunders, a Cleveland native, was back home visiting his dad and carved out time during the trip to have dinner with Griffin. The Timberwolves knew at this point they were going to have to shop Kevin Love during the summer or risk losing him. The Cavs had been interested in Love for years. The feeling, however, was not mutual. Love had expressed no desire to sign an extension if the Cavs traded for him and most everyone in the league assumed Love was headed to Los Angeles when his contract expired. Griffin and Saunders talked about Love in loose terms but certainly nothing was agreed upon at that point.

Griffin entered the lottery armed with Nick Gilbert's trademark bow tie in his pocket and his grandmother's pin on his lapel, which he kept rubbing for good luck throughout the proceedings. Unlike in years past, when the Cavs turned the lottery into their very own traveling concert, this time there was no private jet loaded with Cleveland celebrities. Gilbert didn't even make the trip; he was giving a speech during the lottery. As usual, minority owner Jeff Cohen represented the Cavs in the private room where the drawing was held and Griffin was onstage. That was it. Inexplicably, the Cavs entered ninth and cashed in on a microscopic 1.7 percent chance to win the lottery for an unprecedented third time in four years.

Brett Wilson is a numbers whiz I found while covering the Cavs for the *Akron Beacon Journal*. He graduated from Kent State with a degree in mathematics, and his specialty is probability. He even developed formulas to predict how successful a career a college player will have in the NBA based on his statistics. Wilson is now a software quality assurance tester. I have no idea what that means, but I'm sure it's something smart, because this guy is incredible with numbers. Whenever I need some crazy computation, I find Brett. So when I e-mailed Brett and asked him the odds of the Cavs' winning the lottery three times in four years, this was (part of) his (lengthy) reply.

"Since each lottery has no impact on another they're all independent probabilities, so the probability that [the Cavs] would get 1st in '11, '13, and '14 and not get 1st in '12 is 0.0005 or 0.05%," he wrote. "If you're looking at it solely in terms of LeBron coming back, you might just want to focus on 2011 and 2014. I would argue that what we got out of the 2012 and 2013 drafts didn't make much of a difference in his decision. [The] probability of getting first in both '11 and '14 was 0.0039 or 0.39%."

So basically the Cavs' odds of landing three number one picks in four years was 1 in 2,000—or roughly the same odds that the 18,300 people who applied to be astronauts at NASA faced in 2016. The Cavs, essentially, caught lightning. Griffin knew by winning the lottery, he had enough to go get Love from the Timberwolves because of the value of the number one overall pick.

"I think we're very open-minded," he said after stepping off the stage. "We're going to try to get radically better much quicker. We feel there's a sense of urgency about improving our team as a whole."

Griffin and the front office went to work evaluating talent. Kansas's Andrew Wiggins was the consensus publicly, but the Cavs had other ideas. Griffin believed Wiggins's teammate center Joel Embiid was the best player available, going so far as to call him "a transcendent talent"—the only such player like that in this draft. The Cavs would've happily taken Embiid number one, but there was a problem: Embiid was a mess physically. Foot and back problems prevented the Cavs' medical staff from signing off on him. In fact, they went in the other direction and advised the Cavs to pass on him. He was simply too risky with the top pick.

It was a crushing blow for a team that viewed Embiid as the total package at both ends of the floor. His athleticism and hands were mesmerizing. Had Embiid been healthy, he would've been on the Cavs. Instead, they chose Wiggins over Duke's Jabari Parker. Wiggins was an ultra-athletic wing who was a good defender with a suspect shot. He essentially played the same position as LeBron, but that wasn't Griffin's main concern at the time. Griffin envisioned starting Wiggins at shooting guard alongside Irving and bringing Waiters off the bench in a role that suited him more naturally.

Of course, the reality is they did have the buying power now if James indeed wanted to come home. They now had the trade pieces to acquire Love or another star and surround James with enough talent to win. But trading for Love before getting a commitment from James seemed too risky. Irving, likely, wasn't enough to pique Love's interest, and even his future remained in doubt. Love wanted to play for a team that could contend for a championship. That didn't appear very likely in Cleveland.

Before they settled on whom to choose and what to do with the pick, the coaching search was intensifying. The only problem was that teams that have the worst cumulative record over the previous four seasons—and that fire two coaches in as many years—have a hard time attracting top candidates. Steve Kerr, Griffin's good friend from their time working together in the Suns' front office, declined to meet to discuss the job. UConn men's head coach Kevin Ollie, a former Cavs player and the hottest name among college coaches, also declined. Kentucky's John Calipari and Florida's Billy Donovan passed.

James's free agency was a couple of months away and the Cavs were left to pick their next head coach from a collection of rookie assistants looking for their first job (Adrian Griffin, Tyronn Lue) and guys at the end of their careers looking for another paycheck (Alvin Gentry and Lionel Hollins). Gentry was one of Griffin's three finalists since they'd spent time together with the Suns, but Gilbert overruled him. Griffin preferred Lue, Doc Rivers's rising assistant in Los Angeles. Lue had played eleven years in the NBA, won two championships as a backup point guard, and been surrounded by some of the game's biggest names throughout his career. He was a teammate to both Kobe Bryant and Michael Jordan and he'd been coached by Phil Jackson and Rivers. But he had just turned thirty-seven and had never served as a head coach. Instead, Gilbert went outside the box—six thousand miles from the box, to be precise. The Cavs found their next coach on the other side of the world.

David Blatt was Boston-born and Princeton-educated. He'd spent his adult life playing and coaching overseas, guiding Russia to a bronze medal in the 2012 London Olympics. He'd led Maccabi Tel Aviv to a stunning upset over Real Madrid for a EuroLeague championship in 2014. It was enough to earn him a EuroLeague Coach of the Year award. Blatt was a successful vagabond overseas, rarely staying in one place for more than a few years. He coached in Russia one year and Italy the next. More importantly, he was an NBA unknown, which to Gilbert was more appealing than an NBA retread.

Blatt, a skinny six-footer with a little salt in his mostly pepper hair, convinced himself that he had nothing left to prove in Europe. He'd turned fifty-five in the days after winning the EuroLeague championship in 2014 and he wanted a crack at the NBA. His high school coach, Phil Moresi, cautioned him not to do it. He'd likely have to serve as an assistant coach first, and if he landed on the wrong staff with a trigger-happy owner, Blatt would be out of the league and not have a strong enough name to get another chance. The move was risky. Blatt, however, was undeterred.

Kerr became the head coach of the Warriors after passing on the Cavs job and selected Blatt as his top assistant. The two men shared an agent in Mike Tannenbaum. It was an opportunity for Blatt to ease into NBA culture and learn the league before perhaps one day running his own team. But after the Cavs had rushed into the previous hire in Brown, Griffin wanted to be thorough and present wide-ranging candidates to ownership. With Kerr's blessing, Blatt met with the Cavs and quickly became the coach Gilbert wanted. Blatt bypassed the conventional route of starting as an assistant and zoomed right into the Cavs job. Griffin knew there would be a steep learning curve for Blatt and convinced Gilbert to go get Lue, too, who was the runner-up for the job and Griffin's top choice.

It's unusual for the runner-up to be named associate head coach in any job search, but this was no typical situation. Blatt had no qualified assistants to bring with him. He was relying on the Cavs to supply his coaching staff. That's why a number of assistants were retained from Mike Brown's staff, along with the addition of Lue, who was there to help acclimate Blatt to the NBA and, yes, replace him if necessary.

"David Blatt is going to bring some of the most innovative approaches found in professional basketball anywhere on the globe," Gilbert raved in the team's release announcing the hire. But beneath Gilbert's excitement, there was reason for concern. Blatt was a complete novice to the NBA and before arriving in Cleveland, he was considered supremely arrogant. He lived up to his reputation almost immediately. When he won his first NBA game as a head coach, the players rallied around him and celebrated, presenting him with the game ball for his first victory. Blatt seemed almost offended about the display.

"Not all of you know me that well," Blatt told reporters a few minutes later. "But I've probably won over seven hundred games in my career." Players have far more power in the NBA than they do in Europe, where the coach can be the star. Blatt was slow to grasp that culture from his first day.

"How do you deal with the egos of the players in the NBA? I don't buy that," Blatt said at his introductory press conference. "I've had wonderful discussions with the players from the Cleveland Cavaliers and I find a group of guys that want to be coached, that want to learn, that care about winning. . . . I've coached enough great players to know when guys are happy playing together and seeing that doing it the right way fosters the spirit you need to win, it doesn't make a difference where you're coaching."

Of course, Blatt was referring to a Cavs roster of young players with high ceilings like Irving, Waiters, Tristan Thompson, and rookie Wiggins, the latest number one overall pick the Cavs had drafted. The LeBron factor didn't seem to be part of the consideration at the time, for good or for ill. James was healing from another grueling season that had concluded with an NBA Finals loss to the Spurs five days earlier. Since they had waited this long, there was a thought throughout the NBA that the Cavs wouldn't hire a coach until James chose his next destination. The timing of Blatt's hire, not to mention the choice, shocked most everyone.

"Blatt?" one general manager texted. "That's not going to get it done."

"Get it done" in this case referred to getting James back to Cleveland. Every decision the Cavs made was viewed outside the organization through the LeBron lens. As the summer of 2014 inched closer and closer, agents and executives around the league believed James could return to the Cavs. But now, with his free agency just weeks away, the rest of the league thought their instability and poor season had cost them any chance at getting their king back. Privately, a number of folks within the organization felt the same way.

CHAPTER 10

The Big Three

As 2014 free agency loomed, the final moves were clear. The Cavs, and Griffin, needed to secure Kyrie Irving and use his on-court talents if they had any hope of signing a second star. They still wanted that to be LeBron, but it wasn't clear that was still possible. They needed to prepare for other options while at the same time figuring out how to heal the fractured relationship between Dan Gilbert and James, a task that would be far from easy.

The Irving issue came first. Irving's three years in Cleveland were littered with coaching changes and chemistry issues. His first two head coaches had already been fired and he had problems developing a rhythm with Waiters; the two weren't close at all. He was blamed for being a ball hog, and rival executives thought the losing was getting to him; two separate team executives told me they believed he was pouting on the court. The relationship between Irving's camp and the previous regime was fractured. Jeff Wechsler, Irving's agent, disagreed often with both Brown and Grant. As a result, Griffin didn't know what to expect when free agency began in July 2014. At one point, the Cavs held discussions about whether to build around Irving or trade him, fearing his attitude and defensive lapses would prevent him from evolving into an elite player.

Compounding matters was the fact that Gilbert often regretted the way James had held the organization hostage with his contract. After James left for Miami, Gilbert believed, in hindsight, he should've pushed harder for James to sign an extension prior to his final season in Cleveland. And Gilbert privately believed that if James had refused, he should've traded him. This all seems logical given how it turned out, but the truth is, trading James would've been a public relations disaster, and it would have seemed ludicrous, at the time, to trade the best player in the game.

But the league had learned a great deal from the Cavs' 2010 cautionary tale. Other teams that watched the Cavs unravel feared enduring the same fate. That's why the Nuggets traded away Carmelo Anthony, the Jazz dealt Deron Williams, and the Orlando Magic moved Dwight Howard. All were franchise players, but their teams no longer believed they could re-sign them and wanted to move them while they could still return real value. Gilbert, meanwhile, vowed to never be held hostage by another player or contract.

So when Irving was up for an extension in 2014, no one was quite sure how it would go. The Cavs still held his rights for another year, but if Irving refused to sign the max extension or demanded something shorter, such as a three-year deal, the Cavs would explore trading him.

Even before James, finalizing Irving's fate was their number one priority. That's why Gilbert, Griffin, Blatt, and Lue all met with Irving, his father, and his agent on the first day of free agency. Much to the Cavs' relief, Irving agreed quickly to the max contract, worth $90 million over five years—the most the team could pay him under the league's salary cap rules. The final year was a player option, but Gilbert acquiesced and gave it to him. Griffin didn't spend a lot of time talking to Irving about James because no one knew yet how feasible it was.

"At the time I took over, the most important thing to me was Kyrie has to sign long-term. And building the relationship with Kyrie was really important to me," Griffin said. "That was really what we focused on. When we met with him in free agency, we didn't really talk about LeBron. We talked about the different players we thought we could get involved with, showed them a list of those players. 'Bron probably wasn't even on the list. We went about targeting all of those guys. Kyrie helped us recruit all of them."

Included on that list was Hayward, Utah's restricted free agent. Griffin had long admired Hayward and wanted him on the Cavs, even though it was likely that because he was restricted, the Jazz would match any offer he received and force him to return to Utah. With Irving committed, the Cavs invited Hayward to Cleveland Clinic Courts early in the free agency process with the intent of offering him a max contract. Griffin envisioned Hayward starting at small forward alongside Irving and Wiggins, giving the Cavs a dynamic set of wings (including Waiters) all twenty-four and under. The Cavs had been unable to secure a meeting with James and started to fear waiting around for him while missing out on everyone else, which is what had happened in 2010. And since Griffin had lost hope that James was coming home in 2014, he aggressively pursued Hayward. When James's agent, Rich Paul, found out Hayward was at the Cavs' facilities, he called and told them to be patient and hold off making any decisions. Hayward left Cleveland with no offer in hand.

I had lunch with Gilbert during All-Star Weekend in New Orleans in 2014, less than five months from James's free agency. Gilbert believed then that the Cavs would have a shot at James, even though no one had explicitly told him so. The disappointing end to the season diminished a lot of that hope. But once Paul called and told them to hold off on Hayward, it became apparent the Cavs would at least have a crack at James. They had two main selling points to their pitch: This was home and Gilbert was willing to spend whatever was necessary to win. But there was still one big issue. Even when Grant and Ilgauskas were together in the front office, whenever the topic of James's returning was broached, both men agreed that Gilbert and James would have to at some point bury their differences. That was the biggest hurdle that remained, and the resolution was far from clear.

"When we would have conversations about would he come back or would it be okay, obviously we said he and Dan needed to sit down and talk. They don't need to be best friends, but it's a good business decision for both of them," Ilgauskas said. "Then it was the fans. How would the fans respond? I said stop, the fans will be fine. You'll see a complete one eighty. Don't even worry about the fans. When a player of that caliber wants to come back, you take him back. You make that happen."

The eventual meeting between Gilbert and James was a covert operation few in the Cavs organization even knew was happening. On

Sunday, July 6, a few days after Hayward left Cleveland without a contract, Gilbert flew on his private jet to Miami to meet with James and sort out their differences. A former radio host in Cleveland, Joe Lull, wrote on his Twitter account that Gilbert was flying to Miami to meet with James and it nearly broke the Internet. While Gilbert tried denying the report with his own tweet, Cavs fans located Gilbert's plane on a flight-tracking website and posted to social media its route to Fort Lauderdale.

"We sent Dan down there hoping he'd speak alone to LeBron, but that's not how it went," Griffin said. "They had him outnumbered about five to one. That's wasn't our vision of how it would go. Our hope was, and we requested, we'd sit with him alone."

James had Paul with him as well as other associates. They weren't going to make this easy on Gilbert, not after that scathing letter he'd written on James's way out of town. He'd called him a coward and a narcissist and accused him of quitting on his team. Gilbert apologized for the letter, while James apologized for the way he handled the Decision. The simple reality remains that, as Ilgauskas indicated, Gilbert and James would never be close. But they put enough pieces back together to at least be cordial.

———

The idea of James's returning suddenly began to look promising again. But they had no commitment, and the Cavs needed to take some serious financial, and logistical, risks, even though they were still so unsure of the outcome. Money came first. Part of Gilbert's pitch to

James had referenced the Heat's decision to release Mike Miller prior to the 2013–14 season because owner Micky Arison was unwilling to pay $33 million in luxury taxes. Releasing Miller cut the Heat's tax bill in half, but it also angered James, who lost a good shooter and a piece he needed to win, purely for financial reasons. Gilbert believes money follows; it doesn't lead. That was essentially the Cavs' pitch to James: Come home and we'll spend whatever it takes to win, regardless of luxury taxes. Whatever it takes.

On his way back to the airport, Gilbert held a conference call with his business partners Nate Forbes and Jeff Cohen, and Griffin. It was a matter-of-fact discussion with no real emotion. Neither James nor Paul revealed any clues about whether James was coming home.

"In my view of it now, it was all very boring," Griffin said of the conference call. "Your heart's racing and you hope to God it's good news, but at the end of the day, it was just more box checking. Then at the end of the call, we thought, 'Okay, we need to decide what we want to do next.'"

For Gilbert, the casino owner, the answer was easy. He went all-in.

James left the meeting with Gilbert and flew to Las Vegas for his basketball camp. Gilbert flew home and the Cavs went to work. The Cavs knew James wasn't taking a dollar less than the max to return, so they had to undo the mistakes of the previous summer, which meant clearing Jarrett Jack's salary off their books to have enough cap space to fit him. Jack was a mild disappointment his one year in Cleveland, averaging 9.5 points and 4.1 assists, but he was still a serviceable—albeit overpaid—NBA veteran.

The Nets were interested in Jack and the remaining $12.5 million owed to him, but they had their own bad contract to move. The Celt-ics were called in to facilitate the deal under the NBA's complicated salary cap system, but the Cavs had to pick up the hefty tab: The price was young, promising center Tyler Zeller and a future first-round pick. Zeller wasn't going to the Hall of Fame, but he was a serviceable center with range who would play a long time in the NBA. And the Cavs gave him away for nothing, unsure whether James was really coming home or setting them up for more heartbreak.

"I was very concerned. We made the trade in the dark relative to 'Bron," Griffin said. "We made the trade knowing the only way we get 'Bron is if we have max cap space available. So I had to get to max cap space. Basically it was: We can't be in the game unless I do this, so let's get in the game. But the actual outcome? We didn't know. That's where ownership doesn't get nearly enough credit. They'll take a risk. They'll trust in the process a little bit and they will take a risk. That was a very, very ballsy thing for them to do."

On Wednesday, three days after the secret meeting in Miami with James and Gilbert, James met with Pat Riley in Vegas. Unlike their 2010 meeting in Cleveland, this meeting did not result in a deal.

The Cavs spent Thursday putting the finishing touches on their three-team trade with the Nets and Celtics. After taking a night to sleep on it, James invited *Sports Illustrated*'s Lee Jenkins into his Vegas suite Thursday to collaborate on an essay. Jenkins had written several profiles on James, including a fabulous Sportsman of the Year story in 2012. This time the two spent an hour in close conversation; then Jenkins stitched it all together. After the way it had ended in 2010, after the way James and Gilbert set the organization on fire, there was only one poetic path he could take back to Cleveland: a letter. "In Northeast Ohio, nothing is given. Everything is earned. You work for what you have," James and Jenkins wrote. "I'm ready to accept the challenge. I'm coming home."

With his decision made, James left Vegas and flew to Miami with good friend and now ex-teammate Dwyane Wade. He was in his Miami house Friday when *Sports Illustrated* posted the essay. James spoke briefly with Jenkins, pleased with the day's outcome, while the country shook with the news and Cleveland exploded in jubilation.

I was on United Airlines flight 1174 from Cleveland to Las Vegas to attend Summer League on the morning of July 11. A few Cavs personnel were on my flight and we briefly discussed James's future while boarding. No one had any idea what he was planning or when it would be announced. Our flight was equipped with DirecTV, but I was reading a book when a couple of hours into the flight a man two rows behind me and across the aisle began to repeat, "Oh my God. Oh my God. Oh my God!" Each version grew louder than the last until he was nearly screaming it. People were nervous, turning to look and see why he was making such a commotion. Then he clapped his hands together once and shouted, "*He's coming back!*" I immediately knew what he was talking about and scrambled to activate my seat-back television. By the time the plane landed, my life had changed forever.

The Big Three

Harry Buffalo sports bar is a stiff seven-iron from Quicken Loans Arena. As the man on my flight shouted, *"He's coming back!"* the sleepy lunch crowd at the bar was erupting. Downtown workers flooded in while lines formed instantly down the street at the arena's box office. The Cavs sold out of season ticket packages the same day James announced his return. They probably could've sold out the entire arena for the whole season in a few hours, but they held back some single-game tickets for the general public.

"The night he left with *The Decision,* people in here were running into the streets crying and screaming," Harry Buffalo general manager Caitlin Cassidy said. "When he announced he was coming back, people did not go back to work. They immediately started drinking like it was a holiday. People left work and came in. You couldn't move in here. People were running to the Q screaming with signs. It was really cool."

It felt as if Cleveland had already won a championship. In a sense, it had. The city that had been rejected by so many and neglected for so long was suddenly wanted again.

Griffin was in his office at Cleveland Clinic Courts tying up some last-minute work in free agency. The rest of his staff was already in Las Vegas. He was left behind with only a few lower-level folks, the analytics minds and young guys just breaking into the business. Griffin had the television on in his office when Nate Forbes, one of Gilbert's partners both in business and with the team, called to tell him what was happening. Rich Paul called Gilbert, then Forbes, who quickly called Griffin.

"The king is coming home," Forbes told Griffin just as ESPN was breaking in with the story. Griffin threw himself down on the floor, celebrating on his hands and knees. "It was at once the happiest I had been, and eleven seconds later just this overwhelming sense of, 'Oh my God, now we have to win a championship.' I had no transition. It was literally sheer joy and then sheer panic all at one time."

Ownership threw a celebratory dinner bash that weekend in Las Vegas, but Griffin missed the dinner. His wife, Meredith, landed in time to celebrate. But Griffin flew later in the day and missed everything.

Blatt was holding one of his first Summer League practices in Vegas that Friday morning. He was putting Bennett and Wiggins through drills when a buzz filled the gym. When the greatest player in the game today and one of the five greatest of all time decides to come home, it doesn't take long for word to travel. Griffin called two of his top assistants, Trent Redden and Koby Altman, and told them James was coming back.

As news spread through the gym, Blatt calmly walked over to Tad Carper, the team's vice president of communications, and asked if it was true. Carper said yes. "I kind of feel like I'm jumping from mountaintop to mountaintop," Blatt said.

Shortly after the announcement, James flew to Brazil and watched World Cup soccer with his old-and-now-new-again teammate Anderson Varejao. When he returned, he filmed a movie in New York. He didn't address the media or general public until a rally in early August at InfoCision Stadium, the football home of the University of Akron Zips. Thirty thousand people filled the stadium to welcome LeBron back. Grammy nominee Skylar Grey flew in to sing her hit song "Coming Home." Grey cowrote the song in 2010—the year James departed. It was as if the song had been written with him in mind.

> *I know my kingdom awaits and they've forgiven my mistakes*
> *I'm coming home, I'm coming home*

Grey's chorus echoed throughout the stadium as the sun set and camera flashes spotted the Ohio dusk. James and his family circled the track around the football field as the crowd roared. Finally, he took the stage, held his head in amazement at the scene in front of him, and spoke for twenty minutes. He insisted the basketball aspect was a very small piece in all of this. He was coming back to make a difference in Northeast Ohio. He meant it. Even while he was playing for Miami, James supported his hometown and region by purchasing computers and other equipment for Akron schools. He geared initiatives toward Akron's at-risk youth with a Wheels for Education program (grades three through five) and his I PROMISE network (grades six and up) beginning in 2011, programs he would expand even further after he returned.

"I'm gonna do what makes my city and my state happy," James told the InfoCision Stadium crowd. "That's why I came back. I love you. I'm back."

—

James dropped the mic and walked off the stage as fireworks filled the Akron night sky. The king was back on his throne, but the real fireworks were only beginning. With Irving under contract, James knew he had a perennial All-Star guard to play alongside into his thirties. He had someone to share the load, something he'd never had his first time in Cleveland. Irving had been named All-Star MVP just five months before James's free agency. He held the award on the court in New Orleans, unsure really of what to do with it. Standing behind him, James encouraged him to hoist it high over his head.

"Kyrie is special. It's just that simple. He's a very special basketball player, very smart basketball player," James said during All-Star Weekend. "His ability to shoot the ball, get into the lane, make shots around the rim, he has a total package. And I've always known that. I've always witnessed that, ever since he was in high school. And I'm extremely happy for him."

James likely never would've returned if Irving hadn't agreed to that contract extension at the start of free agency. But he still needed another piece. The NBA is a star-driven league. James had played alongside two stars in Miami and with Irving now under contract, he had the chance to duplicate it because everyone knew the Timberwolves were getting ready to shop Kevin Love.

Love had a reputation as a loner. He's a homebody who often prefers a night on the couch binging on Netflix instead of a night on the town.

He has always been more comfortable walking to his own beat in life. None of that mattered to James, who was enamored with Love's game while the two were teammates at the 2012 London Olympics. They didn't know each other well, but James told Love that he would be the reason the Americans won gold. "He always thought I was blowing smoke," James said.

Love agrees. He wasn't sure how to read James in London. "I would just kind of brush it off and shake it off," Love said. "I was standoffish because I didn't know him well."

When the two were reunited six months later at All-Star Weekend in Houston, James sought out Love to again tell him how much he liked his game. That's when Love knew he was serious. And it came at the right time, because Love wasn't feeling very appreciated in Minnesota. Former Timberwolves general manager David Kahn had previously refused to give Love the five-year max contract extension he and the rest of the league felt he deserved, instead offering four years and the opportunity for Love to be a free agent a year early, in the summer of 2015. Love blasted ownership and management in a December 2012 Yahoo Sports story, just four months after the London games and two months before James and Love saw each other again at Michael Jordan's fiftieth birthday party in Houston.

"I don't know who labels people stars, but even [Timberwolves owner] Glen Taylor said: I don't think Kevin Love is a star, because he hasn't led us to the playoffs," Love was quoted as saying in the scathing piece. "I mean, it's not like I had much support out there. That's a tough pill to swallow."

Love was furious when the story was published, and it changed his relationship with the media for years. He felt betrayed by the piece. The league's collective bargaining agreement forces players to be made available daily to reporters, but all of Love's answers turned into canned clichés that lacked any depth. Still, Love concedes today that the contract offer insulted him.

"I wanted to be locked in for five years. I didn't get it. I got a little upset," he said. "I thought I'd be the franchise tag guy; I wanted to be the face of that."

Kahn was fired at the end of the 2012–13 season and replaced by Flip Saunders, who was respected and adored by many—including Love. But Love was already halfway out the door. He played one more season in Minnesota before making it clear that he wouldn't sign an extension and would explore free agency in 2015. Saunders had a choice: He could trade Love during the summer of 2014 or risk his three-time All-Star walking away and getting little or nothing in return, just as the Cavs did when James walked.

The Warriors explored trading Klay Thompson for Love, which was ironic since Thompson and Love were childhood friends who played on the same Little League team. But the Warriors coaches pleaded with management not to make the deal, believing Thompson fit better with their style and that they were close to a championship. When the Warriors refused to trade away Thompson, it left the Cavs as the front-runners—provided they included Wiggins, the top overall pick from 2014. The Timberwolves weren't interested in Dion Waiters or Tristan Thompson or any other package the Cavs tried assembling. It had to be Wiggins. The Cavs relented, believing Love was finally open to signing long-term in Cleveland because of how aggressively James pursued him.

The Big Three

When James returned to Cleveland, one of his first calls the day his essay posted on *Sports Illustrated*'s website was to Love, who was driving to the gym and pulled off on the side of the road to take James's call. The two spoke for no more than fifteen minutes. Suddenly, all of the seeds James had planted the last two years with him began to bloom. James praised his game during the Olympics and again during Jordan's birthday party. Now James was showing Love how much he meant it all. James knew Love's situation and said he wanted him in Cleveland. Love agreed on the spot. Now it was a matter of getting him there. Cavs officials privately insisted for weeks that they wouldn't trade Wiggins, the über-athletic forward from Kansas who was a long, tenacious defender. But they ultimately relented, sending Wiggins, the disappointing Bennett, and a first-round pick to Minnesota in exchange for Love. Instantly, he joined Irving to give James and the Cavs another prominent Big Three, just as he'd had in Miami with Dwyane Wade and Chris Bosh. Yet for all their similarities (three superstars joining together), there were stark differences as well. James and Wade were close friends when he went to Miami; he had little connection to either Irving or Love. Also, Bosh, James, and Wade were all in the prime of their careers. While James was still in his prime, he wasn't as explosive as he had been in 2010 and Irving was still a few years away from entering his prime. In the span of just a few weeks, the Cavaliers went from bottom-feeders to NBA contenders. It was a triumphant moment, but the Cavs couldn't rest for long. Figuring out how to make all the pieces fit became more difficult than anyone imagined.

CHAPTER 11

The Modern NBA

The modernization of today's NBA began around the new millennium in the waterfront town of Treviso, Italy, where the Botteniga River meets the Sile. That's where Mike D'Antoni was spending his second tour as head coach at Benetton Basket when Phoenix Suns owner Jerry Colangelo flew to Italy to meet with him. Colangelo's son, Bryan, was general manager of the Suns and wanted to bring D'Antoni on as an assistant coach. The elder Colangelo flew with his wife to meet D'Antoni and his wife.

D'Antoni was doing things a little differently in Europe and Colangelo wanted to see for himself. D'Antoni taught his players to push the pace and play fast in a league where, Colangelo believed, that was even more difficult to do than in America. But D'Antoni had proved successful at it. He'd guided Benetton to a 28-8 record in the Italian League and won a championship. He'd also advanced to the 2002 EuroLeague Final Four.

D'Antoni had previously served as the head coach at Benetton for a few years in the mid-1990s, leaving in 1997 for a front-office role with the Denver Nuggets. He was handed the head coaching job for one year in Denver, then promptly fired after going 14-36 during the lockout-shortened 1998–99 season. That was at a time when the Nuggets were burning through a new head coach every year; D'Antoni just happened to be the latest casualty. He bounced around the NBA as a scout and an assistant coach for a couple more years before heading back to Treviso, where Colangelo went looking for him in 2002.

"We felt he was a thinker, he was cerebral, he truly believed in how the game should be played," Colangelo said. "But you have to start somewhere and we started him as an assistant."

Colangelo agreed with his son's recommendation to bring D'Antoni onto head coach Frank Johnson's staff. Johnson was a former reserve guard with the Suns who had the "interim" tag removed after the 2001–02 season. He replaced Scott Skiles during the season and the Suns failed to make the playoffs for the first time in fourteen years. Still, Johnson was handed a three-year contract despite going 11-20 as the interim coach. He was charged with rebuilding the Suns around Stephon Marbury, Shawn Marion, and Joe Johnson. At twenty-five, Marbury was the oldest of the young nucleus.

The Suns indeed returned to the playoffs during Johnson's first full season, but they were quickly eliminated in the first round. He was fired following an 8-13 start to the 2003–04 season and replaced by D'Antoni.

"There's been something amiss all year, in my opinion," Jerry Colangelo said at the time of the firing. "The more I saw on the floor, the more I disliked what I saw as it related to body language, communication or lack of same."

David Griffin was a young executive still working his way up within the Suns organization at the time. He was paying close attention to the way Colangelo structured the franchise, building a family atmosphere of peace, joy, and love. It's the way Griffin envisioned constructing his own teams one day. The pace and space D'Antoni brought, however, were something that no one outside of the Colangelos could've predicted, and it made a huge impression right away.

"It should be exciting the first couple of nights," D'Antoni said at his introductory news conference. "Balls should be flying around. We'll try not to hurt anybody. But hopefully it will make it exciting, anyway."

D'Antoni may not have realized it, but he was starting a revolution in Phoenix. His frenetic style was aimed at pushing the ball on offense so quickly that it would force the opponent to play fast as well. The goal was to get off a shot within the first seven seconds of each possession. Defense was never prioritized; the idea was simply to run teams to exhaustion.

"Offensively we wanted to just wear teams down to where they just didn't have enough in the tank to beat you offensively," said Cavs forward James Jones, who played on a couple of those Suns teams under D'Antoni. "That allowed you defensively to just suppress their numbers. It was all about wearing them down, wearing them down, wearing them down."

And it worked. The Suns won at least fifty-four games in each of D'Antoni's four full seasons and twice won more than sixty. They led the league in scoring three of the four years.

"We knew exactly what the philosophy was, so there wasn't any requirement in terms of ownership, management, and coach to buy in. It was really getting the players on your roster and future players to buy into that philosophy," Colangelo said. "We had certain personnel that made it all happen. Mike had the personnel where this was going to work. That's why it was so successful. It's one thing to say you want to play quick, fast, and push the ball. But if you don't have the personnel to do it, you're killing yourself."

But for all their success, the Suns never won a championship with D'Antoni—they never even played for one. Their best finishes were consecutive appearances in the Western Conference finals, where they lost to the Spurs in five games in 2005 and to the Mavericks in six games in 2006. D'Antoni was fired in 2008 after the Suns won fifty-five games but lost in the first round to the Spurs—the same team that eliminated the Suns from the postseason in three of D'Antoni's four years in charge. At the time, D'Antoni's frenetic style of pace and space and shooting three-pointers was dismissed as a gimmick. Championship teams were built on defensive principles, not the NBA's version of the NFL's run and shoot. But over the next decade, it became the dominant style. In 2017 the NBA is obsessed with pace and space, three-pointers, and layups.

The movement toward pace and space stemmed from a transition toward analytical processes that had been building for quite a few years. It seemed to escalate around 2013 with the introduction of player-tracking cameras in all twenty-nine NBA arenas. Suddenly, every motion on the court was recorded and dissected. While advanced stats such as pace, offensive and defensive rating, and PER (player efficiency rating) had been around for a few years already, now there was even more data to churn through and examine. Some of the league's new-age GMs began to look at the game differently: Why take a midrange jump shot when that is worth the same as a layup? If it's going to be a jump shot, make it a three-pointer. Otherwise get as close to the rim as possible to increase the likelihood of the shot going in. The advanced metrics fell right in line with Griffin, who made his mark in Phoenix initially by poring over statistics and devising his own brand of analytics. It's how he caught the eye of Colangelo and others within the organization after starting out as a media relations intern.

"He was just a young whippersnapper joining the organization. He was wide-eyed. He had arrived being a local kid having a dream and aspiration. He was living his dream," Colangelo said. "The thing that impressed me was he was really a hard worker, very focused, very energetic. Just wanted to be successful. So he was very aggressive in that sense. I think in this business, you need to be."

Griffin learned plenty from the Suns, but he departed the organization in 2010 for a reason. He is not close with D'Antoni, and his relationship with Suns owner Robert Sarver, who bought the team in 2004, remains strained. But Griffin took plenty of lessons from Phoenix, which Colangelo noticed him applying to the Cavs almost immediately.

"I would say just that what he's done, certainly I believe was a reflection of his experience growing up with our organization. And he has said that to me," Colangelo said. "Knowing how David came up, his breeding if you will, in terms of our culture in Phoenix—we had a very, very strong culture. It's hard to pinpoint, but I'm referring to the selection of players, trading for players, signing free agents, and then the things he said to back those things up. It was a little bit of déjà vu in the sense that he may not have been making the calls in Phoenix when he was here, but that's where he got the base. And he's done a terrific job on his own."

Off the floor, Griffin went to work trying to change the Cavs' culture. He muted Gilbert, who stopped doing interviews almost entirely. He prioritized mending the relationship between Irving, Wechsler, and Cavs management. And he began trying to forge a relationship with James after he returned to Cleveland. Griffin had enjoyed the peace, joy, and love culture Colangelo instilled in Phoenix and he did his best to try to replicate it at times in Cleveland—even though that dynamic hasn't always been successful.

"Every team is different. Every group of players calls for a different way to play, depending on your talent. I'm talking about culture and philosophy. That has nothing to do with style of play," Colangelo said. "The culture and putting pieces together and having the philosophy of how you complement your stars. Phoenix was not blessed with a LeBron James. How many teams have had a LeBron? It's totally different with him. Obviously you have to change your philosophy to some degree, but you don't discard your parameters that you've had for years and just say, 'I'm going to do it a new way.' Normally we're creatures of habit. If you believe in something, you're going to stick with it."

Colangelo is a hero in the Valley of the Sun. He rescued the Suns by purchasing the franchise in the 1980s and resurrecting them to thirteen consecutive playoff appearances. He brought baseball to Phoenix and delivered a World Series championship in 2001, which remains the region's lone professional sports championship. He went on to repair USA Basketball after it bottomed out with a bronze medal in

Athens in 2004. One of the first items Colangelo fixed within Team USA is one of the same areas he emphasized in all of his businesses: culture. Build a winning culture and maintain it. It's not so easy to do.

"I think the word is *respect*. I think you have to get the respect of players, and a coach certainly has to have that with his players. In some cases, management can do exactly the same, too. I think we had that in Phoenix. So it starts there," Colangelo said. "Then you agree, usually management and coach agree on how you're going to play and then you have a game plan and stick to it. In the meantime, you create this culture where they feel you really do have their best interest at stake and it's not all about X's and O's and wins and losses. You have to be able to withstand a lot of adversity in the NBA because quite often, plans go astray. What carries you through difficult times is a strong culture."

Yet as Griffin went to work restructuring the Cavs, what no one could've predicted was the quiet empire being erected in the West. The Golden State Warriors' rise to prominence wasn't as loud and dramatic as Cleveland's after James's return, but it was equally as unexpected and impactful. And it seemed to be built on many of the same offensive principles that D'Antoni had applied to the Suns a decade earlier.

Bob Myers was plucked from a successful career as an agent at Wasserman Media Group to work in the Warriors' front office in 2011. Forbes estimates that Myers negotiated more than $575 million in player contracts during his career as an agent, but he left Arn Tellem, at the time one of the most powerful agents in the NBA, to start as the assistant general manager for the Warriors. Myers is well liked around the league. He has the reputation of being humble, almost to a fault. He joined the Warriors following the 2010–11 season when they went 36-46 and finished an anonymous twelfth in the West. He ascended to the top job at Golden State a year later. Much like with Griffin and the Suns, Myers grew up a Warriors fan in the Bay Area. His first NBA game was a Warriors game when he was just a boy.

"This is a great day for me, but what will be a better day is when we get this team to a place when we're playing beyond the regular season and competing for a championship. That's when I'll really be excited," Myers said at his introductory news conference in 2012. "I'm not going to promise anything, but there's a quote I saw that says, 'You cannot ensure success, but you can deserve it.' We're going to work with our staff to deserve to be successful and not stop until we get there."

Myers is a hybrid of the old-school and new-age general manager in the NBA. There was a time when most NBA general managers were former players who retired their way into a front office. And while Myers did play the game at a high level, advancing from walk-on at UCLA to scholarship player to 1995 national champion, he never had much of a chance at a future as an NBA player.

That makes him similar to Griffin, who loved the game growing up but never had much of a chance to play it professionally. They are part of a new wave of analytical general managers taking over the league. Guys such as Daryl Morey, who earned an MBA from MIT and never really played the game, rose to the top of the Houston Rockets. Rich Cho was an engineer, then a lawyer, and then an NBA cap specialist who knew how to construct a roster using algorithms and cost efficiency. In other words, he was the closest thing the NBA had to a Billy Beane / *Moneyball* model. Now he's the general manager of the Charlotte Hornets. The brains, the highly educated, are taking over the sport, just as the Suns-style offense has.

Myers tries to connect with his players and build the same type of culture Griffin was striving to find in Cleveland and Colangelo successfully built in Phoenix. It's the same culture that has made the San Antonio Spurs the NBA's gold standard for decades. After they have fame and riches, Myers has a simple question for his players: What do you want?

"What do you think it takes to win a championship? Because you only get so many years to do it. It's your life. After you're done playing, you can't play anymore. That's it," Myers said during a Sloan Sports Analytics Conference panel in 2017 in Boston. "You have ten years, you have fifteen, twelve. And if you're a superstar, the pressure now to win a championship is tremendous. The emphasis we put on a championship is insane to me. How we value it or devalue it if you don't have one. So these players, these superstars, are under tremendous pressure to check that box. If they're the right-minded type of people, which superstars usually are, they can accept that challenge."

Myers said it isn't so much loving to win but despising to lose.

"If I could give you a test to measure how competitive you are, that's invaluable," Myers said. "It's not liking to win. It's hating to lose. When you're competing, when you are in an intense moment of competition, the thing that drives you to the degrees and depths you don't know you have, what you're trying to do is avoid that feeling of losing. You're not trying to feel the joy of winning. What you're trying to do is, 'I cannot stand what it's like to lose so much that I'm going to dig down and do every single thing possible to avoid that.' You don't win without people like that. That's what drives you to win. 'I cannot picture myself after losing this game, this series, this competition because I know what that feels like and I have to avoid it.' It's not celebrating winning. No, we avoided losing. That's what we did. That's a common thread in successful people. I don't know that it makes the best dinner partners."

That's what Myers strives to find in all his players. He went to work immediately on the Warriors' draft board in 2012, his first draft, looking for competitive winners, and hit home runs with each of his three picks. His best pick, in fact, was his last. Myers scooped up Harrison Barnes with the seventh pick after the Cavs passed on him at number four. He selected center Festus Ezeli with the final pick in the first round and selected undersized power forward Draymond Green with the thirty-fifth overall pick in the second round. Spartans coach Tom Izzo, who nearly took the Cavs job the summer James departed, kept telling Green the Warriors were showing the most interest in him and thought he could wind up at Golden State. The Big Ten Player of the Year his senior year and Michigan State's all-time leading rebounder slid all the way out of the first round.

"I think I'm a little more athletic than I get credit for," Green said at his introductory news conference. "But that's not what I'm going to hang my hat on. I play hard, I'm going to play tough, I'm going to rebound and do those things. I think I'm a better defender than I get credit for as well. That's something I have to continue to prove. If you're going to play defense and you're going to rebound, you're going to find a way onto the court somehow. Defense and rebounding is always going to help you win games, so that's the thing I want to do."

Green ultimately proved to be the steal of the draft and has blossomed into one of the top defenders in the NBA. His fiery temper and tenacity have become trademarks of powerful Warriors teams, although no one could've predicted it at the time. Green and Barnes quickly became starters who complemented a backcourt of Klay Thompson and Steph Curry, two of the league's best shooters. Add in the trades that brought Andrew Bogut, David Lee, and Andre Iguodala and suddenly the Warriors were replicating much of how the Suns played under D'Antoni. There was, however, one stark difference: The Warriors were defending, too.

The frenetic pace, the quick shots, the propensity to take and make threes, however, all looked eerily similar to the style Griffin grew up under in Phoenix. By the 2013–14 season, the Warriors led the league in scoring (110 points per game) while ranking second in three-pointers and pace, which calculates how many possessions a team has per game. The only team that generated more possessions than the Warriors was the Brooklyn Nets.

But much like the Suns the decade before, the Warriors weren't winning, either. They hadn't advanced beyond the second round of the playoffs since 1976, which just happened to be the year after their last championship. It was an exciting brand of basketball and it certainly generated interest, but no one was sure it could generate a champion. After the Warriors were eliminated by the Clippers in the first round in 2014, the team fired Mark Jackson as head coach despite a 98-66 record the previous two years. Despite some success, the relationship between Jackson and ownership became untenable.

Myers quickly zeroed in on Steve Kerr as his choice, stealing him away from Phil Jackson and the New York Knicks. Kerr had presided over Griffin in Phoenix's front office. He'd won championships as a player and he worked as a television analyst. Kerr had the perfect demeanor to lead a team of young stars to prosperity—and it was all happening just as James was returning home.

"He blew our socks off," Warriors owner Joe Lacob said of Kerr. "Steve Kerr and Bob Myers together is my dream team. That is a dream team."

Lacob's dream soon became a nightmare for the rest of the NBA, and particularly the Cavs. James captured the league's full attention with his return home. But no one predicted the Warriors' empire rising out of the Bay Area.

CHAPTER 12

Homecoming King

Rebuilding in the NBA typically is a slow, methodical process that takes years to evolve. The Cavs did it in one summer. There was enormous pressure to get the pieces to work together, ideally immediately. And then there was the LeBron-related pressure. The pressure to coach him, the pressure to surround him with the right pieces. And from the minute James returned, Griffin felt the pressure to win.

James's first home game back inside Quicken Loans Arena was on October 30, 2014, against the New York Knicks. Sure, there were preseason games before it, but this was the one that mattered. This was the first time he'd appeared at the Q in a Cavs jersey for a real game since that horrific night in 2010 when he was booed off the floor following a loss against Boston. And he understood the enormity the morning of the game.

"All of us shouldn't take this moment for granted," James said. "This is probably one of the biggest sporting events that is up there, ever."

Quite a statement, but quite a player. As James jerseys went up in flames four years earlier, as fans booed and hissed him during the years he wore Miami's red and black, this moment had never seemed possible.

Kyrie Irving was introduced first, followed by Dion Waiters and Anderson Varejao. An upbeat instrumental version of Skylar Grey's "Coming Home" played in the background as the crowd roared in the darkened bowl. Kevin Love was introduced next before the music was cut and the arena went eerily quiet, anticipating what was to come. In-game arena host Ahmaad Crump began to growl, "From St. Vincent–St. Mary High School . . . ," as James stood up from his seat, arched his neck and back, and closed his eyes. The crowd roared as their prodigal son took his rightful place on the floor.

The game was far less dramatic than the buildup. James shot just five of fifteen and committed eight turnovers. He scored seventeen points, grabbed five rebounds, and passed for four assists in the 95–90 loss that marked David Blatt's NBA debut. It was the capstone to an exhausting week for James, whose daughter, Zhuri, was born eight days prior to the opener.

"It was a huge night," James said. "I'm glad it was great but I'm also glad it's over. Now we can play regular basketball."

Just like that, another clock was ticking. While Danny Ferry felt James's contract clock always ticking during his first tour in Cleveland, speeding closer and closer to 2010 and free agency, this time, it was his body clock ticking. He had already played eleven years and forty thousand minutes between the regular season and postseason. It was fair to assume James could continue playing at his elite level for about another four seasons before he might start to decline.

"The pressure comes from the fact that I love him, I want what's best for him. I want to see him live the dream he's trying to live out and this is his hometown," Griffin said. "And when you put yourself in that position, you think about the six-year-old version of you. The six-year-old version of me, watching the Suns lose in triple overtime to Boston [in the 1976 NBA Finals]. If I had it in my power to do what he does, and deliver that to them, it'd be the most important thing in my life. So we are part of the most important thing in the life of the most important athlete in America at the given time. He's not the most important basketball player, he's the most important athlete on the planet. We are literally working with Babe Ruth every day. So the responsibility you feel is one hundred years from now, when his story gets written, we were there. We have to give him what the story needs."

And when James first returned, the Cavs needed plenty. They needed shooting, more depth, and a rim protector. Throughout the entire summer of 2014, Griffin didn't really believe James was coming back. He thought all the losing from the last four years and the organization's failure to make a drastic step toward improvement had cost them that chance. There is a plethora of things he would've done differently had he known for sure James was returning. Griffin had believed the most realistic scenario was that James would return to Miami on a one-year deal with a player option for a second year and give the Cavs one more year to get their house in order before seriously contemplating a return in 2015.

While the Cavs finished the 2013–14 season at 17-16 with Griffin as interim GM, they still finished sixteen games below .500 and missed the playoffs in the pitiful East by five games. They were the worst team in the league the four years James was gone—mostly by design—and nobody thought James had any interest in a rebuilding project. James was all about rings and trophies, about chasing down his idol, Michael Jordan, and his six championships. James won only two titles in Miami. He had a long way to go, and by all accounts, so did the Cavs.

"We weren't ready for LeBron when he showed up," Griffin said. "You don't go four years of just horseshit basketball, flip a switch, and become champions. There were going to be growing pains. There were going to be issues."

This, too, was part of the plan. As the Cavs were collecting draft picks and trade assets, Grant always knew some of the personnel wouldn't fit if James indeed returned. That didn't bother him, though, because the pieces that didn't fit would still be valuable commodities that could be moved for pieces that made more sense. And changes certainly were going to have to be made now; Griffin was convinced the Cavs' pieces didn't fit even before James returned. Now it was a matter of figuring out what worked and what didn't. That became clear almost immediately. There were too many dribblers and not enough quality shooters.

In two years together, Irving and Waiters could never find enough oxygen to coexist and thrive. Now they were bringing in the most dominant player in the game. They tried making Waiters into a catch-and-shoot player, but Waiters resisted. "That's not my game," he said. "I can do it, but you know what I'm effective at: pick-and-roll and things like that."

They showed him the numbers from the previous year, when James was still in Miami. Waiters shot an excellent 42 percent on catch-and-shoot three-pointers (72 for 173), which is as basic as it sounds—a shooter stands and waits for the ball, then shoots without dribbling. The number of statistics available to teams, fans, and media now is overwhelming. A

Portland player, for example, has led the league in distance covered on a court every year since the numbers became available for the 2013–14 season. For instance, Nic Batum ran more than 216 miles during games that season, the most ever recorded by the league's data-tracking software. Damian Lillard led the league the following season and C. J. McCollum did during the 2015–16 season. Each player was above 200 miles in distance covered.

There are numbers now to show teams where guys are getting the ball most often on the floor and where they're most effective—they break down a player's elbow touches (when a player reaches the part of the lane where the side line meets the free-throw line) and who most effectively runs pick-and-rolls together. We're in the information era, but it's almost too much information right now. Teams are still trying to sort through what to do with it all.

Teams have analytics departments where smart men who are good with numbers sit in offices and try to decode what they all mean. Teams also have salary cap experts who pore over contracts and the league's complicated collective bargaining agreement searching for secrets and loopholes, such as the fact Baron Davis's contract had a stretch clause in it or that the final year on Brendan Haywood's contract for 2015–16 was worth $10.5 million and it was nonguaranteed. That's why the Cavs had been so eager to acquire Haywood, a fringe NBA player at that point in his career, on draft night in 2014, long before James or Love was in Cleveland. With such a hefty nonguaranteed year, the Cavs believed they could flip him to another team looking to shed salary and obtain a good player in return, since a team could then cut Haywood and not owe him a dime since his contract wasn't guaranteed.

Just as baseball has created a whole new language with terms like WAR (wins above replacement), FIP (fielding independent pitching), and BABIP (batting average on balls in play), the same is now true for basketball. Player efficiency ratings (PERs) and usage rates tell more of the story than just how many points a guy scores. Traditional shooting percentages—how many shots a team takes and how many it makes— have been replaced by offensive and defensive efficiency, which standardizes how many points a team scores and allows per hundred possessions. It's no secret that the NBA has evolved into a pace-and-space league where length and athleticism have replaced sheer size. *Efficiency* is the league's new buzzword. The most efficient shots to take are either at the rim or three-pointers. The midrange game has become obsolete. So, too, are plodding big men who play with their backs to the basket.

Where centers like Patrick Ewing and Shaquille O'Neal once dominated the game—dribble down, set the half-court offense, throw it to the big man in the post, and get out of his way—now that formula is obsolete. Sure, there are still plodding centers (Detroit's Andre Drummond isn't winning a three-point contest anytime soon), but most of the game's centers aren't really centers. Positions in the NBA today, more than at any other time in the game's history, have become interchangeable.

As for Waiters, his 42 percent shooting on catch-and-shoot three-pointers ranked higher than both Love's and Irving's for the previous season. If Waiters could do that, just space the floor and shoot threes while expending the bulk of his energy on the defensive end, he would be an asset. If he didn't, he'd be gone. Instead, on a team with All-Stars like James, Love, and Irving, it was Waiters who led the team in shot attempts in each of the first five preseason games after James returned. Sure, it was preseason and it didn't matter, but it spoke to Waiters's mind-set and his willingness to fit into a system. Waiters wasn't fitting in.

When James first came back to Cleveland, he defended Waiters. He tried mentoring him. All of the veterans did. James Jones told the younger players to stop stretching and sit in their chairs when the head coach was addressing the team. They could stretch before or after he talked. LeBron told them no eating while watching film. As part of the roster makeover, LeBron wanted guys like Jones and Mike Miller, guys who were grown men and who could teach Waiters and Irving how to be professionals.

James believed Waiters had been unfairly labeled as a scapegoat his first couple of years in the league and cautioned the young guard not to pay any attention to it. Yet as the two spent more time together on the court, James seemed to distance himself from Waiters, who dribbled too much and constantly called for the ball. His stunts during his first two years in the league, when the Cavs were terrible and full of rookies, didn't sit well with the new veterans. When Waiters and Irving pounded the air out of the ball during the third game of the season at Portland, James simply stood in the corner in protest, refusing to participate. His message was clear: Keep playing the way you have and you'll keep getting the same results. The Cavs were hammered 101–82.

"There's a lot of bad habits, a lot of bad habits been built up the past couple years," James said after the game. "When you play that style of basketball, it takes a lot to get it up out of you."

Blatt, who was battling his own problems within the locker room, pulled the team together for a film session the next day at Utah. The season was just three games old, but Blatt wanted to establish a food chain. James and Love get to eat first, Blatt told Irving, and as the point guard, it was his job to feed them. Irving could find his own rhythm after the other two got going. Yet when the game ended that night in Salt Lake City, Irving had thirty-four points and zero assists. That aggravated James, who essentially told Irving that could never happen again. The Cavs ended the night with six assists, tying a franchise record for fewest in a game. The Cavs lost at the buzzer, 102–100, and they officially started 1-3 James's first year back.

The problems weren't just centered on Irving and Waiters. Love was a man without a nation his first year in Cleveland. He had made it clear early in the preseason that he was used to playing in a certain style, which included getting a couple of inside touches first before working his way out to the three-point line. No matter how many times he said so, however, he seemed to be ignored. Blatt wasn't interested in making Love comfortable and neither was James. The only person who predicted this, who foreshadowed how badly Love would struggle in his new role, was Chris Bosh.

In a revealing interview with Bleacher Report prior to the season, Bosh had predicted Love was "in for a shock." At the time, he sounded like a scorned ex. Just like Love in Minnesota, Bosh was an All-Star power forward on a team going nowhere BLBJ (before LeBron James). He wanted the chance to win, so in 2010 so he left the Raptors for the Heat in free agency. Days later, James stunned the NBA by joining him and Dwyane Wade in South Beach, forming the superpower that soon became the most hated team in the league.

Bosh's numbers were slashed playing alongside two ball-dominant wings in James and Wade. He looked at the Cavs' roster and predicted the same for Love, who averaged twenty-six points and twelve rebounds in his final season with the Timberwolves. "It's a lot more difficult taking a step back, because you're used to doing something a certain way and getting looks a certain way," Bosh told Bleacher Report's Ethan Skolnick during Love's first training camp with James. "And then it's like, well, no, for the benefit of the team, you have to get it here. So even if you do like the left block, the volume of the left block is going to be different. Now you have to make those moves count. So with me, it was like a chess game. I'm doing this move and thinking about the next move and trying to stay five moves ahead. You're not getting it as much. If you got one or two a game, it's a lot different."

Bosh averaged 24 points, 16.5 shots, and 10.8 rebounds in his final season with the Raptors. He averaged 18.7 points, 13.7 shots, and 8.3 rebounds in his first season with the Heat.

"You just get your entrée and that's it," Bosh warned. "It's like, 'Wait a minute, I need my appetizer and my dessert and my drink, what are you doing? And my bread basket. What is going on? I'm hungry!'"

Bosh's comments were immediately dismissed. Sure, he overhauled his game during his time with James in Miami, becoming much more of a three-point shooter than he ever had been in Toronto. But the comparisons didn't seem to fit because Love was already an adept three-point shooter. Hell, he had even won the three-point contest during All-Star Weekend before arriving in Cleveland. Bosh's comments were also made in the days before the Cavs and Heat played in a preseason game in Brazil. Love concluded the trip to South America with a sparkling performance, scoring twenty-five points in the win over James's former team. He followed it up with another twenty-five-point effort in a preseason victory against the Milwaukee Bucks. Everyone was feeling good about where they stood.

"I'm comfortable and just not trying to, I guess, fit in so much," Love said. "I had a talk with the guys on the plane ride over [to Brazil] and also at different practices off the floor and they told me to fit out. Just be myself . . . You always say check your egos at the door but we also need to bring our egos with us because that's what makes us so great. We wouldn't be here without them."

Just eight days after saying that, Love's tone began to change. He intimated after the preseason finale at Memphis that he was having to adjust his style of play. Those inside touches he'd grown accustomed to having his whole life were no longer there. Now he was a floor spacer but had no role other than to fill in the gaps around the perimeter. He struggled to find his footing in those first few weeks. Just as Bosh predicted, Love was looking for some bread and water. He took six fewer shots and scored ten fewer points per game in his first season in Cleveland than he had in his final season with the Timberwolves. There had to be a better way to use his vast skills, but no one seemed concerned with finding it.

One of Love's low points came in a 103–99 loss at the Indiana Pacers on February 6. He was terrific the previous night, scoring twenty-four points and grabbing nine rebounds in a home victory against the Los Angeles Clippers. But he followed it up against the Pacers by scoring just five points on two of eight shooting and didn't make a basket after the first quarter. He repeated that night what he'd said on so many occasions, that he was just trying to do what the team needed.

"Last game I got the ball in the post a lot and I was able to get myself going early," Love said. "Tonight I wasn't asked to score the ball, but LeBron and Kyrie had it going."

Whether it was Love's remarks or his temperament through the first half of the season, something was obviously aggravating James. He had worked so hard to recruit Love and bring him to Cleveland, but once he got him there, even other folks in the organization noticed the change in his demeanor. The Cavs were off the day following the loss to the Pacers, but James took to Twitter late that evening to fire the tweet heard around the locker room: "Stop trying to find a way to FIT-OUT and just FIT-IN," James wrote. "Be a part of something special! Just my thoughts."

Love was terrific the next day in a rout of the Los Angeles Lakers at home, scoring a season-high thirty-two points and making seven of eight three-pointers. James, of course, was initially asked about the tweet and denied it was related to anything going on with the Cavs. "It was a general thought I had," James said. "Obviously whatever thought I have, people try to encrypt it and *Da Vinci Code* it and all that stuff."

When the pack of cameras and microphones dissipated, a few of the beat reporters hung around James's locker to continue the interrogation. ESPN reporter Dave McMenamin, who used the FIT-OUT/FIT-IN tweet in an October story, pulled up a screenshot of the quote and showed it to James, who read the quote, smiled, and handed the phone back to McMenamin. We told James that was an awfully strong coincidence.

"It's not a coincidence, man," James said while rubbing lotion into his legs and feet. Now we had a problem. Nobody was taking notes and no recorders were rolling. It was just guys standing around talking, so was it on or off the record? No one was quite sure, so I stopped James a few minutes later as he was leaving the locker room to ask him.

"Ain't nothing off the record," he said. "I know everything that comes out of my mouth. If I say it, it's on the record."

Fair enough. James knew what he was saying. It was all on the record. Now, depending on various factors, Love's postgame routine could include weight training, soaking in a therapy pool, or both. He routinely took longer than most to shower, dress, and leave the locker room after games and did so again on this day. He was absent from the locker room while James was talking and had no idea what was being said. Nobody asked Love about the tweet or James's remarks during his usual postgame availability, so I waited until after the scrum dispersed before filling him in on our conversation with James. It was only a matter of time before he saw it on television anyway, so I wondered what his reaction was to all of it. Love has a Twitter account but doesn't spend much time on it and had no idea what I was talking about when I mentioned James's tweet. I showed it to him and told him how James told the couple of us that it wasn't a coincidence. Love felt blindsided.

"I feel like I've done all the right things. I haven't got upset or been down," he said. "There's moments when I hope I would've played better, but it's a long, long season. I don't know really what he's talking about. I feel like I've sacrificed and I think everyone knows that. I'm not trying to downplay what he said, but I think I've done a pretty good job of trying to help this team."

The next day, James walked back the whole sequence on social media and said he wasn't calling out Love, but by then it was obvious.

Even Cavs personnel—including Griffin—later confirmed that James was indeed upset with Love and targeted the tweet at him. After working so hard to get him to Cleveland, James had quickly grown frustrated with Love.

It had started when Love showed up for that first season out of shape. Love hadn't worked out much at all the summer he was traded and he wasn't the player James was expecting. His legs bothered him throughout his first season with the Cavs. His back was hurting. James loves talent and loves playing alongside elite players, but Love's physical condition prevented him from being the type of player James had thought he was getting. So James gravitated toward Kyrie Irving and left Love to twist without a defined role. Blatt did little to help Love adjust, instead bristling whenever the topic of Love's role was broached. When he was asked about Love again in early February after he scored twenty-four points and grabbed nine rebounds in a home win against the Clippers, the Cavs' twelfth straight victory, Blatt had heard about enough.

"You people like to talk about a lot of the things that are, in my mind, less important," Blatt said. "We win twelve games in a row and everybody is talking about Kevin's five-point game. I mean, really, who gives a damn? What's important is that the team is winning and Kevin knows that."

Blatt certainly was correct: Winning is all that matters. At least, that's true in the playoffs. But as James often says, the regular season is all about building the proper habits. And leaving Love without a clearly defined role might have worked to beat the Wizards on a random night in February, but it wasn't going to help beat the Spurs or Warriors in the NBA Finals. Furthermore, Love was entering free agency in a few months. The Cavs had given up a blossoming talent in Wiggins, who could grow into a superstar, to obtain him. Losing him after one season because he didn't fit well with the system would be disastrous.

Love remained adamant that he only cared about winning, but it was fair to wonder what would happen if the Cavs finished the year failing to win a championship while Love continued to flounder in their system. I spoke to one rival general manager who believed Love could leave at the end of the season for the Lakers and Kevin Durant could follow him there the next summer. Love, however, kept maintaining he was committed long-term. After so many years of rumors in Minnesota, he was used to the speculation by now.

"If we lose two or three games in a row, or there's a game where my stats aren't what they should be, people are always going to talk," Love said. "I've said since day one that I'm a Cleveland Cavalier long-term and I plan for it to be that way. I want to grow with this team. If I could end all the speculation now, I would. But people are going to continue to talk no matter what."

His words were reassuring to a certain degree, but problems obviously remained. And Love wasn't the only, or even the biggest, issue facing the Cavs at the time.

CHAPTER 13

Crutches, Calves, and Contracts

David Griffin's first season in charge included navigating plenty of land mines. He had to deal with a coach who didn't know the ways of the NBA, a mismatched roster that didn't have all of the necessary pieces to compete for a championship, and an aggressive owner pushing to win. Fortunately, Griffin's background in public relations is one of his strengths. He is an excellent communicator, both within the organization and when speaking publicly. Where Grant was private and secretive, Griffin was one of the league's most accessible general managers. He believed strongly in winning with peace, joy, and love and even convinced Gilbert to dial back his public appearances significantly.

"Griff," as he's known throughout the league, has been a fighter all of his life. He beat the odds to fight his way up the Suns' organization from an intern to an NBA general manager. He has fought and beaten cancer twice—once in 2006 in Phoenix and again in 2011, shortly after he joined the Cavs. Once the Cavs added Love and James, they supplemented the stars with key veterans such as James Jones and Mike Miller, both of whom had been with James in Miami. James trusted them implicitly and believed he needed them to turn the Cavs' immature culture of losing. By now, however, cap space had become an issue, so they delayed the signings of Jones and Miller and even their draft picks, including Wiggins. Griffin did a terrific job of finding cracks of space and turning them into usable trade exceptions. After the initial flurry of signings following James's return, for example, he took the remaining $1.6 million in available cap room and spun it into a $5.2 million trade exception. He needed four separate trades spread out over two months and eight second-round picks to get there.

The Cavs traded Carrick Felix to the Utah Jazz in July in exchange for Erik Murphy, John Lucas III, and Malcolm Thomas. It was presented as one trade, but it was actually two separate deals under league rules. Felix was swapped for Murphy as one trade, while Lucas III was absorbed into their sliver of remaining cap space. Thomas was making the league minimum and therefore could be traded around without penalty. All players making the league minimum can be traded regardless of the acquiring team's salary cap situation—one of the many complicated exceptions to the league's salary cap structure. The cost for the complex, trivial trade? The Cavs sent away their 2015 second-round pick and $1 million to the Jazz for their trouble.

Now that they were completely out of cap space, the Cavs used a number of other exceptions available under the salary cap rules to sign rookies Wiggins and Dwight Powell along with veterans like Miller, Jones, and Shawn Marion.

In September, they obtained Keith Bogans's contract, which was worth $5.2 million and was non-guaranteed, in exchange for Powell and the three players obtained from the Jazz. They also sent their 2016 and 2017 second-round picks to the Celtics.

They didn't want Bogans or his contract. They wanted a trade exception equivalent to his contract. In the NBA, players can be traded away without taking a player back. Instead, a "trade exception" can be obtained in their place, which is basically like a gift card to use at a later time. So the Cavs called the Philadelphia 76ers, who were flush with cap space, and dumped Bogans's non-guaranteed contract on them in exchange for a $5.2 million gift card they could use in the future on a player they really liked. The Cavs sent the Sixers their 2018 second-round pick basically just to do some paperwork. The Sixers promptly released Bogans and never owed him a dime.

It was all impressive maneuvering by Griffin and the front office and left him with plenty of reasons to be feeling pretty good. Yet his most miserable day as general manager may have been one of his first. In the days before James's regular-season debut, the Cavs were in Memphis for a preseason game. The team hotel in Memphis is directly across the street from FedExForum, so most of the players and staff had cleared out and walked back by the time Griffin was shooting three-pointers after practice. A few minutes later, Griffin came hopping across the court on one leg, cursing, and dropped down next to me on the scorer's table in the empty arena.

"I think I tore something," he said, in considerable pain.

The search was on to find team trainer Steve Spiro. He didn't pick up a call to his cell phone, so another staffer was dispatched to try to find him. Meanwhile, Raja Bell filled in as trainer, and I was his newly appointed assistant. Bell retired from the NBA in 2012 and went to work for the Cavs in a front-office role shortly after the interim tag was removed from Griffin's title. The two had struck up a friendship while Bell played for the Suns, so Griffin offered him the chance to stay in the game and learn about how front offices operate. On this day, Bell's title of "director of player administration" turned into "dude who finds the ice bags."

Bell had dealt with enough calf injuries in his playing days to know Griffin needed ice. He searched the court and came up with a couple of watered-down, half-melted ice bags the players had previously used and discarded following practice. I held Griffin's right leg by his ankle while Bell positioned the melted bags around his calf and wrapped them in cellophane. Then we waited on Spiro, who was eventually located and returned to the arena. Within seconds, Spiro told him the calf was torn. He found some crutches in a back room of the arena and Griffin crutched his way across the street and back to the hotel. He was soon fitted with a walking boot.

It was the first of many obstacles he had to navigate as boss. The chemistry issues weren't getting any better with Blatt or Waiters, whose attitude and game had soured his teammates. A few weeks after the game at Portland, when James did little more than stand in the corner during the second half, Waiters nearly broke the rim on an ill-advised three-point attempt. James closed his eyes and walked off the baseline in disgust while play continued in the other direction. Griffin kept preaching patience, telling James he just needed time to fix the roster. There wasn't much to be done about the coach, however.

The best players Blatt had ever coached in Europe were, at best, NBA journeymen. He had never guided a collection of talent quite like this. After a career driving around used Hondas, Blatt suddenly had the keys to a Ferrari. He quickly burned out the clutch. Early in their first training camp together, James began identifying more with Lue, the former NBA player, than he did with Blatt. James likes to say he is coachable and will play for any coach, although he certainly has a way of making life miserable for some of his coaches. He made Erik Spoelstra's first year in Miami difficult and made it clear early on Blatt was going to have to earn his respect. But while Blatt certainly wasn't a name that enticed James home, he hadn't been enough to deter him, either.

James briefly texted Blatt after announcing his decision to come home, but the two didn't actually meet for another three weeks. Even then, Blatt had to fly to New York and visit the set of the movie *Trainwreck,* which James was busy filming, in order to have a sit-down with his star. Blatt admitted once that while James was obviously the most talented player he had ever coached, he was also the most difficult. Blatt was accustomed to being revered by his players. The slew of veterans who had recently joined Cleveland had all previously enjoyed varying degrees of success in the NBA, and little reverence was forthcoming. It seemed obvious that no one was overly impressed with their coach.

James at times tried to say complimentary things about Blatt, but his actions rarely supported them. One scout from an opposing team watched in disbelief during their first season together as Blatt approached half court during one road game shouting to get James's attention, to no avail. Instead, he returned to the bench and sent Lue out to the court to deliver the message.

In truth, regardless of what team Blatt was brought to Cleveland to coach, his learning curve was significantly steeper than anyone expected. The organization considered firing him two months into his first season and he barely made it through Christmas and New Year's. The Cavs were blasted by a bad Detroit Pistons team at home, 103–80, and followed it up with a loss at Atlanta when James and Love spent most of the evening in the locker room nursing injuries. The pressure on Blatt intensified following a lethargic 96-80 home loss to the Milwaukee Bucks on New Year's Eve when James and Love sat out again with injuries, making the Cavs losers in three straight and four of their last five games.

But it was a tough call. After having fired two coaches in two years, dismissing a third within twenty months would present the image of a franchise in disarray. With Blatt under fire publicly, the Cavs remained silent for more than a week, contemplating what to do while speculation over his future swirled. With the head coach under siege, the team announced on New Year's Day that James was taking two weeks off to rest knee and back injuries. James had never dealt with a significant injury and the two-week break marked the longest stretch he had been sidelined throughout his career—although one person who knows him well categorized it as a mental break as much as a physical one. He'd gone on a rigorous diet the summer he announced he was returning to Cleveland and shed about ten pounds. Whether it was the weight loss or the knee and back problems, James was lacking his trademark explosiveness. He returned to Miami to sit in the sunshine and receive an injection to help the back pain.

With James away from the team, Love and Irving combined for fifty points the next night and the Cavs beat a bad Charlotte Hornets team on the road, 91–87. It was an otherwise uneventful game against a bad opponent, but shortly after that victory, Gilbert made up his mind. He chose to keep Blatt. When the Cavs returned home, Griffin (that gifted public speaker with a media relations background) called an impromptu press conference before a Sunday afternoon game against the Dallas Mavericks to support Blatt and blast the media for ever questioning his future.

"This narrative of our coaching situation is truly ridiculous. It's a non-story, it's a non-narrative. Coach Blatt is our coach, he's going to remain our coach," Griffin said, pausing for effect. "Do not write that as a vote of confidence. He never needed one. It was never a question. So don't write it that way. . . . We're like traveling with the Beatles. I'm not surprised, but I've been disappointed the slant has been an attempt to be so negative all the time. This is exactly what we said it's going to be: It's a work in progress and we're going to continue to get better every day."

Griffin's impassioned defense of the coach he never wanted was rather impressive but did little to inspire his team. With James away, the Cavs were blistered at home by the Mavericks, 109–90. It triggered a six-game losing streak that included a miserable West Coast trip that also infuriated team officials and again nearly cost Blatt his job. A particularly dreadful 103–84 loss to the woeful Sacramento Kings exactly one week after Griffin's public defense of Blatt left the Cavs at 19-19. During a difficult postgame press conference, he fired back at Cleveland.com reporter Joe Vardon, who rightfully asked why the team was struggling so badly despite having two max players on the floor in Irving and Love.

"Well Kev's not a max player yet, is he?" Blatt countered. It was as if the record had scratched and the music stopped as we all looked around in disbelief. It could easily be interpreted, even if it wasn't Blatt's intent, that he was implying Love wasn't worth max contract money. It was a bad moment, particularly since Love had had so many problems getting a max contract in Minnesota and was struggling to fit in with his new surroundings.

Blatt's dealings with the media were often combative. He told me once he was conditioned to be that way because the media overseas can be vicious. Show weakness, he said, and they'll tear you apart. Head coaches have to talk to reporters three times a day on some game days, so it can be tedious and the questions certainly can get repetitive. We've all asked our share of stupid questions and all coaches botch answers at some point. Most coaches try to have a cordial relationship with the reporters who cover them every day, although a few go to war. Blatt seemed to always choose war, to the point where those who worked for the Cavs were often shaking their heads in disbelief at his behavior. Successful coaches can get away with being arrogant, but guys who are in over their heads, who aren't ready for the job in front of them, when they're arrogant, it comes off as insecure.

Blatt's response that night had nothing to do with Love's ability as a player and everything to do with trying to tighten up Vardon over a question Blatt didn't like. The unintended consequence of saying Love wasn't a max player was that he stung one of his best players, who was already struggling to fit in and could be a free agent in a few months. Team officials were seething; one told me the next day that Blatt was "a fucking moron" for saying it. Blatt tried to clean up his mess the next day.

"My comment was either misunderstood or misconstrued," he said. "I was simply saying that with our team he does not have a max contract because we're not allowed to talk to him about anything until after the season is over."

A few days later, Gilbert joined the trip in Los Angeles and wanted to meet with Lue at a hotel to discuss replacing Blatt as coach. Lue, fiercely loyal to Blatt, declined the meeting for fear of how it would look if anyone saw them together. It was one of three times the Cavs approached Lue about taking over as coach, but he kept refusing the job out of loyalty to Blatt. Stick with us, Lue told Cavs officials, we'll figure this out.

James returned during the trip and promptly shoved Blatt back to his own bench while arguing with an official in Phoenix; Blatt was screamed at by Jack Nicholson in Los Angeles for blocking the Hollywood star's courtside view during a game against the Lakers, and he was caught in the awkward position of having to defend himself over the team's use of time-outs—all in a span of about ten days. Opposing scouts looked on incredulously as Lue repeatedly called time-outs from the bench during Blatt's first season. The head coach is the only person allowed to call a time-out from the bench, yet it was Lue often making the calls. "If one of my [assistants] did it," one rival head coach said, "I'd kill him."

It's important to understand that Lue was in a difficult spot and never operated behind Blatt's back. Lue genuinely liked Blatt and supported him at every turn. Up and down the organization, he has been praised for the difficult position he was thrust into with a head coach who wasn't prepared for the job. Before he joined Blatt's staff, Lue discussed the situation with Clippers coach Doc Rivers, who is Lue's coaching mentor. Although it was going to create a huge hole on his own staff, Rivers encouraged Lue to take the job. It was going to be awkward because Lue was the runner-up to Blatt, but Rivers believed Lue needed to get away from him to really grow as a coach. Plus, the Cavs were willing to make Lue the highest-paid assistant in the league.

"For Ty, I thought it was the exact right thing to do," Rivers said. "I knew he was going into a tough situation, but I also told him, it's not *that* tough of a situation. As bad as it's going to be, you're going to win fifty games. No matter what happens, you're going to do well record-wise. Where you have to make sure is that you give David the correct support and never, ever, ever make anyone think that you're coaching the team. I thought he did a great job with that."

Since Gilbert was forced to give Blatt the season, Griffin went to work trying to fix the roster. He dealt Waiters to Oklahoma City in a three-team trade on January 7, 2015, that brought Iman Shumpert and J. R. Smith from New York to Cleveland.

"We had to do something to augment the group and it probably had to come at the expense of Dion because we didn't need another ball-dominant play creator. It was just a really bad fit," Griffin said. "We needed what J. R. provided much more because we already had the ball dominance and play creation. It was just really a matter of fit. The Dion piece was obviously the misfit."

Crutches, Calves, and Contracts

It goes back to the general assumption the Cavs operated under when they began the rebuild: If James comes back, not all of the pieces will fit. But they all held enough value to help find the pieces that would fit. In a vacuum, teams might have preferred Waiters over Smith because he had less baggage, he was younger, and he was still on his rookie contract. But for what the Cavs needed, Smith was the much better shooter, making him the much better fit.

The key to the deal initially appeared to be Shumpert, a terrific perimeter defender with an inconsistent shot. Shumpert had torn his ACL in a playoff series against James and the Heat in 2012, and scouts believe he has never quite been the same player since. In order to get Shumpert, the Cavs were forced to take Smith and the balance of his $6.5 million deal. Knicks president Phil Jackson was trying to clear his books and wanted to get rid of Smith, who owned a player option for the following season. Jackson didn't want to risk Smith's picking it up and was willing to give away Shumpert just to be rid of Smith. Shumpert was also in the final year of his contract and was seeking a new deal starting around $10 million a season. Jackson did not want to pay it, which made him expendable.

Smith came with more baggage than Delta. At the start of the 2016–17 season, Smith had missed twenty-seven games in his career—the equivalent of one-third of a season—due to suspension, the most serious being a seven-game ban for killing his friend when he ran a stop sign in 2007 and flipped his SUV. The friend died two days later from head injuries. Smith spent thirty days in jail for it and had his license suspended. He has been suspended for drugs, for punching players on the court, and for poor decisions on social media. He has paid fines totaling about $500,000 throughout his career. But he can shoot, and what the Cavs desperately needed more than anything was a shooter.

"I would not have taken J. R. There's no chance," a rival front office executive told me in the days after the deal. "Shumpert is not good enough for us to take J. R. Not even close. But I get it from Cleveland's perspective. If I was in Cleveland's shoes, I might have done the same thing."

Prior to finalizing the deal, Griffin informed James of the plan. Smith is a year behind him in age, but the Cavs' star was familiar with him because they worked out together the summer before Smith entered the NBA. James didn't care about his reputation or what the rest of the league thought of him. LeBron knew Smith was one of the best shooters in the league. He was ecstatic to have him.

"I was like, 'What? They're going to throw J. R. into the deal?'" James said. "I was like, 'Okay. I've got him. I've got him.'"

Smith had won the Sixth Man of the Year Award as a member of the playoff-bound Knicks in 2013, proof he could contribute to a winning team. He was also better defensively than his reputation. Smith was described by other teams as someone who needed guidance. If his team wasn't winning and the locker room lacked leadership, Smith would be a detriment. But if he was part of a winning culture with a strong leader above him, he would be fine. In Cleveland, Smith had all of that and more.

"If J. R. fucks up, it'll be off the court," one Cavs executive said prior to Smith's debut in Cleveland. "Dion was fucking us up on the court."

Griffin wasn't done. In addition to Shumpert and Smith, the Cavs received a much-needed first-round draft pick from the Thunder in exchange for Waiters. Two days after the first trade was complete, Griffin sent the pick he received from the Thunder along with another first rounder to the Nuggets in exchange for Timofey Mozgov. Griffin targeted Mozgov early in the season because he was enormous (seven foot one, 275 pounds), he was making only $4.6 million, and he had another year on his contract. They used the $5.2 million trade exception Griffin created prior to the start of the season to fit Mozgov's salary under the cap.

Trading two first-round picks for Mozgov sounded like a drastic overpay. In the last few years, players who had been traded for two first-round picks were Dwight Howard, Steve Nash, James Harden, Andre Iguodala . . . and Mozgov. All of the others were franchise cornerstones. Mozgov never was and never would be. But he was a massive body that filled the lane and protected the rim—something the Cavs desperately needed. He was also relatively cheap.

Griffin would have preferred to combine the two trades into one enormous deal just for the optics, but that would've been illegal under league rules. So instead they had to break it into two separate trades. The Cavs never looked at it as giving up two first-round picks for Mozgov. They viewed it as trading Waiters and their own first-round pick in exchange for Smith, Shumpert, and Mozgov because the second pick came from Oklahoma City in exchange for Waiters. They just simply transferred it from the Thunder to the Nuggets. The trades were a home run. With the roster better suited now to fit around James, Lue went to Blatt and told him he needed to adapt or he was going to be fired. The players were bucking Blatt's offensive system. Lue told Blatt to let the players run what they wanted on offense. Defensively, with

Blatt's blessing, Lue overhauled the schemes. Blatt struggled with drawing up plays coming out of time-outs—one of Lue's strengths. So he often handled that, too.

The Cavs erupted, ripping off a twelve-game winning streak shortly after Smith and Mozgov arrived (Shumpert didn't get on the court until a few weeks later since he was still recovering from a separated shoulder). The winning silenced the rhetoric around Blatt, who had been under fire basically since the day he was hired, but the players still never really bought into their coach.

"At the end of the day, when we hired David he was hired to coach a different team, and that fit became increasingly bad as we went along," Griffin said. "When you're around our team as much as I am, I wasn't seeing any accountability. When we made the J. R. Smith trade, that didn't get any better, we just got a whole lot better. Guys were joyful being part of the process again, which masked some of those issues. But those issues were there the whole time. And they continued to be throughout the playoffs."

As the Cavs were about to discover, making it to the playoffs for the first time since 2010 wasn't enough. The plan was almost complete, but the weeks and months ahead would show there was still much to do, and big questions to answer.

CHAPTER 14

Shoulders, Slings, and Fighter Pilots

I t was only fitting that the first playoff opponent the Cavs faced upon LeBron's return to Cleveland was the Boston Celtics—the same Celtics who ended the Cavs' postseason in 2008 and then chased James out of Cleveland in 2010. Both teams looked vastly different, particularly since Paul Pierce, Ray Allen, and Kevin Garnett had all left Boston. Still, it was the green-and-white and the Garden and all the memories of past clashes. The Cavs, after all, had ended Larry Bird's career in the second round of the playoffs in 1992.

For all of the problems and dysfunctions with Blatt, the Cavs still entered the playoffs 53-29. They caught fire after obtaining Smith, Shumpert, and Mozgov and went 34-9 to close the season with their new pieces, the best record in the East over that stretch, after bottoming out at 19-20 in January. James downplayed the significance of facing the Celtics, the team with which he had so much personal postseason history.

"I think we're past that. Both cities," he said. "Both teams are extremely different from the battles that we had in the past."

For all the problems Love had fitting in during the season, he was terrific against the Celtics. He had a double-double in Game 1 with nineteen points and twelve rebounds; then he made six three-pointers and scored twenty-three points in Game 3, breaking the game open late with consecutive three-pointers to give the Cavs a commanding 3–0 series lead. He averaged 18.3 points and nine assists through the first three games of a series that was growing more and more physical. Almost overnight, the Cavs' Big Three finally began playing the way it was envisioned they would when this team was assembled.

"He's been highly criticized this year," James said of Love during the Celtics series. "When you have a Big Three, they've got to find someone. When I was in Miami, Chris Bosh was that guy at one point. I've seen it before. When you've been in a position where you have your own team, and now you come and join forces, at one point in Miami we were nine-eight and they start pointing fingers at anybody. They've got to find somebody. Kevin was the guy they tried to find and tried to tear him down. The one thing about him, he's always stayed positive. I've always believed in him."

James's comments were laced with revisionist history. It was reminiscent of the cult favorite football movie *Varsity Blues,* in which head coach Bud Kilmer spent all season destroying Mox, his backup quarterback, right up until the moment he needed him. "I'm behind you," Kilmer told Mox. "Let's go!" Now that the Cavs' Mox was starting to shine, their Kilmer finally stopped whipping Mox's helmet with a whistle.

On the off day prior to Game 4, Love sat on the scorer's table inside the Garden stretching his legs and tying his shoes. He was talking to me about his future again, something that was a recurring talking point throughout the season. Yes, Bosh was right. Yes, his transition into this system was more difficult than expected. Yes, James seemed to be hard on him at various turns. The relationship between the two stars had been scrutinized almost to silly lengths, such as skeptics wondering why Love never seemed to appear in the group photos James posted to social media throughout the season. Of course, Love didn't help his case when he went on a national radio show and selected his college teammate Russell Westbrook as his MVP instead of James.

"It hasn't been as bad as you think," Love said about his season of scrutiny. "Sure, there are times I fought it or it might have been a little tough because I'm so used to playing efficient and consistent, but it never wavered my love for basketball or playing with these guys. We have a great group. We have a fun group. You guys don't see that every day, but we've got some really good people here. It's been great."

Love was unwavering that day on his commitment to re-sign with Cleveland. Things were looking up, and no one had any idea in that moment that his season was about to end. Jae Crowder missed a three-pointer badly during the first quarter of Game 4 and Love, tangled up with the Celtics' Kelly Olynyk, chased after the rebound. Olynyk had no real chance at getting to the ball, so he pinned Love's left arm between his arm and chest and yanked Love away from the ball. Love's shoulder immediately dislocated, and in excruciating pain, Love grabbed at his arm and ran directly to the locker room. The Cavs were furious with Olynyk—most notably Love.

"I thought it was a bush-league play," Love said after the game, his arm in a sling. "I have no doubt in my mind that he did it on purpose.

That's just not a basketball play. The league will take a look at it and it better be swift and just."

Love was incensed that after waiting seven years just to make the playoffs, his postseason was over after less than four games. Tension on the court was high, and the Cavs appeared to take their frustration out on Jae Crowder, who irritated Cavs players after just two games in the series.

"Nobody on their team is intimidating," Crowder said despite being in an 0–2 deficit. By the time Love was out in Game 4, the Cavs were ready to fight. Kendrick Perkins clobbered Crowder while setting a screen and J. R. Smith knocked Crowder out when he hammered him with a closed fist while fighting for rebound positioning. Crowder crumpled to the court and fell so awkwardly that he sprained his knee.

Following that sequence, the Cavs' locker room after the game was somber. Griffin quietly strolled through, his arms folded and a tired look on his face. By then, he knew Love was going to miss a fair amount of time and assumed Smith would likely be suspended, too. The Cavs were advancing, but no one could feel particularly good about it in that moment.

Smith was ultimately suspended the first two games of the conference semifinal series against the Chicago Bulls, a series the Cavs trailed 2–1, and they were in danger of falling behind 3–1 when Blatt nearly ruined the season and bought his own ticket back to Israel. James Jones burned the Cavs' last two time-outs during the final minute of Game 4 while trying to get the ball inbounded. After a basket by Derrick Rose tied the game at eighty-four, Blatt stepped onto the court with 8.5 seconds left and signaled for a time-out he didn't have. The entire coaching staff saw it, but only Tyronn Lue was close enough to grab Blatt and pull him back before the officials saw him.

After so much attention was paid to the Cavs' bench throughout the season and the way Lue was calling time-outs instead of Blatt, it was ironic that Lue had to save Blatt and pull him off the court over a time-out fiasco. Had the officials spotted him, it would've been a technical foul and the Bulls would've received a free throw and possession of the ball. That would've been the end of the game—and likely the Cavs' season.

"I almost blew it," Blatt acknowledged afterward. "Good thing they caught it, my guys."

And yet the time-out issue wasn't even the most embarrassing thing to happen to Blatt that day. James drove the length of the floor on the ensuing inbounds play, but the ball went out of bounds with eight-tenths of a second remaining. Officials had to stop play to review the call, giving Blatt an opportunity to huddle his players and draw up a play despite not having a time-out. Blatt wanted James to be the in-bounder. Most everyone in the huddle rejected that idea—including James, who was quick to out his coach.

"To be honest, the play that was drawn up, I scratched it," James said. "I told Coach, 'Just give me the ball. It's either going into overtime or I'm going to win it for us.' . . . . There was no way I'm taking the ball out unless I could shoot it over the backboard and go in. I told him, 'Have somebody else take the ball out, get me the ball, and everybody get out of the way.'"

Seconds later, James shot a buzzer beater and the Cavs tied the series 2–2. The scratched play was still a hot topic the next day. Blatt was forced to address it again and grew defensive, offering a ridiculous comparison that only added to his trouble.

"A basketball coach makes one hundred fifty to two hundred

critical decisions during the course of a game, something I think is paralleled only by a fighter pilot," he said as the organization collectively groaned and grimaced. He'd managed to say the wrong thing at the wrong time yet again.

The Cavs won Game 5 at home and the series shifted back to the United Center for Game 6. Coincidentally, the NBA combine was in Chicago at the same time, meaning the rest of the league was in town to interview all of the prospective draft prospects and watch them work out. The combine was buzzing with league folks talking about Blatt's tough week. Flip Saunders, who only a few months earlier had traded Love to Cleveland, agreed that James should never be the inbounder in that situation and instead suggested Mike Miller, a little-used veteran who is widely considered one of the league's smartest and best inbounders. An agent at the combine laughed at Blatt's fighter pilot remark.

"For who?" he asked. "Malaysia Airlines?"

Blatt was clearly under fire and so were the Cavs, who beat the Bulls in six games. Along with Love's shoulder injury, Irving was now hobbling around on a bad knee. He played just twelve minutes in a decisive Game 6 victory. Cleveland won easily, 94–73, after the Bulls seemed to accept their fate. It was a stunning turnaround for a team that had trailed 2–1 in the series and was one blown time-out away from going home.

It was Matthew Dellavedova who had helped save the Cavs when Irving was fighting tendinitis in his left knee. Dellavedova was a gritty guard who went undrafted in 2013. The Cavs held two first-round picks that year, yet it was the little-known Dellavedova who turned out to be their best find. After the '13 draft was over, Chris Grant had reclined in his chair when one of his assistants, Trent Redden, ducked in to talk about which undrafted players they should pursue and who they should sign for their Summer League team. *Dellavedova* was the name scribbled atop the whiteboard in Grant's office that night. "I love that kid," Grant said with a wide smile.

Dellavedova was a bruising, physical Australian guard out of St. Mary, which is coached by Randy Bennett, who was an assistant at the University of San Diego when Grant and Brown were there. Bennett was the one insisting to Grant he needed to take a look at Delly, who left St. Mary as the all-time leader in points and assists. When the Cavs brought him in for a predraft workout, they paired him with guys more talented and more athletic. Yet Delly's team won all of the three-on-three scrimmages. So the Cavs changed up the teams. Dellavedova's team still won.

"By the end," Brown said, "every one of those motherfuckers was looking at Delly and doing what he said. Delly was leading them."

Philadelphia 76ers coach Brett Brown coached the Australian national team when Dellavedova was on it. He twice cut Dellavedova from the national team before he was ignored and went undrafted by the NBA.

"I count that as being cut," Dellavedova said.

Grant and Brown knew Dellavedova was likely to be ignored on draft night because the NBA is always seeking athleticism and high ceilings with their draft picks—guys who have room to develop and grow. Delly had neither, but he had a toughness that allowed his teams to win.

"When you start talking about the character and DNA of people, he ticks the right way," Brett Brown said. "He's a country Victorian, a true Aussie that is a headbanger. He plays with reckless abandon. There's a physicality to him and a toughness you fall in love with. He at times might not be pretty, he's a little bit Neanderthal in how he goes about his business, but he's for real. I loved coaching him."

Yet the Cavs spent the trade deadline in 2014 trying to upgrade the position. Dellavedova was the only backup point guard behind Irving, but Griffin wanted a point guard more offensive-minded who could score. He also didn't want to be one injury away from elimination, and at the time an injury to Irving seemed devastating. So they looked around the league and overseas for another playmaker. When they couldn't find one, they were left with only Dellavedova. It turned out to be a blessing. He played thirty-four minutes and scored a career-high nineteen points to close out the Bulls, but Irving's availability against the Atlanta Hawks in the conference finals was unknown.

Irving had six days off to rest his ailing knee between the semifinals and the conference finals, but it was still bothering him. He'd had an MRI earlier in the postseason, which revealed nothing wrong structurally. Still, Irving was tentative, to the frustration of the organization. The strong inference was that Irving just had to suck it up and play through the pain, which he wasn't doing to their liking. When he re-aggravated the knee on a drive to the basket in Game 1 against the Hawks, he wound up sitting out three of the game's last eighteen minutes.

Instead of playing Irving in Game 2, the team flew him to Dr. James Andrews in Florida for another opinion, to again reassure him there was nothing wrong structurally with the knee.

"Everyone's pain tolerance is different," said James, who was dealing with an ankle injury of his own. "My responsibility is much higher than a lot of guys', not only this team but a lot of guys in professional sports. I take it very seriously being out there with my guys. If I'm able to play at seventy, sixty, fifty percent I feel like I can give something to the team. If I'm hurting the team then I'm gonna sit down, but if I can give something to help them I'll be out there for them. I think my presence alone can help us more than anything."

Even with Irving hobbling, the Cavs made quick work of the Hawks, who had won sixty games during the regular season but seemed to peak too early. Irving played a total of forty-nine minutes in the series, but Cleveland swept Atlanta, including a dominant 118–88 win in a clinching Game 4 celebration at home that sent the Cavs back to the NBA Finals for the second time in their history and first since 2007. The sweep, coupled with Irving's knee problems, took the focus off Blatt about the time he could use a reprieve. NBA analyst and former front office executive Isiah Thomas ripped Blatt to me prior to the series and even picked the Hawks to win because of the imbalance in coaches.

"As we saw in the last series, there's a learning curve that is still going on and the players on the floor are compensating for it," Thomas said, referring again to the time-out gaffe against the Bulls and James's scratching Blatt's play call. "But how long does it happen before you can't compensate for it?"

Apparently, it turned out, at least one more round. As the Cavs celebrated in their locker room for winning the East, James walked toward James Jones and Mike Miller and put one arm around each of them while holding a bottle of champagne in his left hand.

"The Big Three," James whispered quietly before taking a swig of champagne. The three stood together, silent. These were the two veterans James had handpicked to come with him and help turn around an ailing franchise. These were the two he relied on to teach a young roster how to be professionals. They'd advanced to the NBA Finals together as teammates in Miami; now they were going back as teammates in Cleveland.

"*Thanks* is a powerful word," Miller said. "I thank him every time."

The sweep of the Hawks meant more time off to get Irving's knee healthy. He had nine days from the end of the conference finals until Game 1 of the NBA Finals at Oracle Arena against the mighty Golden State Warriors, who had come out of nowhere to win sixty-seven games and win the Western Conference. Cavs officials did their best to sandbag before the game, insisting to any reporter who would listen that Irving was still hobbling and would be limited.

Privately, however, Griffin was optimistic the knee problems were finally behind them. Irving had been compared to a Ferrari throughout the postseason, and it seemed the torque he generated on his cuts was causing a lot of the problems. Plus the location of the tendinitis, the Cavs said, was a bad spot in the back of the knee. Add it all up and Irving had been limited in every round. Now, however, the Cavs were hopeful he was healthy.

He was sensational in Game 1, scoring twenty-three points, grabbing seven rebounds, and passing for six assists. The Cavs had a chance to win the game in regulation, but James missed a fadeaway jumper from the wing with 3.9 seconds left. Iman Shumpert gathered the rebound and flipped up a second attempt at the buzzer, but the shot missed by inches. Luke Walton, a former Cavs player under Scott and now a Warriors assistant, was standing directly in line with Shumpert's shot and was convinced it was going in. "I don't know how it rattled out," Walton told me.

It's hard to say how much of that series would've changed if Shumpert's shot had gone in. The Cavs obviously would've led 1–0, but more importantly they may have had Irving for the rest of the series. Irving's troublesome left knee, the one that had bothered him throughout the playoffs, finally gave way for good in the overtime session. Irving was trying to dribble to the basket when he collapsed on the court, his left knee fracturing when it appeared to collide with Klay Thompson's right knee. Irving limped off the floor with trainer Steve Spiro in obvious pain and slammed his jersey into the tunnel in frustration. His season was over. If the Cavs were going to win a championship, James would have to deliver it himself. Love and Irving were now both out with injuries.

Back in the locker room, Irving's father was furious. He was in a private room with his son; Irving's agent, Jeff Wechsler; and the Cavs' medical staff. After a few minutes, Drederick stormed out of the room and slammed the door behind him.

"There was a lot of mistrust from them toward us at the time," Griffin said later, refusing to provide details. "We had a lot of work to do to repair that relationship."

They had even more work to do on the court. With little help around him, James was magnificent throughout the series. The Cavs turned into street fighters. They slowed down the games and beat the hell out of the Warriors physically. The plan was always to go right at Steph Curry, to be physical with him and take him out of the game. It worked.

In Game 2, Curry shot just five of twenty-three and missed all eight of his shots while Dellavedova was guarding him. Delly had picked up a reputation as a "dirty" player in earlier series against the Bulls and Hawks. Against the Warriors he played to exhaustion and hounded Curry from baseline to baseline. James had thirty-nine points, sixteen rebounds, and eleven assists for the fifth triple-double of his Finals career and the Cavs beat the Warriors 95–93 in overtime for their first Finals victory in franchise history after they were swept by the Spurs in 2007.

"It's the grit squad that we have," James said. "It's not cute at all. If you're looking for us to play sexy, cute basketball, it's not us right now. Everything is tough."

James was going it alone throughout the series, both in personnel and in coaching. James shocked Warriors coaches and players by blatantly ignoring Blatt's play calls. Teams scout each other enough that they know all of the other team's play calls by June. The Warriors watched Blatt call out a play, only to have James ignore it and run whatever he wanted. It happened throughout the Finals. James was taking matters into his own hands.

The Cavs beat the Warriors 96–91 at home in Game 3 to take a stunning 2–1 series lead. James again dazzled with forty points and Dellavedova again roughed up Curry and again played to exhaustion. The formula was simple: Never leave their guards. The Cavs' guards were under strict orders to never leave Curry and Klay Thompson alone.

200

If there's a loose ball, let the bigs dive after it. It seemed to be working, right up until the fourth quarter, when Dellavedova was exhausted and Curry found his rhythm. He tied a Finals record by making five three-pointers in the fourth quarter and he scored seventeen points. Cavs executives were ecstatic to be up 2–1 in the series but nervous that the fourth quarter awakened Curry after he had been a nonfactor in the series.

"I think I found something when it comes to how I'm going to be able to attack their pick-and-rolls and even certain iso situations," Curry said after Game 3. "I'll keep that in the memory bank going into Game Four, and hopefully it has a trickle-over effect into the first quarter of the next game."

Perhaps not so coincidentally, Curry got hot just as Dellavedova was cramping up. Delly had to leave the game with cramps and he left the arena on a stretcher, dehydrated after playing thirty-nine grueling minutes. Dellavedova spent the night at the Cleveland Clinic, but he was never the same player the rest of the series.

Even without Love and Irving, James dragged the Cavs to a Game 6 against the healthy Warriors. James became the first player in Finals history to lead both teams in points, assists, and rebounds and made a strong case to earn the Finals Most Valuable Player award even in a losing effort. The only other time that occurred was 1969, when Jerry West won the MVP despite his Lakers team losing to the Celtics.

James played at least forty-five minutes in every game of the series except Game 4, when the Cavs were blitzed at home by the Warriors 103–82 to even the series 2–2. But ultimately, James couldn't do it alone. The Warriors won the final three games of the series to win their first championship since 1975. Just like the Spurs in 2007, the Warriors won the championship on the Cavs' home court. James said he wasn't interested in winning the MVP award if the Cavs lost the series, yet he still nearly won it anyway. The final MVP vote was 7–4. Andre Iguodala won it over James, but not by much, considering James was on the losing team.

I was one of the eleven voters for Finals MVP and I was working for the *Akron Beacon Journal,* James's hometown newspaper, at the time of the series. Somehow that fact required me to vote for James, at least in the minds of Cavs fans, who subsequently lost their minds upon learning I voted for Iguodala. My Twitter mentions quickly filled up with angry/bitter fans who thought it only right for me to fire myself, kill myself, or preferably do both.

When the league had asked me to be a Finals MVP voter earlier in the day, I knew the scenario I'd be facing. In my mind, James had to get the series to a Game 7. If he did, win or lose, he had my vote. West took the Celtics to a seventh game in 1969 before ultimately falling. In my mind, James had to stretch the series out as long as it could possibly go in order to earn an MVP in a losing effort. Secondly, I had a hard time giving it to a player whose team lost three consecutive games.

As for Iguodala, his impact on the series was overwhelming. When he was off the court, James shot 44 percent and the Cavs outscored the Warriors by thirty points. When Iguodala was on the court, he was James's primary defender. James shot 38 percent in those instances and the Warriors outscored the Cavs by fifty-five. If Golden State didn't have Iguodala, they wouldn't have won the series. That was pretty valuable in my eyes.

James, however, was physically, mentally, and emotionally exhausted after the series. While the Warriors were busy draining hundreds of bottles of Mumm Napa Brut Prestige champagne down the hall in Dressing Room H, James couldn't move. Nearly an hour after the game ended, he remained reclined at his locker with a towel wrapped around his head and his hands holding it in place. He was an exhausted giant who had just been struck with a final stone. After he showered, dressed, and walked down the hall to the podium, James wasn't feeling any better.

"Of course you question it, especially when you get to this point," James said. "I always look at it, would I rather not make the playoffs or lose in the Finals? I don't know. I don't know. . . . I'm almost starting to be like, I'd rather not even make the playoffs than to lose in the Finals."

James concluded his interview, said his good-byes, and staggered into the warm summer night. He had been to five straight Finals, but he had lost the last two, and three of the five. His overall Finals record slumped to 2-4, and most painfully, Cleveland's championship drought dragged on. Not even LeBron James was powerful enough to overcome more than five decades of misery. At least, not yet.

CHAPTER 15

Pool Views

Jensen Karp is a Hollywood comedy writer who was invited to visit a friend at the posh Peninsula hotel rooftop pool in Beverly Hills one sunny day in late June, just a couple of weeks after the Cavs' loss to the Warriors. Karp, an avid basketball fan, spotted James getting a massage in one of the hotel's twelve private cabanas. He later told a Cleveland radio station he didn't think much of it but kept his eye on James as he continued chatting. Soon, he saw someone who looked like Love grab a chair and join James in his cabana. This was confusing, because James wasn't expected to try to recruit Love back to Cleveland.

Love was now a free agent after opting out, as expected, of the final year of his deal. By now everyone knew the score, and the challenges ahead. After some of the tensions Love and James had throughout their first season together, it was fair to question whether Love was going to follow through, despite repeating for months that his intention was to remain in Cleveland.

The pool at the Peninsula is sixty feet long and offers breathtaking views of the Los Angeles skyline. But it was the view inside that shocked Karp. He walked closer to the pair, snapping a picture of Love as the Cavs star was grabbing a chair. Unsure what to do with it, Karp sent it to a friend to verify that it was really Love. When his friend confirmed it was, Karp thought about what to do for another ten minutes or so before finally electing to post the picture on Twitter. It was retweeted a couple of times, and Karp didn't think much of it. A few minutes later, however, his phone began vibrating from all of the retweets and it wouldn't stop. The photo was retweeted more than five thousand times. Karp had unexpectedly kicked off summer free agency.

As I, and the rest of the press, later found out, Love had pursued the meeting with James to try to clear the air. His mind was still made up—he was returning to Cleveland—but changes had to be made to their relationship. Love, however, insists there was never any sort of ultimatum.

"More than anything I just wanted to see what he thought about where the team was going and what we wanted to accomplish," Love said. "It was always 'we' or 'us.' It was never like, 'You need to tell me this.' Never."

The two met for no more than an hour, but Love's message had been delivered. He followed through on his in-season promises to re-sign with the Cavs, announcing the five-year, $110 million deal on the first day of free agency—the most the Cavs could pay him.

He arrived for his second season in fantastic shape. He spent the summer in Park City, Utah, with Alex Moore from the Cavs' training staff. Moore is no stranger to Park City. Before he was hired by Grant in 2013, Moore spent the previous six years as the strength and conditioning coordinator for the US ski team. In one of his final moves as general manager the summer before he was fired, Chris Grant brought in Moore to help overhaul the Cavs' training staff. Grant believed American medicine was well behind the world and team trainers had become reactive to injuries instead of proactive. They did well at taping ankles and treating sprains and tears, but there wasn't enough done in the way of injury prevention. So he went and found Moore.

Australia's population is about twenty-four million—roughly the size of Texas. In order to adequately compete in the Olympics, Australia has become the world leader in studying athletics and the human body. The Australian Institute of Sport was created in 1981 to give the country's elite athletes a place to train and to learn about nutrition and recovery. American officials agree there is nothing like AIS in this country, which helps explain why Moore was here. By the summer of 2015, Moore had become a fixture in Love's training regimen and now spends most of the year with him—even during summers.

Moore is the unofficial mayor of Park City after his time there with the ski team. With an elevation of nearly seven thousand feet, it's the perfect place to work out. But these workouts consisted of paddleboards, yoga, and hiking trails that carried them to heights of nearly nine thousand feet, along with more traditional weight training and exercise bikes. They were workouts for mind, body, and spirit, a much-needed cleansing after the torn labrum prematurely ended his season and the Cavs fell short of the championship.

A typical training day included a stretch, followed by sixty to ninety minutes of weights and then recovery, followed by more training.

On-court basketball work occurred in the evening. Moore was taught that living and training in that high an altitude for a month will alter the body's hemoglobin mass, essentially allowing the body to carry more oxygen in the blood. Therefore, the body will be capable of doing more work when it returns to sea level.

After his time in Park City, Love arrived for the 2015–16 season in the best shape of his life. If he wanted a bigger role in the offense, he was about to get it. With Irving sidelined to start the 2015–16 season while recovering from knee surgery, the Cavs were going to have to rely on James and Love for at least the first couple of months. James began saying things like Love would be the focal point of the offense and "We're going to ride his coattails."

"He's going to have a hell of a season," James said. "He's going to get back to that All-Star status. He's the focal point of us offensively."

In all his years in the league and with all the teammates that he had played alongside, never had James called another player a focal point or admitted to riding another man's coattails. Not Wade, not Bosh. Certainly not anyone from his first tour in Cleveland. There was little chance James actually believed it—Love even knew he didn't really believe it—but James appeared to be sending a message: You want it? You got it. Love was eager to prove he could do it.

"We talked about that I can do more," Love said. "From a comfort standpoint, I feel a lot better."

It didn't take long into their second year together for people within the Cavs to finally admit the first year between the two stars did not go as planned. All of Love's 2015 ailments—his back, his legs, his general conditioning—were connected, and none of his body parts were firing properly. James had been right to be frustrated. This wasn't the player he'd thought he was recruiting to join him in Cleveland.

James loves challenges and the Cavs believed he took on Love as his own project in their second season together in an effort to build him up and empower him. That's what James has always done on the court. He empowers his teammates and makes them better than they really are—and Love was already an All-Star without him.

"Some of the finer points and perhaps things people overlook is how he influences his teammates and how he influences the flow of the game just by recognizing what helps other guys function better when he trusts in something or someone on the court," Blatt said at the time. "'Bron also understands this is a long season and the more he empowers those around him, the better it's going to be going down the line."

Love averaged 17.3 points and 10.5 rebounds while Irving was rehabilitating. He shot 44 percent and was no longer just a decoy and a floor spacer. He was also getting about eight shots a night that were not three-pointers. The Cavs were 17-7 when Irving returned just prior to Christmas, and the coaches and front office hoped the team would continue playing so well with Love and James that Irving would fall in line. As feared, however, Love's production again fell off. His scoring dropped to thirteen points a game the first month Irving was back and he shot just 38 percent from the floor in those first seventeen games. Love was very clearly the third wheel again, lodged behind the two guys who had the ball in their hands most nights.

But the Cavs were winning and Love was now locked in long-term, so Blatt wasn't terribly concerned with making sure Love got his numbers. He was rightfully more concerned with making sure the Cavs got their victories. James, meanwhile, shifted his focus to getting his All-Star point guard back up to game condition. All of which led to one fascinating afternoon in Dallas in early January.

The Mo Williams Academy is tucked away in a nondescript strip of warehouses in a nondescript section of Dallas. Williams, the veteran point guard who'd returned to Cleveland prior to the season after playing alongside James during his first stint with the Cavs, was tired of paying high-priced trainers to work with him during the summer months, so he created a gym near his offseason home to fit his hectic schedule. Williams is a husband and father and sometimes can't get to a court until the middle of the night. His gym allows him access whenever he wants. He built the facility in 2011 and now has family running it year-round.

"I tell guys all the time—we go out and we buy all the nice cars and big houses and these things like that. Invest in a gym," Williams says. "That's your craft. You can do what I did, which is the cheaper route [on a house] and have your facility. This is what you do for a living. Splurge on that."

What started as a personal luxury grew into something more significant. Now Williams sponsors summer Amateur Athletic Union basketball teams comprised of middle school kids and has worked with some of the game's brightest young stars, such as Julius Randle and Emmanuel Mudiay. One of his more recent pupils, Billy Preston, was milling around the facility as one of the nation's top high school players the day the Cavs were there. Preston would later be recruited by Kansas.

Since opening his facility, Williams has played for the Clippers, Jazz, Trail Blazers, Timberwolves, Hornets, and now the Cavs. His NBA teams routinely use the facility when they're in town to play the Mavericks, and so it was in January 2016 that the Cavs made the short drive to Leston Street for an off-day practice just hours before Alabama beat Clemson to win college football's national championship. At the time, Irving was about a month into his return from the fractured kneecap he suffered in the Finals. He needed surgery to repair the fracture and spent six lonely months rehabbing.

Irving had turned twenty-three in March, three months before his knee injury. Turning twenty-three is significant. It's referred to as "the Jordan year," named after Michael Jordan's number 23 jersey. It's even more significant when you play in the NBA and your birthday falls on the twenty-third. As Irving was celebrating his twenty-third birthday on March 23, his friends and family kept insisting this was going to be his golden year, his Jordan year. That's what Irving kept thinking about as he lay around with his knee in a cast. He did a lot of reading, he worried about whether he'd be the same player when he returned, and, yes, he watched the play where he was injured.

"I knew at that moment I was done," he told me. "I knew it." The moment it happened, Irving had sat on the court feeling his right knee, then his left. The left one didn't feel the same. He told Steve Spiro, the Cavs' trainer, he needed to go back to the locker room.

"As I'm walking and my adrenaline and my body started to slow down, I'm like, 'This is it right here,'" he said. "'I'm done.'"

Long before the knee injury, Irving had developed a reputation for making big shots in big moments. His first game winner occurred during his rookie year, back when he was nineteen and Byron Scott was still joking that his breath smelled like the baby formula Similac. Irving dribbled around a screen, split two defenders, and flipped in a left-handed layup over a late-arriving Paul Pierce with 2.6 seconds left at the Garden to stun the Celtics, 88–87. His father, Drederick, who had starred collegiately at Boston University, pumped his fists in excitement from the stands.

Irving lacked confidence growing up, but it's now one of his greatest strengths. Irving concedes that his father worried whether Kyrie would ever develop an ability to destroy his opponents. Early in his career, Scott wasn't sure whether Irving had that "killer" gene. Chris Paul had it. Scott was Paul's first NBA coach and he spotted it as early as his rookie year. Scott used to joke that Paul would tear an opponent's throat out to win a game. He wasn't sure Irving had it.

"It's going to be scary to see him in four or five years," Scott said toward the end of Irving's second season. "When he figures out this league and the game really slows down for him, it's going to be scary."

Irving fought injuries throughout his career, first his toe and then shoulder, wrist, and facial injuries. He also struggled with learning how to lead. He was asked to carry a heavy load while James was in Miami. He was a point guard who rarely passed and was considered a ball hog by most everyone—including his teammates. Irving insists he was doing what was asked of him to try to win games, but one of James's first goals after arriving was teaching Irving how to be a distributor.

Once James chose to return to Cleveland, he began watching film of Irving. He knew Irving was a great young talent, but he wanted to learn his tendencies. Film study may not reveal a player's personality, but it will expose how much a point guard can help his teammates. James saw Irving wasn't doing much in that regard. It's part of the reason he took the ball out of Irving's hands early in their first year together. James was teaching Irving how to be a point guard in the NBA, when to pass and when to attack.

"I just wanted him to understand that he could mean so much more to our team by also being a playmaker for the guys that can't play-make for themselves," James said. "Obviously, he's able to go through two and three guys every single possession if he wants." Referring to their first year together, James said, "My game was all predicated on figuring out how to get these guys, and mostly Kyrie, to understand how important it is getting other guys involved. And he's a good student. Little hardheaded at times. [Young guys] all are, which I expected. I expected that."

Now, as Irving dribbled and shot on the court inside Williams's academy, James was subtly teaching him another lesson. The Cavs had rebounded from their crushing Finals loss and survived injuries to both Irving and Iman Shumpert to start the season 17-7. Shumpert missed the first six weeks recovering from a fractured wrist he'd suffered just prior to the start of training camp. Irving returned from his knee injury December 20 against the Philadelphia 76ers.

Before and after his return from knee surgery, Irving routinely remained on the floor long after the formal portion of practice had ended, working on his shot and rhythm. James often joined him. On this day, while Irving threw up shot after shot—from the wing, the three-point line, the corner, and all points in between—Williams spoke for more than an hour about his gym: the office space, the full laundry services, and the small lounge.

What it lacked, however, was showers. So while Irving and James remained on the floor shooting and shooting, the rest of the sweaty Cavs stood on the sidelines or sat in the bleachers and waited. As the minutes swelled into an hour, their patience waned. Sasha Kaun, an NBA rookie, was the first to be visibly irritated. Anderson Varejao saw how mad Kaun was getting and laughed at him.

"He doesn't get it," Varejao joked with me. "This is life with LeBron. Sometimes you wait."

Yet after about twenty more minutes, Varejao wasn't laughing anymore. Now he was annoyed, too. Love fidgeted with his phone. Assistant coaches made dinner plans. James and Irving, however, never flinched. They simply kept shooting.

"I will never leave the court without him," James told me. "Meaning if he's the only person in there shooting, I'm not going to leave. I'm not. And he knows that."

James knew teammates and coaches were getting upset, but he didn't care. The shooting session went on so long that even Tyronn Lue, still Blatt's lead assistant, stormed back into the gym as James and Irving were concluding. "Let's go!" Lue shouted across the gym. "This is fucking rude and disrespectful!" James chuckled and told him not to get so upset in front of the media, even though there were only a few of us there at the time.

"They can leave us. They don't have to wait for us," James told me later. "We know the way back."

With LeBron, there is almost always sound reasoning behind a display. In that moment, he wanted the rest of his teammates to see how hard the two stars were working, and the more pissed they got, the more they'd remember.

"At the end of the day, late in games, the ball is going to be in our hands," James told me. "We've got to be able to trust each other and our teammates have to be able to trust us. If they see us working like they always do, it gives them more trust in us. And then we have to come through for them."

He was right. One hundred and sixty-one days later, Irving would have the ball in his hands in the last minute of Game 7 of the NBA Finals.

CHAPTER 16

Christmas Mourning

The life of an NBA writer is equal parts exhilarating and depressing, fulfilling and fruitless. It's earning Marriott platinum status while living out of a suitcase eighty nights a year, answering four A.M. wake-up calls to get to the next city, and choking down bad arena food (usually lukewarm pasta or something fried, things that are cheap to make and that can be cooked in bulk) before tipoff. Catch a quick nap and risk getting beat on a story; let your cell phone die at the wrong time and it's career suicide. I was out to dinner with my family one fall night when my cell phone died. In the twenty minutes it took to finish eating, pay the check, buckle the kids in the car, and plug my phone in, Tristan Thompson ended his holdout and agreed to a five-year contract. I was the last to know.

Baseball was always my first love, but the life of a baseball beat writer is personal-life homicide. With a wife and three kids, the grind of a baseball season (45 days at spring training *and then* a 162-game season) is even harsher than that of basketball. At least with the NBA, I'm home most of the summer when the kids are out of school. I've done college football and the NBA, but family is a big reason why I stayed in this lane and never pursued a career covering baseball. It's difficult at times choosing between career and family. David Blatt has been forced to continually make that decision year after year. He also has a wife and four children, although his kids are grown now. When they were younger, however, Blatt was rarely with them. He bounced from Israel to Russia to Italy to Turkey for various coaching jobs while his wife and kids remained in Israel. Even when Blatt took the Cavs job, his family stayed behind.

In 2015, I skipped the Christmas Day game at Golden State to watch my kids open presents. I caught up with the West Coast trip the next day in Portland, where the Cavs were scheduled to play the Blazers that night. Shortly after I landed, it became clear something was wrong. Players were angry with the way the Cavs lost at the Warriors on Christmas Day and they were taking it out on Blatt.

"It's hard when you go from playing overseas where you're playing one or two games a week, kind of like in college, to come here where you're playing four games in five nights," former Cavs center Brendan Haywood said. "You can't play LeBron, Kevin Love, and Kyrie all these minutes. You've got to play a Mike Miller or develop him for later in the season. Maybe it's Joe Harris. Somebody. You have to develop your bench during the season. You can't burn these guys out during the regular season and that's something eventually he was going to learn, but he didn't understand that."

Richard Jefferson didn't play at all in the loss, which upset some of the veterans. Blatt's approach, which was to treat every night like a Game 7 and win at all costs, rather than trying to develop a consistent rotation and style of play, was aggravating the players. So was the way he refused to hold James accountable in film sessions and seemed to be intimidated by his star.

"I saw the tepidness in how he was trying to correct LeBron at times. In film it was uneasy," Haywood said. "As a coach, you have to have control of your team. That's what T-Lue does very well. There's no uneasiness. He says, 'LeBron, I need this.' When you dance around hard topics with your upper-echelon players, the middle tier and lower tier guys see it. Then what happens is it slowly eats away at your credibility. I think that's what happened to David."

"He's losing them," one person told me the day after the Cavs lost at Golden State. In truth, he never really had them. Even at 19-8 and first place in the East, a mutiny was mounting. The Cavs played one of their worst games of the season the next night at Portland. James seemed disinterested, rarely engaging on either side of the ball and spending most of the night half-heartedly jogging up and down the floor. The Blazers were without star guard Damian Lillard, but that didn't even matter. The Cavs trailed 34–12 after the first quarter and it never got better. The team with one of the highest payrolls in league history was embarrassed 105–76.

"We got kicked in the keister," Blatt said.

James was more direct and even hinted at some of the players' frustrations over an ever-changing lineup and rotation.

"For the first eight weeks, we had built chemistry, we knew who was playing, we knew who wasn't playing. We had rotations. Coach had rotations down, so we've got to get back to that," James said. "We have no rhythm. We have some guys who don't know if they're going to play and it's hurting our rhythm a little bit."

Suddenly it became evident that the record didn't matter anymore. The players were sick of their coach. They tolerated him when they won and blamed him when they lost. His inability to stand up to James was just one of his many issues. These holidays were happy for no one. The entire locker room was fed up.

"They're going to fire him, aren't they?" one person who knew the team well asked me during that Blazers game. It was a stunning turn of events. David Griffin was standing in the corner of the locker room with his arms folded when I approached him after the game.

"Guys are pissed," I said, and he nodded in agreement. I told him the players were done with Blatt and revolting against him. Griffin didn't say much, but he didn't deny it. I asked if Blatt was going to be fired. He said no.

But he was going to be fired, actually—just not yet, because Griffin had yet to convince Lue to take the job. At some point in December, the Cavs again approached Lue about taking over as head coach. He refused, instead calling Rivers, his mentor, and telling him he couldn't do it.

"People didn't know the behind-the-scenes that they had already asked him a month before and he said no," Rivers said. "Ty called me and said, 'I'm not taking this job. This is just going to make me look terrible. I'm loyal to David.'"

So the Cavs trudged on with Blatt in charge. It was an unusual situation, certainly, but everything with Blatt was unusual. No coach had ever been fired with his team atop the conference. But while the Cavs had beaten the easy teams, they struggled to beat the league's elite. They won eight straight after the embarrassing loss at Portland but lost to the Spurs on the road in a close game to end the winning streak. Then the Warriors returned to Cleveland on January 18 for a much-anticipated rematch of the Christmas Day shootout. The Warriors swaggered in with a glistening 37-4 record, but they had been drilled two nights earlier at Detroit. No matter. Steph Curry said he hoped the visiting locker room in Cleveland still smelled like champagne from the hundreds of bottles of Mumm Napa Brut Prestige the Warriors had drenched Dressing Room H in the last time they were here. The champagne comment irritated James, who was further rankled when the media didn't ask him about it the morning of the game. James had a retaliation ready, but no one ever heard it because of what happened that night.

The Cavs were dismantled by the Warriors 132–98. They showed no fight and no heart. The energy was lacking for such a pivotal game—one of the few of consequence in a monotonous eighty-two-game march through the regular season. The Warriors were terrific defensively, packing the paint to cut off drives while staying with the shooters on the wings. With all of their options neutralized, the Cavs were reduced to isolation, with James and Irving dominating the ball while the Warriors built a forty-three-point lead early in the fourth quarter. It was the largest deficit James had ever faced during his twelve years in the NBA.

"They came in and just kicked our ass," Irving said.

James's criticisms were getting more pointed. When I asked him before the game about the possibility of facing the Warriors again in the Finals, James shook his head in disgust, saying it was "absurd" and "ridiculous" to be thinking about June in the middle of January. The Cavs had plenty of issues to fix before they could worry about the Finals. A few hours later, the Warriors exposed them all.

"Against the top teams, you want to play well. And we haven't done that," James said after the beating. "We're oh-and-three versus the top two teams in the West. We've got to play better basketball."

Despite Lue's resistance, the decision was made. The loss to the Warriors was the knockout punch. David Blatt was going to be fired. If Lue didn't want the job, they'd go find somebody else. But Blatt's time in Cleveland was over. Knowing how close Lue was to Rivers and how much he admired his mentor, a high-ranking Cavs official called Rivers the day after the Warriors loss to tell him Blatt was going to be fired.

"That's when I knew it was definite," Rivers said. No one from the Cavs ever explicitly told Rivers to convince Lue to take the job, but Rivers didn't see any other way to interpret the phone call. "When I've got them calling me to say, 'Hey, this is going to happen,' I think that was their message. They didn't say that at all, they just said, 'We've got crazy stuff, we're going to let David go.' I'm no dummy. I knew."

Blatt stayed on long enough for the Cavs to beat a terrible Nets team two nights later, and Griffin maintained he didn't like the way the locker room felt after the victory. It was dead inside, even after a win.

"Their heart was gone," Griffin said. "It was completely undermining the team."

The truth is, the decision to fire Blatt had been made even before that game in Brooklyn. Rivers and the Clippers came to Cleveland the night after that win against the Nets for a back-to-back. Rivers walked into the Q already knowing Blatt's fate.

"It was actually a tough game coaching against David because I like him," Rivers said, but ultimately he did as the Cavs wanted. He convinced Lue to take the job. He had no choice.

"You've got to take the job," Rivers told him. "They're going to fire David. Whether that's right or wrong, they're going to fire him. And if you don't take it, someone else is going to take it. You have to take this job. You're getting a great job. Now go do the job."

At 30-11, with the best record in the East at the exact midpoint of the season, Blatt was fired the day after the Cavs beat the Clippers. He was then replaced by Lue in an announcement that shocked the league.

"I'm embarrassed for our league that something like this can happen," said Dallas Mavericks head coach Rick Carlisle, who is also the president of the coaches' association. "It just leaves you with a bit of an empty feeling because Blatt's a great guy and he did a great job there."

Other coaches, such as Gregg Popovich and Stan Van Gundy, also took shots at the Cavs over the firing. The faux outrage across the league was widespread and nauseating. Some of the coaches feigning shock and disappointment at Blatt's firing were the same ones crushing him privately during his first season in charge.

"What the hell is he doing?" one rival head coach had asked me during Blatt's first week on the job, when he bragged about how he delivered a tongue-lashing to his team before his second game as a head coach. Coaches around the league were surprised at his demeanor, the way he interacted with the media, and his confounding substitutions and use of time-outs. Now, however, they were going to stick up for him. After all, the Cavs had reached the Finals with Blatt in charge and again owned the best record in the East. If he could be fired, then none of them were safe.

"We just really caught fire in a unique way during those playoffs and found a way to overcome. It's because that team dealt with adversity so incredibly well, I almost think the David fit being bad was the adversity that they needed," Griffin said. "But it wasn't David's fault. You can't run a team that's trying to win a championship that has the best player in history on it and not be a gangster. It's just not going to work that way. Especially when you have two other kids who were as good as Kyrie and Kevin. That's a lot of personalities, it's a lot of talent, and it requires a very strong hand. And it just wasn't the right fit."

Lue, however, was the gangster Griffin needed.

The annual Fourth of July party Tyronn Jamar Lue throws is one of the perks to living in Mexico, Missouri. Well, that and the Miss Missouri pageant, which is held there every year. Lue was born and raised in the small rural town about 110 miles northwest of St. Louis and returns there every summer to throw a daylong party that concludes with a fireworks show—paid for by Lue. He began the tradition early in his playing career and now thousands attend.

Lue rents out the city pool that day so all the kids can swim for free. He hires a blues band for entertainment and purchases hot dogs and hamburgers to feed the entire city and even folks from neighboring communities. The town proudly considers itself the "soybean capital" and even has a soybean festival every summer, but a biodiesel refinery serves as its biggest industry now. The coach, however, remains their finest export.

Lue played for seven teams during his eleven-year career as a backup point guard. He wore cornrows as a player but shaved them before he went into coaching. Now his blunt honesty and charming smile are his trademarks. He was listed as a six-foot guard during his playing days, although those height measurements are known to be generous. What Lue lacked in size he compensated for with smarts and grit.

"Sometimes you've got to see the game a step or two ahead and he's got that," Cavs assistant coach Larry Drew said. "We'll be sitting on the bench during games and things will be happening and he could dissect the play. We would go through the options of our play and as it's happening, he would see things that would be there as the fourth and fifth option. Guys like that, man, they're rare. They're rare."

Lue broke into the league as a backup with the Lakers. He was part of the reserve unit scrimmaging the starters one day near the end of practice when Kobe Bryant drove baseline while Lue was standing at the elbow—the area on the court where the free-throw line meets the lane line. Lue met Bryant at the rim and pinned his shot against the glass for a clean block. Devean George made a layup at the other end and Lue's team won. Bryant was furious.

"Kobe wanted to fight me at first," Lue said. "Second, he wanted to play one-on-one after practice. I said, 'No, I'm not playing you one-on-one.' After that, every day we stepped onto the court, he just went after me. Every single day. It was crazy."

Rivers coached Lue for only one season in Orlando and was so enamored with him, Rivers gave him an open invitation to join his coaching staff whenever Lue retired. Five years later, Lue took him up on the offer. He remained with Rivers for five years, working his way up the coaching bench before the Cavs stole him away to be Blatt's top assistant. His job was to acclimate Blatt to the NBA, and while no one ever said it out loud, it was clear that Lue was also the break-glass-in-case-of-emergency if the Blatt experiment went off the rails.

Now the time had come. The glass was broken, and Lue was in charge of a first-place team with championship aspirations. And the organization was behind him in every way, both publicly and privately. "I feel like we won't miss a whole lot," Griffin said when he made the change. "But I do feel like we're going to gain a lot in some areas that were critical to us."

The most important of those areas was accountability. Blatt never stood up to LeBron, either publicly or privately. The most uncomfortable he ever made James was the one night he emerged from his office after a game wearing only a towel. "C'mon, Coach," James said. "I can't talk to you like this." But they did. After a brief chat, James turned and walked toward Tristan Thompson. "That man was naked," he said.

Lue was respected and revered around the league. In seemingly every arena he enters, players and former players seek him out to say hello. That credibility extends to superstars such as James. In his first few days after taking the job, Lue criticized the players for not being in proper shape, and told his Big Three to stop worrying about their brand and focus more on winning.

"If you win, everybody's brand is better," Lue said. "We still have a young group of guys. Just gotta keep instilling that message. If we win, everybody is taken care of. That's the message."

Lue vowed to hold LeBron accountable. He called out James's mistakes during film sessions and addressed his chummy on-court behavior with Dwyane Wade after the Heat whipped the Cavs in a March road game. He was also the one who had cussed out James, back when he was still just an assistant, for staying so long at Williams's facility and forcing the rest of the team to wait.

But he also had problems of his own. One of his biggest issues was trying to implement Love into the offense. James's talk of making Love the focal point had slowly dwindled after Irving returned, and he again looked lost on the court. When the Cavs suffered an embarrassing 104–95 loss at Brooklyn during Easter weekend, the wheels were threatening to come off the cart again just a week before the playoffs. Firing Blatt from a first-place team left a target squarely on Griffin, who wondered whether he would be fired at the end of the season.

Rumors about Tom Thibodeau began to resurface. Gilbert has long had an affection for Thibodeau's defensive style of coaching. The Cavs had asked the Bulls for permission to speak with Thibodeau prior to hiring Blatt. The Bulls denied them, then fired him anyway at the end of the season. Whispers were growing louder that if the Cavs failed to make the Finals, another housecleaning would be in order. Blatt's firing was all on Griffin. If this went sideways, Griffin and Lue could be out, and Thibodeau would be in, with the title of president and head coach. He would have full control and answer only to Gilbert.

It was a long night within the organization following that loss to the Nets. That was also about the time that Lue got in Love's face and told him to start playing like an All-Star. Love scored eleven points and grabbed twelve rebounds against the Nets but shot five of fourteen and missed all five of his three-point attempts. Lue was tired of watching how passively Love was playing. He wanted Love to be more aggressive and demand the ball. The gangster in Lue that Griffin loved so much came firing out. He wanted Love to shoot with confidence and to stop hesitating.

"You're a bad motherfucker," Lue told Love. "Play like it."

Love ended the regular season averaging 18.9 points and 9.9 rebounds. He shot a dazzling 46 percent from three-point range. There were only nine games before the end of the regular season, but Love got back to playing the way Lue wanted. The Cavs ended the regular season 27-14 under Lue, three games worse than they were under Blatt. No one cared about the record. Griffin believed when he made the coaching change that the Cavs might regress before taking a step forward. The record indicated they had, but everyone within the organization believed they now had a chance to win. Lue, meanwhile, was simply saving his finest coaching performances for when they mattered most.

CHAPTER 17

Gambling Man

Tyronn Lue insists he's never smoked and doesn't touch alcohol. If he has a vice, it's gambling. He loves the tables in Las Vegas and can often be found there during Summer League or even during the All-Star break. That helps explain why he was so quick to bet on himself after replacing Blatt as head coach. Gilbert fired Mike Brown one year into a five-year deal and he fired Blatt less than two years into a four-year deal. Lue, however, didn't like the figures the Cavs were offering and chose instead not to sign. He'd coach the team, but he wasn't signing a new contract. Part of it was money; part of it was not wanting to look like he was undermining Blatt and negotiating a new deal behind his back. So he bet on himself and a team that finished the season 57-25, tops in the East. He took his chances with a deep postseason run to prove he was worth more.

Lue had more confidence in himself than many others. *Sporting*

News ranked him fourteenth among all sixteen head coaches entering the postseason. The only ones below him were the Thunder's Billy Donovan and the Rockets' J. B. Bickerstaff, who were also rookies. I was near the back of the media scrum one day shortly after the rankings were released when Lue threw his shoulder into me on his way by. "Fourteen," he muttered, glaring at me. Lue often likes to joke and body-check me on his way by, so I didn't think much of it, but I had no idea what he meant by "Fourteen." A few days later he signaled "fourteen" to me with his fingers and shouted at me from across the practice court on his way into his office. Again, I had no idea what he was talking about, so I walked over to talk to him.

"Man, you ranked me fourteenth out of all the coaches!" Lue barked. I laughed and told him he had the wrong guy. It wasn't me. "He told me you did!" Lue exclaimed, driving the bus over Cavs assistant coach Damon Jones, who immediately denied culpability. Regardless, it didn't take long for Lue to outperform the ranking as the fourteenth-best coach of the playoffs.

He outcoached highly respected names like Stan Van Gundy and Mike Budenholzer in the first two rounds. The Cavs entered believing the Pistons could be a bad matchup to begin the playoffs. The pick-and-roll combination of Reggie Jackson and Andre Drummond was dangerous because of the fear it would expose Irving's deficiencies defensively, while the undersized and athletic Marcus Morris at power forward was a bad matchup for Love.

The Pistons were not a prolific three-point-shooting team, but after they made ten in the first half of Game 1 and led the Cavs 83–76 on Reggie Bullock's three-pointer early in the fourth quarter, an uneasiness filled Quicken Loans Arena. Eight years earlier, Van Gundy had brought an underdog into the Q and stunned the Cavs by spreading the floor with four shooters around one dominant big man. The Orlando Magic had eliminated the Cavs in the conference finals in 2009, inching James a little closer to his ultimate exit. Now Van Gundy was eleven minutes away from replicating that formula and taking a stunning 1–0 lead against the heavily favored Cavs.

Lue flipped the game—and the series—when he called a time-out following Bullock's three and rolled out a smaller lineup when the game resumed. James began the fourth on the bench because he needed a quick breather after playing nearly all of the third quarter. When Lue reinserted him at power forward and shifted Love to center with 11:04 to play, the Cavs erupted. The game was tied in less than two minutes and they scratched out a 106–101 win. Lue was praised for his lineup maneuvering while Van Gundy left the arena second-guessing his decision to stick with ineffective Tobias Harris so long and leave rookie Stanley Johnson on the bench.

"The first thing that comes to my mind is things I could have done differently to give us a better chance to win the game," Van Gundy said. "I'm not really looking to stay close, that's not my objective here. We're here to try to win games and we didn't get it done tonight and I think I had a considerable amount to do with that."

Johnson made quite an impression in the series, but not all of it was for his play. The brash nineteen-year-old went right at James on and off the court in the series, insisting after Game 2 he was in James's head.

"He jabbers. He moves his mouth sometimes. Their whole team does, kind of like they're little cheerleaders on the bench," Johnson said.

"Every time you walk in the right corner. They're always saying something like they're playing basketball, like they're actually in the game. There's only seven or eight players who play. I don't see why the other players are talking. They might as well just be in the stands, in my opinion."

It's nothing new for young guys to try to make a name for themselves against James, particularly in the playoffs. DeShawn Stevenson tried and failed with the Washington Wizards; then Lance Stephenson tried engaging James in the postseason. Stephenson infamously blew in James's ear during an Indiana-Miami playoff series and James responded with an eye roll and head shake. By now, he was used to inferior players using him to make headlines. He had consistently responded the same way: by not engaging.

"The game is played in between the four lines," James said. "Everything outside that means absolutely nothing."

While Van Gundy was addressing Johnson about his comments and trying to get him to quiet down, Lue was impressing with his quick-change lineups and play calls. Lue had the awareness to get James and J. R. Smith back into the game for an out-of-bounds play with 1.6 seconds left in the first quarter of Game 1, a foreshadowing of things to come. James made a layup to give the Cavs the lead in what was the first of many out-of-bounds plays Lue drew up that worked perfectly. Plays drawn up after time-outs, or "ATOs" for short, are crucial in playoff series.

Lue has kept a notebook that dates back to his playing days full of different notes, scribbles, and play ideas. Within the notebook is a full section on ATOs. Van Gundy changed the Pistons' defensive schemes on ATOs during the series and Lue knew he needed a counter, so he sat down with Larry Drew shortly before Game 3 to brainstorm. "We've got to be able to burn them," Lue told Drew, and the two spent about ten minutes scribbling out ideas. Three hours later, they flipped Kevin Love and LeBron James's positioning on an inbounds play and it worked. Irving made a crucial three-pointer in the corner in the final seconds and the Cavs took a commanding 3–0 series lead.

The Cavs led 95–90 with forty-five seconds left when Lue gave the ball to Matthew Dellavedova to inbound from the far corner of the court. Irving began the play at the elbow, then turned his back to the play and set a screen on Harris to create a mismatch. When the bigger, slower Harris switched onto the guard, Irving flashed to the far corner on the other side of the court. Dellavedova heaved a perfect pass about forty-five feet to a wide-open Irving, who made the corner three-pointer to seal the victory and essentially the series.

"It's crazy that play right there sealed the deal for us," Lue said. "And we worked on it right before the game."

Much like the first-round series with Boston a year earlier, however, the series with the Pistons was growing more physical with every Cavs victory. They felt Detroit was targeting James at one point, repeatedly hitting him with hard elbows around the neck and body with no fouls called. Drummond caught him twice in the series and Morris hit him once—on one play during Game 2, they hit him at the same time. It was Love's turn in Game 4. Morris picked up Love on a switch and twisted his right arm behind him before throwing him down to the court. Love was furious in the locker room over that play.

"Was he trying to even me out?" Love asked, referring to his surgically repaired left shoulder. If he thought the Olynyk arm bar was bush league, then this certainly was. Nothing about it resembled a basketball play and it spoke instead to Morris's threat after Game 1, when he said the Pistons wanted to rough up Love. By the time Morris wrenched Love's arm and threw him to the ground, however, it was too late. The Cavs swept the Pistons with a 100–98 victory in Game 4 and were moving on to the second round.

"We're able to get hit and keep moving forward," Lue said. "We've been harping on that all season—not to drop our head, not to have bad body language when teams make runs. This series we got down a lot. Every game we were down and we just kept pushing, kept moving forward. That's the biggest growth of this team right now—staying with it and not giving in when things get tough."

Beyond the X's and O's, Lue was masterful with his lineups throughout the postseason. He surprised the Pistons with small lineups, then came back to surprise the Hawks with a bigger lineup in the conference semifinals. The Cavs had swept the Hawks out of the postseason in the conference finals the year before when Love was out and Irving was hurting. Now that both players were healthy and the Cavs were making shots, the Hawks had no chance.

Lue is friendly with Bill Belichick from his time as an assistant coach with the Celtics. One of Belichick's best attributes as a coach is his ability to eliminate an opponent's greatest strength. The same is true of Lue, who forces teams to beat the Cavs left-handed. Whenever the

Cavs face the Warriors, they'll run multiple defenders at Steph Curry. Guards are given explicit instructions never to leave Curry's side. Loose ball? Don't leave Curry; let someone else get it. Marreese Speights open on the wing? Don't leave Curry. Ever. They treated Kyle Korver and the Hawks much the same way in every playoff series with the Hawks.

It wasn't an identical duplication of the schemes used against Curry and the Warriors because Curry is Golden State's entire engine; Korver is simply the Hawks' best shooter. The key was not to leave him alone in transition, where he does most of his damage on threes. Korver shot 40 percent from three-point range during the regular season and shot 55 percent in the final six games of Atlanta's first-round series against the Celtics. He shot 50 percent in the conference semifinals against the Cavs, but he took two three-pointers or fewer in three of the four games. Much like the year before, the Cavs successfully eliminated Korver from the Hawks' plans.

"They don't leave Kyle anywhere," Hawks coach Mike Budenholzer said. "They'll send two people at him, they'll send three people at him and leave other people with opportunities. A lot of the shots we get, we'll take. We'll continue to take the same opportunities and if they're going to run two, three guys at Kyle, other guys are going to have good looks and good opportunities."

With Korver neutralized, Cleveland dared the rest of Atlanta's roster to win games and it couldn't. Dennis Schröder made five threes and scored twenty-seven points in Game 1, both career postseason bests, but the Cavs took Game 1, 104–93.

When the Cavs set an NBA record with twenty-five three-pointers in Game 2, it became clear the Hawks still had no idea how to defend so much shooting. The Cavs and Warriors seemed to be locked in a subtle battle of one-upmanship. The Cavs matched the previous record of twenty threes in a game—shared by the Warriors—in their win in the first round against the Pistons. When the Warriors countered by making twenty-one three-pointers in a playoff game four nights later, the Cavs reclaimed the record with a booming night of deep balls against the Hawks.

"It's on them now," Love joked of the Warriors. "It's not like we're going out there saying we've got to beat them on what they're doing or play their type of game. We're just going out there and playing our game."

J. R. Smith made seven three-pointers in the game, including one off one foot while spinning and falling out of bounds. James made four. Even Moondog, the team's mascot, made a half-court shot by heaving the ball underhand, with his back to the basket, on his first try. And after it was over, after the assault was complete, James insisted the Cavs weren't really a three-point-shooting team—even though at the time they led all teams in three-point shooting in the playoffs.

"We're not a three-point-shooting team. We don't want to be labeled that," James said. "We're a well-balanced team that's capable of making threes. . . . Obviously we've got guys that can knock down shots from the perimeter. It's been key to our success, but we have to continue to understand that we have to be very balanced offensively."

Hawks coach Mike Budenholzer was named the Coach of the Year in 2015. He is a disciple of Spurs coach Gregg Popovich, one of the greatest coaches in NBA history, and shares the same philosophies regarding ball movement and defense. Lue may not have liked being ranked fourteenth in the league at the start of the playoffs, but he clearly was the underdog in coaching going against Van Gundy and Budenholzer. Yet Lue made moves that left both coaches spinning.

After his ATOs and lineups caught Van Gundy off guard, Lue surprised Budenholzer and the Hawks with another lineup combination they never prepared to see. Lue was hesitant to play reserve center Channing Frye next to Love because of the defensive issues it caused. Neither player was known for being a strong defender. As a result, they'd appeared together in a game just nine times counting the regular season and playoffs prior to Game 3 of the series against the Hawks. They totaled just thirty-eight minutes together on the court.

With the Cavs trailing 91–85 entering the fourth quarter, Lue rested James and paired Frye and Love together with Irving. The result was an offensive eruption. Frye and Irving scored Cleveland's first fourteen points of the fourth quarter and the Cavs beat Atlanta 121–108 to take a commanding 3–0 series lead. It was their tenth straight win over the Hawks and pulled them within one more win of yet another sweep. Afterward, the Hawks appeared emotionally and mentally defeated. By that point, they knew they couldn't compete.

"We didn't prepare for that," Hawks center Al Horford said of the Love/Frye pairing. "They took advantage."

The Cavs finished off the sweep in Game 4 and ended the series by making 77 three-pointers—easily the most any team has ever made in a four-game series. They made 134 three-pointers through the first two rounds, the most of any team in the league, and they did it in the fewest number of games (eight). And after storming out to a 2–0 lead in the conference finals against the Toronto Raptors, winning the two home games by a total of 50 points, James's sixth consecutive trip to the NBA Finals seemed inevitable.

"We're not giving up until they put us under, until that final buzzer goes off," Raptors coach Dwane Casey said after the Cavs beat Toronto 108–89 in Game 2. "If we do that, we're in the wrong business. Why are we here? I don't see quit. They beat us two games, okay, but it's not over with yet."

Lue's ten consecutive wins to start the postseason was the most in history for a rookie coach, surpassing Pat Riley's nine straight with the Lakers in 1982. James orchestrated a sneak attack in the Cavs' locker room to celebrate the achievement. Before Lue entered, James instructed all of his teammates to grab two water bottles and wait for his signal. After Lue addressed the team following the Game 2 victory, he told the players to meet at the plane at one P.M. the next day to fly to Toronto. They'd watch film at the hotel. As Lue started to leave, James said only, "Congratulations to Coach Lue," and Lue was mauled by at least thirty water bottles. His designer suit, and the carpet in the locker room, were both drenched.

"There are a lot of nights we don't get a lot of rest, a lot of sleep," Lue said. "You're dreaming of ATOs and plays you can run and things that happen, so a lot of sleepless nights, but the way things are going right now, it's worth it."

They were also dreaming of another trip to the Finals, but Casey was right. The Raptors weren't giving up. They won the next two games at home to end the Cavs' momentum and return the series to Cleveland tied at two. No one on the Cavs seemed overly rattled by the consecutive losses.

"Everything is going to be all right," Richard Jefferson said. "We're fine."

Love, yet again, took the brunt of the criticism for the two losses. Often the target of scrutiny since arriving in Cleveland, Love had been terrific through the ten-game winning streak, but he struggled badly during the two losses at Air Canada Centre. He shot just five of twenty-three, including three of eleven from three-point range in games the Cavs lost by a total of twenty-one points.

On an off night in Toronto between Games 3 and 4, a few of the writers went to Real Sports Bar in Toronto, which boasts a thirty-nine-foot HD television. We arrived during the first half of the Oklahoma City Thunder's impressive 133–105 dismantling of the Warriors in Game 3 of the Western Conference finals. James, Love, Dahntay Jones, and a few other players and Cavs personnel watched the game from Real Sports, too, reserving a walled-off portion of the restaurant just above us for a private viewing. Love and James sat together throughout the night and watched midway through the second quarter as Draymond Green swung his right leg wildly while going up for a shot. He kicked Steven Adams in the groin for the second time in their series, leaving the league with a difficult decision to make.

The NBA had already suspended Jones for one game following his nut shot on the Raptors' Bismack Biyombo the day before in Game 3 of the Eastern Conference finals, but no one on the Cavs—including James—expected the league to suspend Green. Sure enough, his kick on Adams was ruled a common foul during the game and upgraded to a flagrant 2 by the league the next day. More importantly, it allowed Green to avoid a suspension. It did, however, leave him one more flagrant foul shy of an automatic one-game suspension. Green knew he had to be on his best behavior for the rest of the Warriors' postseason run.

When the Eastern Conference finals shifted back to Cleveland, Channing Frye told Love to stay positive, that no one is immune to struggling at times in the playoffs. In order for the Cavs to be successful, Frye told him, Love needed to be aggressive. He responded with twenty-five points in twenty-four minutes and the Cavs reestablished their dominance with a 116–78 victory at home in Game 5—their most lopsided postseason victory in franchise history. They broke a record that stood for only eight days. The old mark was set during the opening game of the series, a 115–84 win. The Cavs finished the series outscoring Toronto by a staggering eighty-eight points in the three games at the Q.

"I give [Frye] a lot of credit for staying on me and staying vocal," Love said. "Just needed to respond."

Now one win away, another trip to the Finals seemed inevitable. James, after all, has never failed to close out a series throughout his sparkling career when given more than one chance to eliminate an opponent in the postseason. The Raptors were no match for them in Game 6, either.

James was terrific again, scoring thirty-three points for his first thirty-point game of the postseason. He played thirty-five of the first thirty-six minutes and left the game for good with three minutes remaining, when he could begin hugging teammates and opponents alike in celebration of what was to come. James advanced to his sixth consecutive Finals, the longest streak in the NBA since Bill Russell carried the Celtics to ten straight appearances in the 1950s and '60s.

Irving, Love, and James combined for eighty-three points, twenty-seven rebounds, and nineteen assists in the closeout game. James had said since returning to Cleveland that the Cavs would go as far as their Big Three would take them. For the second straight year, the stars shined all the way to the Finals. Lue helped guide them there. With the pressure of knowing his future beyond the season wasn't guaranteed, Lue dazzled throughout his first postseason with rotations and lineups that befuddled opposing coaches. He drew up key inbounds plays at critical times and, most importantly, he empowered Love to play like an All-Star again. There were mistakes along the way, sure, but Lue quickly proved that indeed, that ranking of fourteenth on the coaches' list was far, far too low.

"It was tough at first because taking over midway through the season, you really don't have a chance to have a lot of practices and no time to really put your stamp on this team," Lue said after winning the East. "But I thought every day my coaching staff really did a great job of just keep honing in on, 'Let's be a team, playing the right way and playing together and moving the basketball and trust.'"

James, meanwhile, has never been one for reflection in the moment. Ask him about his dizzying list of accomplishments and James will always revert to some form of the same answer: He has been fortunate to play for two great organizations and alongside a number of wonderful teammates, and one day when he's old and retired, he'll crack open a bottle of his favorite red wine and sit on a porch somewhere reflecting on all the good memories with his closest friends. Until that time, however, there is still work to be done.

And so it was in the visiting locker room at the Air Canada Centre, when the Cavs didn't have champagne with which to celebrate so they improvised with water instead. Just as they bathed Lue for winning ten straight to begin his coaching career, they baptized each other now with ice buckets and water bottles. For guys like Jefferson, it was the capstone to a long wait to get back to the top. Jefferson had gone to the Finals (and lost) each of his first two years in the league with the New Jersey Nets. He'd never come close to reaching the Finals again.

The only reason he was in Cleveland now was because DeAndre Jordan changed his mind and re-signed with the Los Angeles Clippers after committing to the Mavericks. Jefferson agreed to re-sign in Dallas when he learned Jordan was coming, but after Jordan changed his mind in a dramatic theater scene played out over social media, the Mavericks were gracious enough to let Jefferson out of his verbal agreement with Dallas owner Mark Cuban's blessing. At thirty-five years old, Jefferson was running out of time. He wanted to find a place that gave him a legitimate chance to win a championship and chose Cleveland.

"This is the most talented team I've ever been on, and just really built for what you need," Jefferson said. "I'm the one guy that probably didn't have the biggest smile on my face. I've been here before. It's been thirteen years since I've been here and I'm enjoying this, I'm definitely having fun, I'm relaxed. But you want to see a smile on my face and tears in my eyes? Talk to me after four more wins."

The trophy for winning the East is a silver statue in the shape of a basketball. Players took turns celebrating with it and cradling it in the locker room. When J. R. Smith was done holding the trophy, before he headed off to the shower, he placed it above his locker as onlookers cautioned him not to drop it.

"I'll be right back," Smith told the trophy. "I'm going to get your sister next."

CHAPTER 18

Go West and Strangle the Media

Those men who had last witnessed a Cleveland sports championship, those watched Jim Brown storm through the Baltimore Colts in 1964, many of them were dead by 2016. Those who remained, those who could vividly recall Frank Ryan's touchdown pass to Gary Collins, were old and gray. Pain and scars had stained most of those memories, wounds from failed regimes and terrible ownerships, from Red Right 88 and the Drive and the Fumble and José Mesa and John Elway, from Kevin Love's dislocated shoulder and from Kyrie Irving's broken knee. The common denominator in the lineage of Cleveland sports was always heartbreak and defeat. No matter how the plot twisted and turned, ultimately it ended in some sort of magnificent disaster.

But Richard Jefferson grew up in Arizona. He didn't give a damn about any of that when he signed in Cleveland and he certainly didn't care about it on the eve of the NBA Finals rematch with the Warriors, who had stormed back from a 3–1 deficit for a stunning victory against the Thunder in the Western Conference finals. Jefferson was six months old when Sipe threw the interception in the end zone. He had just learned to drive when Mesa blew the World Series. He was in Dallas playing for the Mavericks when Love's arm was in a sling and Irving was on crutches. None of it mattered to him now.

"That means absolutely nothing to me," Jefferson said of the city's title drought. "I mean no disrespect to the city of Cleveland. We're doing this for the team. We're doing this for our guys. We're doing this for our families. We're doing this for the people that believe in us, and we're happy to be doing it in Cleveland. We're happy to be doing it for the fans who want it as bad as we do. People say, 'Are you doing this for the fans?' It's like, 'Man, I've been working my entire life. I grew up in Arizona. I don't know what the Cleveland history is.' Yeah, it's great to be a part of that. It's great to do it for fans who want it as bad as we do, but for the most part, when you're locked into the battle, when you're locked into the guy next to you, picking him up, that's what we're really doing it for. We're doing it for our families. We're doing it for ourselves. We're doing it for our teammates."

For twelve months, Cleveland had wondered how the 2015 Finals would've transpired if James had had a little more help, if Love and Irving hadn't been injured. James had dragged the Cavs to six games essentially by himself. The city of Cleveland believed adamantly that with three stars, even just two healthy stars, the Cavs would've toppled the Warriors and ended the city's title drought the year before. Now they had their chance. The Warriors may have stormed to a 73-9 mark during the regular season, the best in NBA history, but the Cavs weren't intimidated. They knew they'd led this same team 2–1 in the Finals the year before with a wounded roster and now they were healthy. Steph Curry had suffered a knee injury earlier in the playoffs, but other than that, both teams entered these Finals relatively healthy. Privately, however, the Cavs remained concerned about Love.

Love's second season in Cleveland was better than his first, particularly after Lue replaced Blatt. He finally had a role now. He was creating a comfort zone. Against twenty-eight other teams in the league, including Detroit, Atlanta, and Toronto in the playoffs, Love was a devastating weapon. Even with the two bad games at Toronto, Love averaged 17.3 points and 9.6 rebounds throughout the postseason. He was shooting 45 percent on three-pointers. But the Warriors were the one team that gave him fits. Love had never been known as a great defender and the Cavs were convinced he couldn't guard Draymond Green. They might be able to slide him over onto Andrew Bogut on the defensive end, but when the Warriors went to their famous Death Lineup of Steph Curry, Klay Thompson, Andre Iguodala, Harrison Barnes, and Green, there was nowhere for Love to hide.

"He may have to be our David Lee," one team official told me in March in anticipation of a Finals rematch with the Warriors. It was in reference to the '15 Finals, when Lee, the defensively challenged former All-Star, made $15 million to come off the bench for the Warriors. He didn't play in either of the first two games of those Finals against the Cavs, but Warriors coach Steve Kerr turned to him in Games 3 and 4. Now, three months before the Finals, Cavs executives were already contemplating whether Love would have to accept a similar role and how he would respond to the idea.

After the Warriors won the last three games of the 2015 Finals, they extended that streak by winning the first two games at home again. Neither Curry or Klay Thompson played well in Game 1, but Shaun Livingston scored twenty points and the Warriors' bench outscored Cleveland's 45–10 in a choppy game that lacked much rhythm. It was the first time Livingston led the Warriors in scoring all season and it was particularly painful because he was a former Cav the organization let slip away.

Livingston had rejuvenated his career during the second half of the 2012–13 season after he was released by the Clippers. He appeared in forty-nine games for the Cavs and played well, but they moved on from him because they believed they could do better. So they signed Jarrett Jack, which turned out to be a mistake, and they had to give away a first-round pick and a young center in Tyler Zeller just to get out from under his contract and clear the necessary space to be able to offer James a max-level contract. Now Livingston was back to punish the Cavs for their mistake, but he wasn't the only one whipping them.

The Warriors mauled the Cavs 110–77 at Oracle Arena in Game 2 to take a commanding 2–0 series lead. Curry was a nonfactor yet again, making the losses particularly deflating. He totaled twenty-nine points through the first two games, which is how many he averaged in the nine previous playoff games since returning from that knee injury. The Cavs were determined to make others on the Warriors' roster beat them—and they were. The cumulative forty-eight-point difference was the most through two games in Finals history. The Warriors were simply too fast, too long, too strong, and too athletic for the Cavs to match them. Writers who follow Golden State scoffed at the results, insisting the Thunder gave the Warriors a more competitive series than anything Cleveland could muster.

"We didn't win anything," James said while surveying the stats sheet after Game 2. "No points of the game did we beat them in anything. They beat us to fifty-fifty balls, they got extra possessions, they got extra tip-ins. They beat us pretty good."

The more pressing matter was the health of Love, who had taken a forearm to the back of his head from Harrison Barnes while boxing out for a rebound and suffered a concussion. The Cavs knew it was unlikely he was going to be available for Game 3, which at least temporarily solved their riddle of what to do with him in this series. But they were going home with no momentum and no wins through the first two games of the series. Even in 2015, without Love and Irving, James and the Cavs had still salvaged a split in the first two games at Oracle. Now they were heading home in a deep hole.

"It's a must-win for us," James said of Game 3. "We can't afford to go down three-oh to any team, especially a team that's seventy-three and nine in the regular season and playing the type of basketball they're playing. So it's a do-or-die game for us and we understand that."

Love's absence in Game 3, however, provided Lue with a chance to change his lineup. He started Richard Jefferson at small forward and shifted James to Love's spot at power forward. That meant James would have the assignment of guarding Green, who had punished the Cavs with twenty-eight points, seven rebounds, and five assists in that Game 2 beat-down at Oracle. James gathered his teammates together in the tunnel before taking the floor for Game 3. His instructions were simple.

"Follow my lead and do your fucking job!" he said. Then he roared during the conclusion of the national anthem and roared again when Kerr was forced to take a time-out just two and a half minutes into the game, when the Cavs showed life for the first time in the series and stormed out to a 9–0 lead. James finished with thirty-two points, eleven rebounds, and six assists. Equally important, Green was neutralized to just six points on two of eight shooting. The Cavs pounded Golden State 120–90, handing the Warriors their worst loss of the postseason, and now were just one win away from tying the series.

But just as the Cavs weren't shaken by one loss at Toronto in the conference finals, neither were the Warriors concerned about one loss in Cleveland in the Finals.

"They came out and played like a team with a sense of desperation, like their season was on the line," Green said. "We came out and played like everything was peaches and cream."

The larger question that loomed over the Cavs and Lue was what to do with Love for Game 4. He was going to be cleared to play, but the new lineup with Jefferson starting and James guarding Green seemed to change the series. Lue stuck with what worked, and what the Cavs were privately wondering about in March was suddenly coming true in June. Kevin Love was going to be a bench player for the first time in six years.

The lineup that worked so well in Game 3, however, sputtered in Game 4. The Warriors' switch-everything defense on pick-and-rolls ground the Cavs back into their old ways of isolation basketball, with Irving and James dribbling far too much at the top of the key. That's easy to guard for a swarming defense such as Golden State's, and the Warriors swallowed up the Cavs in the fourth quarter of Game 4 for a

108–97 victory and a commanding 3–1 lead. Love's role in the game was irrelevant, and the bigger detriment was James and Irving combining to take thirty-three of the Cavs' thirty-eight shots in the second half.

James was wrapped in a towel, soaking his feet in a bucket of ice, when I approached his locker. He is a student of the game and knew full well no team had ever rallied from a 3–1 deficit to win the NBA Finals. The Warriors hadn't lost three straight all season. In fact, the last time they'd lost three consecutive games was November 2013. They had played more than 280 games since then. The Cavs' and James's quest to bring a title to Cleveland was officially on life support.

I wondered how someone of his caliber could play forty-six minutes, spend most of that time in the lane attacking the basket, and shoot just four free throws. It didn't seem possible. One of the biggest complaints involving James is how often he gets fouled and there is no call. Blatt had done his best to stick up for James while he was the coach, and Lue did, too.

"He's the Shaq of guards and forwards," Lue said earlier in the postseason. "He's so strong and so physical, when he goes to the basket, guys are bouncing off of him. Those are still fouls, but he doesn't get that call. We used to tease Shaq all the time about soft fouls. He said, 'Listen, if I pinch you, it feels the same way when you pinch me. No matter how big I am, it feels the same.' I never thought about it like that. That's kind of how LeBron feels."

James was furious with how Game 4 had been officiated. He felt Curry slap him on the forearm during one of his drives to the basket in the first quarter. No call. It would've been Curry's second foul, forcing him to the bench and changing the entire complexion of the

game. I told LeBron I was going to ask him about the fouls and officiating when he went to the podium for his postgame press conference.
He laughed and said I could ask whatever I wanted, but he would be
cooled off by then, so I shouldn't expect a juicy response. Fine. But I
wanted to give him the opportunity to address it. Sure enough, after
James showered, dressed, and walked down the long corridor from the
locker room to the interview room, I asked him about the officiating.

"It's been like that all year for the most part," he started. "I'm not
quite sure what I can do personally to get to the free-throw line. I'm
getting hit, but the refs are not seeing it that way. But I've got to continue to be aggressive for our team. That's who I am, that's what opens
up the floor for a lot of our shooters, and just worry about the results
afterward. You know, it's tough playing forty-six minutes and only
going to the line four times, as much as I attack the rim. It's just a tough
situation for our team."

Lue had maintained since taking over as head coach that he didn't
argue with officials. He didn't as a player and he wouldn't get baited
into doing it as a coach. Yet even Lue was fined $25,000 for complain-
ing in his postgame press conference about how James was treated in
that Game 4 loss.

"He never gets calls," Lue said. "I mean, he attacks. Outside of
Russell Westbrook, he's one of the guys that attacks the paint every
single play. And he doesn't get a fair whistle all the time because of his
strength and because of his power and guys bounce off him. But those
are still fouls and we weren't able to get them."

The locker room was eerily quiet. It usually is when dreams are
dying. The Warriors had won eight of the last nine meetings between

these teams dating back to the 2015 Finals and now the Cavs were headed back to Oracle Arena, where they had lost four straight, facing elimination. In order to win, they had to do something no other team had done in the sixty-six-year history of the NBA Finals. The grave was dug and the obituary was written, but there was a path, a narrow, hidden path out of the wilderness. And it was up to the league office to help the Cavs find it.

In the final minutes of Game 4, James and Green became tangled near half-court and Green fell to the floor. James had plenty of ways around Green, but he chose the most direct route—right over the top. His step-over on Green remains one of the lasting images in the series. James said afterward that he was just trying to get back in the play and will forever maintain that, but incensed Warriors players believed he was trying to bait Green into losing his temper—which is exactly what happened. Green jumped up, called James a "bitch," and punched him right in the crotch, something Green had shown a penchant for doing throughout the playoffs. James was incensed at the name-calling as much as anything else.

"I'm all cool with the competition. I'm all fine with that, but some of the words that came out of his mouth were a little bit overboard," James said. "And being a guy with pride, a guy with three kids and a family, things of that nature, some things just go overboard and that's where he took it, and that was it."

Now that the Warriors were one win away from completing the

greatest season in NBA history (they did, after all, win a record seventy-three games during the regular season), Green had placed both his team and the league office in a difficult spot. After his kick to the Thunder's Steven Adams's groin during the conference finals, any sort of retroactive flagrant foul or technical foul now would result in Green's being suspended. While NBA players maintained Green's kick was not a typical basketball move, it at least had occurred in the midst of game action. Intent could at least be debated. On his punch to James, the intent seemed clear. Both men were far removed from the action on the floor. It seemed evident that Green's punch was retaliation for James's step-over. Much like with the kick on Adams, however, James steadfastly believed Green would not be suspended. He was wrong.

The Warriors were nearing the end of practice the day before Game 5 when the league announced Green's one-game suspension. Green's teammates were furious. Many believed that James had concocted the whole thing and gotten exactly what he wanted.

"It's a man's league and I've heard a lot of bad things on that court, but at the end of the day it stays on the court," said Klay Thompson, the most outspoken of all the Warriors' players. "Obviously people have feelings and people's feelings get hurt even if they're called a bad word. I guess his feelings just got hurt."

The Warriors practiced first that Sunday and did media right after. Then the Cavs followed the Warriors and did media first before practicing. James was in disbelief when he heard that Thompson had basically called the four-time MVP a wimp.

"Oh my goodness," James said. "It's so hard to take the high road. I've been doing it for thirteen years. It's so hard to continue to do it, and I'm going to do it again. At the end of the day, we've got to go out and show up and play better tomorrow night. And if we don't, then they're going to be back-to-back champions."

Indeed, even without Green, the buildup to Game 5 felt like the walk down the fairway on eighteen. The Warriors were tipping their caps and waving to the crowd already. Victory felt assured, and after dousing Dressing Room H at the Q the year before, players were dreaming of celebrating this championship with their home fans. Similarly, James's dismal 2-4 Finals record seemed destined to drop to 2-5. The thought that it was somehow James's fault infuriated Warriors executive Jerry West, who had befriended James in 2011.

James called West after the Heat lost to the Mavericks in 2011, when he fell to 0-2 in Finals series. If anyone could relate to him, James figured, it was West, who had so often failed to topple Russell's dynasty in Boston. West retired a ghastly 1-8 in NBA Finals, even becoming the only player to win a Finals MVP in a losing effort—something James nearly duplicated in 2015. The Finals losses are the only blemishes on West's otherwise sparkling career. He remains one of the greatest players in league history and his silhouette remains the NBA's official logo. But West stood on the court at Oracle, his team comfortably ahead in the series, defending James's brilliance from what he thought were unfair criticisms over another losing Finals record.

"That's the most ridiculous thing. If I were him, frankly, I'd probably want to strangle you guys [the media]. It's ridiculous. He's carried teams on his shoulders," West said.

Indeed, James had dragged the Cavs to the Finals in 2007 with a magnificent performance against the Detroit Pistons in the Eastern

Conference finals, scoring twenty-five consecutive points and twenty-nine of their last thirty in a 109–107 Game 5 win in double overtime. He was equally remarkable in 2015 against the Warriors when injuries ravaged the Cavs' roster. In all of James's Finals series, the only time he truly did not play well and could take the blame was 2011, when he responded by reaching out to West. Otherwise, James had been sensational in guiding his teams to the Finals for six straight years.

"How many times have they been the favorite?" West asked. "None. Zero. Okay? Grossly unfair to him. I don't want to sound like Donald Trump, but it's hard for me to believe that someone doesn't recognize his greatness. It's hard for me to believe. This guy does everything. He's like a Swiss Army knife. He does everything, and he's competitive as hell. Frankly I wish people would leave him alone."

James said during the playoffs that his Finals record bothered him, though it wasn't because of his critics. It was simply his competitive nature.

"If I lose in a game of H-O-R-S-E to my son, it's going to bother me," he said. "But as far as how people look at it, that doesn't bother me. My career will speak for itself when I'm done with it, no matter what my Finals record. Some people never get here at all. I'm at seven [Finals appearances] up to this point. Heck, that's over half my career I've been in the Finals. So that doesn't bother me."

Falling behind 3–1, however, certainly bothered Griffin. The Cavs' general manager was inconsolable when he went to bed after the Game 4 loss. All the hours, weeks, and months to get back to the Finals were four quarters away from vanishing yet again. The Cleveland jokes would soon return, as would hecklers poking fun at James's lousy record in the Finals. Since James had returned to Cleveland, Griffin felt the pressure not to screw this up, not to waste the years of his prime when he was trying so desperately to deliver to his city what it craved. These Warriors hadn't lost three in a row all season and Griffin felt like the series was over when he went to bed. By the time he woke up, he was giddy with joy.

"We're going to win," he told his wife, Meredith. "Think about it: Everything we've ever done is record breaking and history making. Everything we do is loud. We don't do anything easy. We've basically put ourselves in the only position we should win from. You know how people say, 'Why not us?' This group is, 'What the fuck else would we do?'"

Griffin continued to ruminate on that as he showered and drove in to the office. When he arrived at his desk, he sent an inspirational e-mail to everyone in the organization, concluding it with: "I think all of this will mark the weight for our Game 5 victory in Oakland, followed by a Game 6 win at home and our ultimate triumph in an epic Game 7 in Oakland. More reality to you than a dream. This is going to happen."

As the team boarded the plane headed to California for Game 5, James read the e-mail to himself before he was even seated.

"I knew in my heart," Griffin said, "it was done and we were going to win."

Opponents seemed to be targeting James throughout the Cavs' playoff run. His reaction to Klay Thompson, however, was far different.

255

Thompson is a great player, but he's not in James's elite class. Yet the Warriors felt so comfortable with their positioning in this series—and really, why shouldn't they have?—that Thompson felt confident enough to verbally punch James in the groin again with his "It's a man's league" remark while reserve forward Mo Speights tweeted an emoji of a baby bottle.

"Draymond being suspended fueled that whole thing. That's really what helped us. The e-mail had jack to do with it. If I send the e-mail and Draymond's not suspended, I don't look very good right now," Griffin said. "I don't know that I necessarily think it would've been over in five, but they wouldn't have had the same fractured effort thereafter."

Since he was suspended, Green was prohibited from being inside Oracle Arena during the game. But the Warriors wanted to keep him nearby so he could participate in a postgame champagne celebration, so they set him up in a suite across the walkway at an A's home baseball game. How close are O.co Coliseum and Oracle Arena? Commissioner Adam Silver was made available to the media during the Finals in the baseball stadium. Green could walk, particularly with a police escort, from one venue to the other within minutes.

That suspension, however, changed the dynamic of the series. Not only did the Cavs have the opening they needed, but the Warriors had committed the deadly mistake of provoking the game's best player. James's overall numbers were terrific: He had averaged 24.8 points, 11 rebounds, and 8.3 assists through the first four games of the series, but he was averaging nearly six turnovers a game and shooting just 31 percent from three-point range in the series. He had not been at his best in these Finals. That was about to change.

For days, the Cavs' mantra centered around the fact they had to fly back to Cleveland regardless after Game 5. Why not make the Warriors get on a plane and come with them? Then James scored forty-one points, grabbed sixteen rebounds, and passed for seven assists in a 112–97 Game 5 victory to extend the series one more day. It was lost on most everyone in the moment because of Thompson's comments, but James had arrived to practice prior to Game 5 wearing an Undertaker T-shirt from the WWE. The irony in the message seemed clear: Bury us if you'd like, but we're not dead yet. Irving matched James's forty-one points, making them the first set of teammates to score at least forty in a Finals game. The Cavs were indeed flying back to Cleveland. And now the Warriors were going with them.

Even before Green was suspended, before Cavs players left the Q following that crushing Game 4 loss, there was a belief within the locker room that if they could steal Game 5 on the road, they weren't losing Game 6 at home. Steal 5, get to 7. Now the Warriors were returning to Cleveland for an unexpected Game 6, and while they'd have Green back from suspension, they were going without their starting center. Bogut was injured during Game 5 and was lost for the rest of the postseason to a left knee injury.

"[Green's] being out of the lineup that day created the opportunity for us to win that day, but it also hurt them a little bit moving forward," Griffin said. "They had to use up more of what they had left. The Finals are always a war of attrition and we won the war of attrition. Draymond being out and them having to pick up the pieces around him took more out of their other guys. So they had less in the tank for Games Six and Seven."

Prior to Game 6, just as he did before every playoff game, James gathered his teammates in the tunnel between the court and the Cavs' locker room. This time, however, his message was much more subdued: stay focused, stay together.

The Cavs followed through with a 115–101 victory to force a Game 7. They mauled the Warriors in the first quarter, outscoring them 31–11. It was the lowest first-quarter total by any team in the Finals in the shot-clock era. James was again magnificent, with forty-one points, eleven assists, and eight rebounds. He scored or assisted on twenty-seven consecutive points in the second half, including scoring eighteen straight.

Curry scored thirty points and shot the Warriors back into the game in the fourth quarter, but he fouled out with 4:22 left on a questionable foul and was so incensed he uncharacteristically rifled his trademark mouth guard into the seats—striking the son of minority owner Nate Forbes on the shoulder. Curry quickly regained his composure and apologized, but the evidence was overwhelming: The Warriors were cracking. Maybe it was the pressure of the seventy-three-win season or the pressure of becoming the first team in history to blow a 3–1 lead. Regardless, the Warriors were unraveling with one game to go.

CHAPTER 19

Seven

When the Cavs were chasing a championship during James's final season in Cleveland in 2010, Doc Rivers quietly believed his Celtics were better. So after Boston beat the Los Angeles Lakers at Staples Center on February 18, 2010, Rivers demanded $100 from each of his players, coaches, the trainer . . . everyone. Then he stuffed $2,600 into an envelope and had security sequester the team in the shower so no one could see what he was doing. The only other person included in his plan was assistant coach Kevin Eastman. Together, they scoured the visiting locker room at Staples Center looking for a place with no plumbing, no wires, and no reason for anyone to go looking in the ceiling. When he found the right spot, Rivers called for the team to rejoin him.

"There's money in this arena," Rivers told his team. "The only way we get it back is we have to return. This team is going to be in the Finals."

At the time, no one outside of that locker room realistically expected the Celtics to get through both the Cavs and the Magic in the East and make the Finals. But that's exactly what they did.

"I've got to tell you, when we got there for Game One and the bus pulled in, I watched all the guys sprint by me to get to the locker room. I just kept walking. I knew they'd never find it," Rivers recalled. "When I got to the locker room, the place was in shambles. Those fuckers had looked everywhere. I knew exactly where it was at. I walked in and punched the ceiling and the money fell out. I wasn't sure if someone had found it or not. When that money fell out, it was awesome."

Lue was in his first season as Rivers's assistant when he pulled the money stunt. In the euphoria of the Cavs' Game 5 win, standing in another visiting locker room in another California arena, Lue followed his mentor's lead and did the same thing. He collected $100 from each player and staff member. If a staffer didn't have $100 on him, one of the players covered him. Lue gathered all the bills and hid them in the ceiling of the coach's office inside Oracle Arena, just as Rivers did in Staples Center six years earlier. The only way players would get their money back, he told them, was if they returned for a Game 7. The Cavs' home victory in Game 6 sent them flying across the country again, four quarters from ending the city's fifty-two-year drought. Rivers spoke to Lue a couple of hours before the game to go over his pregame speech.

"I just told him to keep them focused on the fact that they were going to win and the dream that they've all decided, whatever that dream is. Keep them focused on that, not the game," Rivers said. "The game will take care of itself. But you've got to be able to make them see where they were supposed to be at the end of the game."

Rather than take them to the end of the night, Lue instead brought them back to the beginning of the night before. The day before Game 7, Lue took some staff members and assistant coaches, like Larry Drew, Damon Jones, and James Posey, twenty-five miles north of Oracle Arena on I-580 to San Quentin State Prison. Lue barely knew his father, Ronald Kemp, who was a Missouri playground hoops star before he went to prison for drug trafficking. Now Lue regularly visits prisons and has done so for years.

On the eve of the biggest game of his coaching career, Lue walked the yard at San Quentin. When the buzzer sounded and the doors opened, suddenly the visiting Cavs personnel were surrounded by convicts. Unfazed, Lue shot baskets alongside rapists and murderers. The prison warden told him 75 percent of the men imprisoned would never commit another crime, but what they did was so heinous that they needed to be locked up anyway. When he gathered his players in the locker room prior to Game 7, Lue told them of his trip and reminded them that any of them could've been in one of those cells.

"Where we come from, the environments we come from, it could've been any one of us in prison. One bad night, one bad car ride, somebody got drugs on them, or one bad night and you get into a fight and someone dies, whatever," Lue said. "One bad night could change your whole life."

One good night could, too.

One of Griffin's favorite lines throughout this turbulent season was that the Cavs functioned their best amid dysfunction. It wasn't the way he envisioned it when he assembled this $100 million payroll, the highest in the league and among the highest in the game's history. Griffin thrives on peace, love, and joy, and this team was the exact opposite. By the end of the regular season, after the Blatt drama and the never-ending LeBron scrutiny, Griffin finally seemed ready to embrace it.

He was standing outside the Cavs' locker room before Game 5 at raucous Oracle Arena, with his team trailing 3–1, when I asked whether he had a good feeling about the game. Griffin never bothered to look up from his phone.

"The only way this city's drought can end," he said, "is with the greatest, most historic comeback in NBA history."

I meditated on that brief exchange while watching the Cavs punch their way back in a Game 5 victory. Then Curry fouled out and threw his mouthpiece near the end of Game 6 and the Warriors were back inside Oracle, not celebrating a title but preparing for a Game 7. It quickly became clear that none of them had expected to be in that position when they were up 3–1 a week earlier.

"Coming into Game Five, we just expected it to be over," Draymond Green said prior to Game 7. "Fans, players, everybody just expected it to be over. And it wasn't."

"I don't think people imagined it this way, the route that we've taken, and that's fine," James said, laughing. "Like I always say: Every day is not a bed of roses and you have to be able to figure out how to get away from the thorns and the pricklers of the rose to make the sunshine. So we've put ourselves in a position to do something special."

The Cavs trailed the Warriors 49–42 and were twenty-four minutes away from making it a fifty-three-year drought, from adding another chapter of heartbreak to a city already devastated by championship-game miseries. The same team that had set a playoff record with twenty-five threes in a win against Atlanta shot just one of fourteen on three-pointers in the first half of Game 7. James had twelve points, seven rebounds, and five assists, but he also committed four turnovers. Green, meanwhile, was crushing the Cavs with twenty-two points. He made all five of his three-point attempts.

When Griffin fired Blatt and gave the job to Lue, he did so believing Lue would hold his star accountable during the most important moments. "You gotta be better!" Lue barked at James during the half. "If we're gonna win, you gotta be better. Your legacy is on the line!"

James was exhausted and fuming. He vented at teammates and coaches. He'd scored forty-one points in consecutive games just to get the Cavs to this point, and now of all the guys in the locker room to go at, Lue had picked him. Lue knew exactly what he was doing.

The Cavs and Warriors were tied at eighty-nine with 4:40 left in Game 7 when they began a scoreless four-minute duel that took them into the final minute. A beautiful series built on seismic momentum shifts came down to the final few minutes. Guys were exhausted and simply out of punches. Curry flipped a lazy behind-the-back pass out of the reach of Klay Thompson and out of bounds. The Warriors' terrific motion offense predicated on pace and space ground down on one crucial possession, with four guys standing around watching Thompson dribble frantically before hoisting a desperate three-pointer. Harrison Barnes, who struggled terribly throughout the Finals, missed an open three-pointer from the corner.

Curry had become the first player in league history to make four hundred threes during the regular season and he was also the NBA's first unanimous Most Valuable Player. He shot 48 percent from deep during the regular season and 45 percent in the postseason when the nearest defender was at least four feet away, but when the Cavs blew a defensive coverage and left Curry with a wide-open look with 4:06 left, he clanked it off the front of the rim.

The Cavs, however, weren't faring any better. With the game still tied at 89, James missed a contested jumper from just inside the three-point arc, the worst shot in basketball in terms of efficiency. They kept running pick-and-rolls with the ball in his hands, trying to create mismatches by getting either Festus Ezeli or Curry to switch onto him. Even when it worked, nothing was falling. James missed another jumper in the lane over Curry, then later drove past Curry but was blocked at the rim by Andre Iguodala.

After Irving missed an off-balance runner in the lane, Iguodala grabbed the rebound and the Warriors had the numbers as the clock ticked under two minutes. Iguodala and Curry led the break, with nothing but J. R. Smith standing between them and a potential championship-winning basket. Just as he crossed the half-court stripe, Iguodala fired a pass ahead to Curry while James sprinted to catch up. Curry gave the ball right back to Iguodala on a bounce pass and Smith was helpless to stop the two charging lions. James was still trailing at the three-point line when Iguodala caught the pass from Curry at the free-throw line and attacked the basket. With 1:51 left, the Warriors were poised to regain the lead.

This is the moment when television executives teed up the Cleveland heartbreak reel. From Sipe's interception in the end zone to Byner's goal-line fumble in the AFC Championship game, Mesa gagging away Game 7 of the World Series and Michael Jordan's buzzer-beater jumper over an outstretched Craig Ehlo, Cleveland sports fans can sing about heartache better than Sam Smith.

Iguodala jumped from the right side of the lane toward the basket while LeBron took flight from the left, soaring across the lane and pinning the ball against the backboard for a championship-saving block with one-eighth of a second to spare. It was one of the defining moments in James's brilliant career.

Had Iguodala's layup touched the glass before James's right hand arrived, it would've been goaltending and the basket would've counted. ESPN's *Sport Science* group calculated that Iguodala was seven feet closer than James was to their eventual meeting point when he caught the bounce pass from Curry, but James closed the gap by sprinting twenty miles per hour down the court and soaring so high his hand was eleven and a half feet above the floor when he blocked the shot. Smith disrupting Iguodala's direct line to the basket bought James an extra 0.15 seconds, which is all the time he needed to close the gap. Flight 23 was a tourniquet blocking fifty-two years of scars and sadness. Cleveland had waited two score and twelve years to celebrate a major sports championship. Now the Cavs were one score away. This was why James came home. This was why Lue pleaded with him at halftime to be better.

A pair of misses by the MVPs, one each for James and Curry, left the ball in Irving's hands. James inbounded to Irving coming out of a time-out, but Lue was out of magic ATOs. This time, the plan was simple: Get the ball to Irving and get the hell out of his way. Smith set a screen, forcing Curry to switch onto Irving and creating the matchup the Cavs wanted. After the defensive switch, Cavs players spread the floor. Smith stood on the wing opposite Irving while Love, James, and

Richard Jefferson flattened out the baseline. The wide spacing prevented the Warriors from switching a better defender into the play.

At twenty-four, Irving had already won six games with baskets at the buzzer and had made enough clutch shots that television play-by-play man Fred McLeod nicknamed him "Mr. Fourth Quarter." Irving ended the regular season tied with Kevin Durant in scoring with the game on the line, which the league defines as a game within three points and with twenty-four seconds or less to play. He led the league in clutch scoring (last five minutes and the game within six points) his second year in the league and is third in his career in clutch scoring behind Durant and LeBron.

"He's special. He's that special, man. He's much better than an All-Star. Much better than an All-Star," James had said after Irving returned from knee surgery earlier in the season. "If he continues to play the way he's been playing, he can do something that's very special around this league. I know in my head what he can become."

Irving received the inbounds pass from James and worked his way over to the right wing as time melted off the clock. He took six dribbles before Smith set the screen on Thompson, forcing the Curry switch. He dribbled eight more times with Curry defending him, first backing away from the basket before reversing direction and inching closer and closer to the three-point line. He dribbled between his legs once, then twice, followed by a quick crossover and a jab step. He was home. With fifty-five seconds left in the game, Irving raised up high above Curry and released one single shot to erase fifty-two years of darkness.

The best players in the league make the biggest shots at the most important times. Irving had barely slept since the Game 6 win. He had lain awake in bed, rolling over every scenario his mind could conjure. This was his first Game 7 experience, and advice from Game 7 veterans like James Jones or LeBron helps only so much. But if James truly can see things happen before they develop, as his teammates have always insisted, he proved it in that moment in Mo Williams's Dallas gym back in January.

"At the end of the day, late in games, the ball is going to be in our hands," James had said. "We've got to be able to trust each other and our teammates have to be able to trust us. . . . And then we have to come through for them."

Swish.

Irving's shot in the final minute, off the wrong foot, touched nothing but the net. The Cavs were less than a minute from victory.

James had delivered his moment with the block and Irving had delivered the game-winning basket. Now the Cavs needed one more stop. The action was coming right at Love, their maligned former All-Star who was concussed and forced to come off the bench in this series. The Cavs had dreaded for months how he would fit against the high-powered Warriors, if his defensive shortcomings would be exposed at the worst possible times. Now in their switch-everything defensive scheme, Love was about to be given the defensive test of his life.

Iguodala set the screen that left Love on Green, and Green set another screen that sent Love onto Curry. One of the team's weakest defenders was now stuck guarding the game's best shooter. Curry moved left, then stepped right. He crossed over and stepped back. Love stayed with him stride for stride. Curry passed off to Green, who gave it right back. Love had been great once, but now he had to do it again. Curry started left, then crossed over. Love's hands were up the whole time, first the left and then the right.

Throughout our postgame conversations during the regular season, particularly after embarrassing losses, Love was adamant. "When it's win or die," he said repeatedly, "we will win."

As precious seconds ticked away, Love stayed with Curry stride for stride. It was indeed time to win or die. Love was winning. Curry launched and missed.

"Everything that happened from the concussion to him sitting out, to be able to respond like he did in Game Seven, that's what real men do," James said. "They respond in the most adverse times."

After the final second ticked off the clock, Love ran into James's arms. Then James collapsed to the court, sobbing. He had not cried after either of his championship celebrations in Miami, but now the emotions came roaring out of him. He had come home to lift up his hometown, to give the inner-city kids of Akron a chance at a better life, and to give his truest fans a taste of the greatness they deserved. It was a heavy burden for one man to carry, but in that moment he accomplished it all. On his hands and knees, James pounded the court. Lue, whose mother and grandmother had missed the entire postseason because they were both fighting cancer, sat alone on the bench and hid his face in a towel, sobbing.

James eventually made his way to the podium and clutched the trophy. This was his third championship, but this one felt different. Yes, this one meant so much more. He ended it with a triple-double, with 27 points, 11 rebounds, and 11 assists. After nearly winning the MVP in a losing effort in 2015, this time James was the unanimous choice. He averaged 36.3 points, 11.7 rebounds, and 9.7 assists over the final three games of the series.

"I knew what we was capable of even being down three to one versus the greatest regular-season team ever. Everyone counted us out and that's when we strive the most, when everybody counts us out. That's definitely when I strive the most, when everyone counts me out," James said. "This is what I came back for. I'm home."

For Mesa and Ehlo, Sipe and Colavito; for Bernie, Belle, and Byner; for the Drive and the Dawg Pound, the Shot and the Fumble; for burning jerseys and burning rivers; for the blue collars and the rust belt. Cleveland—yes, Cleveland—was a city of champions.

CHAPTER 20

Larry

Jeff Cohen navigated the champagne-soaked visitor's locker room carrying a three-liter bottle of Moët & Chandon made specifically for him. Cohen, Nate Forbes, and Dan Gilbert had each received a giant bottle with their name embossed on it, compliments of Moët, when James returned to Cleveland in 2014.

"We've waited two years to open this motherfucker," Cohen said on his way out of the locker room. He was saving it for the flight to Las Vegas. Yes, Vegas. The Cavs flew from California to Vegas because that's where all high rollers go to celebrate achievements. The Vegas stop was poetic for James, considering he had been in Las Vegas when he chose to return home and begin this two-year quest.

I was sequestered with Cohen in the lottery room the night the Cavs won the right to draft Irving first overall. Fast-forward 1,862 days and it was Irving, not James, making the biggest shot of the night to end

Cleveland's fifty-two-year title drought. But it was James who guided them there.

"Just knowing what our city has been through, Northeast Ohio has been through, as far as our sports and everything for the last fifty-plus years," James said. "You could look back to the Earnest Byner fumble, Elway going ninety-nine yards, to Jose Mesa not being able to close out in the bottom of the ninth, to the Cavs went to the Finals—I was on that team—in 2007, us getting swept, and then last year us losing four to two. And so many more stories. And our fans, they ride or die. The Browns, the Indians, the Cavs . . . They continue to support us. For us to be able to end this, end this drought, our fans deserve it. They deserve it. And it was for them."

J. R. Smith, maligned throughout his career and weighed down by his reputation as a team cancer, broke down on the podium. With tears streaming down his face, he thanked his family for always standing by him. He hadn't always made life easy for them given his reputation, his suspensions, and all his fines, but sitting on the podium crowned a champion, Smith felt redeemed.

"I've been in a lot of dark spots in my life, and if it wasn't for them, I wouldn't be able to get out of it," Smith said through the tears. "But they are who they are. They fought with me. They yelled at me, they screamed at me, they loved me, they hugged me, they cried with me, and they always stuck by my side no matter right or wrong."

When the Cavs had the opportunity to acquire Smith from the Knicks, Griffin had gone to James to see what he thought. James never hesitated. Go get him, he told Griff, and I'll take care of him. In return, Smith helped James win his third championship ring, leaving him halfway to Jordan's six. His performance in these NBA Finals, particularly in dragging the Cavs back from the ledge, makes it clear he is still the most dominant player in the game.

"He's the best player in the world. I think he showed that," Cohen said. "He removed all doubt. I don't know how anybody can argue that. Everybody said he's past his prime, that the face of the NBA today was Steph. Steph is a great player, but LeBron is still the greatest player in the world."

Before the playoffs began, James Jones had the idea to create a puzzle. Sixteen pieces in the shape of the Larry O'Brien trophy—one for every win the Cavs needed to win a championship. After each playoff win, a different player on the fifteen-man roster took a turn fitting in the next piece. When Love missed Game 3 against the Warriors with a concussion, he was able to place that piece after the game because James told him they'd win it for him. The players kept the puzzle quiet throughout the postseason, waiting for the cameras to leave before pulling it out after each victory. Finally, after Game 7 of the Finals, it was Lue's turn to place the last piece, shaped like the state of Ohio. The puzzle was complete, and it was time to party.

Before Game 7, Cavs fans had jammed into the Q to watch the game on the Jumbotron. There were so many people that the viewing party spilled out into the plaza between the arena and Progressive Field. When it was over, the real party started. I joked for years that if Cleveland ever won a championship, the city would burn off the map and fall into Lake Erie. While other major cities have been plagued by crime, fires, and violence during sports championship celebrations, Cleveland again shined. It was a peaceful, passionate party.

Thousands met the Cavs' charter flight at the airport early the next afternoon to greet a team of exhausted, hungover players. James was the last to emerge from the plane, hoisting the Larry O'Brien trophy high above his head. He took a lap around the fence so the screaming fans could catch a glimpse of what a real trophy looks like. Flights into the city quickly sold out, as did hotel rooms across downtown. After waiting fifty-two years to throw a party, no one wanted to miss it. People who had grown up in Cleveland and moved away over the years flew home for the show; some traveled in from other countries just to be part of the celebration.

City officials warned folks to arrive early and take public transportation. Lines for buses and the rail system stretched into the hundreds by seven A.M.—hours before the parade began. By nine A.M., the estimated wait time to catch a train from the airport into downtown was five hours. City and team officials scrambled to create a parade route, construct a stage, and think of every last detail. They nearly had a catastrophe when nobody thought to order a few hundred portable toilets, a clutch save nearly as important as James's late-game block on Iguodala.

The streets of downtown were flooded with an estimated one million people—nearly triple the city's population of about 390,000. Aerial shots of the city were breathtaking. A sea of humanity stretched a half mile south along Ontario Street from the arena past Progressive Field, across Carnegie Avenue, and a mile north on East Ninth toward the lake. People were hanging out of parking garages and scaling the world's largest rubber stamp, a twenty-eight-foot-tall statue spelling out FREE in Willard Park, just to get a good view.

Police never bothered to barricade the parade route and bystanders spilled into the streets, blocking the path and delaying the start of the parade. The one-and-a-half-mile stretch of road was only supposed to take about an hour to travel, but the parade took four hours to complete because police had to clear the roads inch by inch in order for the caravan to pass. Players shook hands and gave high fives. Smith, Iman Shumpert, and Mo Williams spent the day shirtless—Smith wore his uniform shorts and went about three weeks without ever wearing a shirt, judging by social media pictures. Love carried around two WWE-style championship belts with a cigar in his mouth. When the caravan passed the ten-story LeBron James banner that hung across the street from the Q, James stood, arms outstretched, mimicking the banner, creating one of the most iconic images from the day.

James concluded the celebration by taking the stage and delivering a notes-free speech that lasted sixteen minutes. He addressed each of his fourteen teammates individually, thanking each one. He credited Tristan Thompson for his durability (he possessed the longest active consecutive games streak in the NBA), Love for his resiliency, and Irving for his potential. "He thought I was blowing smoke up his ass early in the season when I said he could be the best point guard in our league and also be an MVP in our league," James said. "And I know every single one of you watched that Finals. You all saw what this guy's capable of doing. And he's only twenty-four. Oh, my goodness. He's only twenty-four." James was funny and unfiltered, cursing throughout a speech that was carried live on television. "It still hasn't hit me what actually happened," he said. "And for some crazy reason, I believe I'm going to wake up, and it's going to be like Game Four all over again. I'll be like, shit, we're down two to one still."

The day ended with James and Hall of Fame icon Jim Brown holding the championship trophy together, the long-ago past meeting the delicious present in Cleveland. Gilbert had vowed when he purchased the franchise in 2005 to deliver a championship, although he never could've imagined it taking this long or this path. Plenty of mistakes were made. Coaches and general managers were fired, superstars came and left and came back. And along the way, the Cavs created their own path to glory. League executives have known for years it's impossible to win in this league without a superstar, so the Cavs planned for years to lure back their ex. They drafted and developed a new star, then compiled a war chest of trade assets to go trade for another one once James returned. And the analytics component identified the proper supplementary pieces to round out the roster.

And when it was all over, after the plan was executed, the championship celebrated, and the parade complete, James descended the stage and saw me out of the corner of his eye. He turned and flashed a thumbs-up and walked into the arms of immortal greatness. He was still cradling the Larry O'Brien trophy. He might never let go. He doesn't have to.

Epilogue

Fifteen days after the Cavs exited Oracle Arena as champions, LeBron James was vacationing in Spain during the Fourth of July holiday when Kevin Durant shook the NBA universe by joining the Warriors. A team that won seventy-three games during the 2015–16 season now boasted an MVP winner and arguably the NBA's second-best player.

Dan Gilbert, meanwhile, was busy cutting checks. The championship season cost him about $161 million in payroll and luxury taxes, which meant Gilbert took a loss of about $50 million on the season, according to people privy to such information. He can afford it. Forbes estimated his net worth in the spring of 2017 at $5.9 billion, a $1.3 billion increase over his net worth from the fall of 2016, making him the wealthiest resident of the state of Michigan. But the championship also meant other teams were now highly interested in chipping away at the champs.

Prior to the 2015–16 season, the Cavs had an opportunity to lock up Matthew Dellavedova on a reasonable three-year, $10 million deal. But since they still controlled his rights at the time, they declined and forced him to play out the season on a one-year, $1.1 million contract before he could reenter free agency. Dellavedova agreed to a four-year, $38 million deal with the Milwaukee Bucks after the championship, and although the Cavs had the opportunity to match it, their tax situation made the feat virtually impossible. Letting the scrappy Dellavedova go, and failing to sign him for the long term when they had the chance, hindered them throughout a turbulent 2016–17 season.

Dellavedova departed to Milwaukee, while center Timofey Mozgov left in free agency for the Los Angeles Lakers. Mo Williams compounded the Cavs' problems when he called GM David Griffin the day before camp opened to announce his retirement. The void caused by the departures of Dellavedova and Williams left the Cavs scrambling without a viable backup point guard to Kyrie Irving. It was also the first sign that the Cavs' title defense was going to be more difficult than they had imagined.

First, however, was the chance to celebrate. The Cavs received their championship rings on a historic October night in Cleveland while the Indians opened Game 1 of the World Series across the street against the Chicago Cubs. A city that waited fifty-two years for just one championship had the chance to win two within five months. While that made for a bustling downtown—lots around the facilities were charging $110 for parking (about five times the normal rate)—the atmosphere inside Quicken Loans Arena, for the season opener against the New York Knicks, was electric.

Epilogue

J. R. Smith cried during the ring ceremony because that's what he does. James also wiped away tears after addressing the crowd, and Kyrie Irving ran off the floor to embrace his father and present him with the championship ring.

"We just have a very, very unique relationship which goes deeper than almost life itself," Irving said. "Just a culmination of a lot of emotions as a kid kind of watching him sacrifice as much as possible to allow me to have the freedom to play basketball every single day, but also understanding how basketball correlates to life and vice versa. How he always related it back to me being an even better man every single day. It's just very, very, very fulfilling in terms of giving it to him and I'm glad he got it."

The next eight months, however, constituted one of the strangest seasons of James's career. Smith got a late start when his contract dispute dragged into the preseason, and then he missed nearly three months after breaking his thumb just before Christmas. He returned in March, a few weeks after Kevin Love went down with a knee injury that cost him a month. In all, Cavs players missed 186 games during the regular season to injuries, illnesses, rest, and other excused absences, the sixth-most in the NBA. Even coach Tyronn Lue fell victim to illness, missing time with bouts of vertigo.

"It's been a strange season, probably one of the strangest I've been a part of from the simple fact of just having the chemistry and camaraderie out on the floor," James said in March. "From the coaches to the players, guys have been in and out. We've had a lot of injuries."

Chris Andersen was lost for the year in December to an Achilles injury. Channing Frye mourned the devastating losses of his mother and father, who died just a month apart. Andrew Bogut was signed in March, but his career with the Cavs lasted less than a minute. Bogut broke his left leg just fifty-eight seconds into his debut after a freak collision with Miami's Okaro White. Griffin spent most of the season searching for a big man and another point guard. Meanwhile, the losses mounted.

Griffin privately believed this team was even more explosive than the team that won the championship. At one point, he thought the Cavs were talented enough to flirt with seventy wins. Instead, they coasted through the regular season at 51-31, which wasn't even good enough for the top seed in the weakened Eastern Conference.

They were embarrassed in Chicago in early December, surrendering seventy-eight points in the paint defensively en route to their third consecutive defeat—the first time they had lost three straight games since Lue took over as head coach. The Cubs' Game 7 victory back in October cost the Indians a World Series championship and forced James to arrive at United Center that night wearing a full Cubs uniform to pay off a bet he made with good buddy Dwyane Wade. He left the arena that night, however, wearing a scowl.

"We've got to get out of the honeymoon stage," James said. "You've got to battle every night like we ain't won nothing. Last year is last year and after ring night, it's over with. Now it's a new season and everybody is gunning for us every night and we have to understand that. The honeymoon stage is over and it's time to play some real ball."

James was just getting warmed up. After the Cavs acquired sharp-shooter Kyle Korver in early January, James used it as an opportunity to remind people they still needed another point guard. And when I asked LeBron a few weeks later why he was throwing so many more passes to Korver than anyone else on the team, James shrugged.

"Who the hell else is going to throw him the ball?" James said.

The Cavs and Warriors spent most days with one eye on what the other was doing. When James hosted his annual Halloween party for his teammates, the drum set had a special 3–1 LEAD decal and he handed out cookies of tombstones with Warriors players' names on them. But James also respected the roster and talent assembled in the Bay Area and the number of players who could dribble, pass, and shoot. The Warriors are full of playmakers, while the Cavs rely heavily on James and Irving.

By the trip to New Orleans in late January, James was fed up with it. He had privately grumbled for weeks about his team's inefficient play, and a loss that night to the Pelicans, after falling behind by twenty-two points in the first half, was their fifth defeat in seven games. James hadn't gone 2-5 in a seven-game stretch in nearly three years. This was the loss that broke him.

"We're not better than last year, from a personnel standpoint . . . we're a top-heavy team," James said. "I just hope that we're not satisfied as an organization. How hard it was to do that shit. I just hope we're not satisfied."

James fumed for the better part of fifteen minutes, but he made it clear that he wasn't angry with the job Griffin did in assembling the roster.

"I ain't got no problems with the front office," he said. "I told [Griffin] to his face, so it ain't like I'm telling y'all to put it on record. I see Griff all the time. One thing about me, if I got something to say, I'm going to tell it to your face. We need a fucking playmaker."

Griffin was angry that James made his complaints so public. And even though James made it clear his comments were not directed at the GM, that didn't stop Griffin from firing back. He directed the complacency at the players, not ownership.

"The comment about the organization being complacent I think is really misguided," Griffin said. "Organizationally there is absolutely no lack of clarity on what our goal set is. We are here to win championships and there is no other solution, there is no other outcome that is acceptable and there never has been. But in terms of the on-the-court complacency, I've seen a lot of that."

Nearly a month to the day following James's rant, Griffin found his long-sought point guard and playmaker in Deron Williams. The Dallas Mavericks bought out the remaining few weeks on his deal and released him so he could sign with a contender. Williams quickly chose the Cavs. He was thirty-two and a five-time All-Star. On paper, he was the ideal complement to what the Cavs needed. He might have lost a step or two, but he could still run pick-and-rolls, he could still shoot, and the Cavs only needed him to play fifteen to twenty minutes a night. But the signing fell flat. Williams never really adjusted to the reserve role.

Until Williams signed, James was essentially the backup point guard. Lue tried guys like DeAndre Liggins, Jordan McRae, and rookie Kay Felder at the spot. But of the three, Felder was the only natural point guard, and he was too inexperienced to really help. Using James as the primary ball handler behind Irving forced Lue to juggle a number of elements. James averaged a league-high 37.8 minutes a night, a number that caused plenty of consternation during the season. James insisted he felt great and wanted to play that many minutes. His trainer, Mike Mancias, gave his blessing, so Lue obliged and kept him out there.

But it came with trade-offs. The Cavs rarely practiced, sometimes going weeks with nothing more than shoot-arounds the mornings of game days. Lue also sat James plenty of nights for rest purposes, which at times angered the league. By the time the regular season was over, James had missed eight games and had logged just eighty-five more minutes than he had the previous season.

But that wasn't the end of the concessions. Whereas previously James often guarded an opponent's best player, that couldn't continue. Lue was asking James to do so much offensively that he pulled his defensive assignments, and he often left James on weaker players so he could save his energy for the offensive end. All of those factors, along with Lue trying to hold back some of his better schemes for the post-season, caused the Cavs' defensive game to deteriorate dramatically. They habitually coughed up big leads, fell into bad defensive habits, and often lost focus. They got distracted too easily and couldn't be bothered to play hard on many nights.

They ranked ninth in the NBA during the championship season in defensive rating, which standardizes how many points teams allow per hundred possessions. In the 2016–17 season, they tumbled to twenty-first.

Why was that so important? No team had finished outside the top ten in defensive rating and still won a championship since the 2001 Lakers. Lue was a reserve guard on that team. Like the Cavs, those Lakers were defending a championship and dealt with complacency and some injuries during the season. Lue promised things would improve during the postseason, and for a while he was right.

The Cavs' collapse at the end of the regular season, when they lost their last four games, handed the number one seed and home-court advantage in the playoffs to the Celtics. That meant the Cavs would have to open the conference finals on the road, but privately no one in the organization thought the Celtics had a realistic chance of beating the Cavs, so they weren't overly concerned.

The Cavs won their first ten playoff games, including sweeps of the first two rounds, just as they did during the championship season. They improved dramatically defensively by following Lue's intricate blitz schemes, which they rarely showed during the regular season. Lue's focus was to eliminate an opponent's best player. They caused fits for the Pacers' Paul George in the first round and Toronto's DeMar DeRozan in the conference semifinals by sending two defenders at them and forcing the ball out of their hands.

The Pacers had a chance to steal the playoff opener at the buzzer when C. J. Miles missed an open jumper, but then the Pacers blew the biggest halftime lead in playoff history when the Cavs rallied from a twenty-five-point deficit to steal Game 3 at Indiana. But each victory in the postseason seemed to strengthen the Cavs. Although they blew Game 3 at home against Boston, spoiling their perfect march through the East, the Cavs had little trouble eliminating the Celtics in five games—just as most everyone in the organization had predicted.

James surpassed Michael Jordan as the NBA's all-time postseason scoring leader in that Game 5 victory, turning James's seventh consecutive trip to the NBA Finals into an homage to Jordan.

Epilogue

"For my name to come up in the discussion with the greatest basketball player of all time, it's like, wow," James said. "I did pretty much everything that M. J. did when I was a kid. I shot fadeaways before I should have. I wore a leg sleeve on my leg and folded it down so you saw the red part. I wore black and red shoes with white socks. I wore short shorts so you could see my undershorts underneath. I didn't go bald like Mike, but I'm getting there. But other than that, I did everything Mike did. I even wore a wristband on my forearm. I did everything Mike did, man."

And now James was chasing that ghost to the Finals again, seeking his fourth championship in an effort to match Jordan's six rings. But he was going to have to do it against those same mighty Warriors, who stormed through the West playoffs with an average margin of victory of 16.2 points. And now they had Durant. Even losing coach Steve Kerr to health concerns in the first round couldn't slow them. The Warriors swept through the twelve wins behind acting head coach Mike Brown—the same Brown the Cavs had fired three years earlier. The same Brown whom James credits with teaching him the importance of defense early in his career. And the same Brown to whom owner Dan Gilbert will pay severance checks until 2020.

But the Warriors were much more than Brown. They were perhaps the most talented team ever assembled and they had been plotting their revenge against these Cavs for the past year. After all of the "Warriors blew a 3–1 lead" jokes; James's Halloween party shenanigans; and another Cavs victory in this series on Christmas Day, when Irving made yet another shot in the final seconds to give Cleveland another stunning win in basketball's best rivalry, these Warriors were ready to unleash their anger.

"If Cleveland comes out of the East, I want to destroy Cleveland," outspoken Warriors forward Draymond Green told NBA.com in October. "No ifs, ands, and buts about it. But I also know that there's steps to get to that point. And if and when we get to that point, I want to annihilate them."

Green finally got his chance, and the Warriors didn't disappoint. The Cavs privately hoped the nine-day layoff would disrupt Golden State's rhythm, but it didn't. The Warriors outscored the Cavs 33–20 in the third quarter to win the opener 113–91 and extend their postseason record to 13-0. When the Cavs forced twenty turnovers in Game 2, but the Warriors still scored 132 points and won by 19, everyone in the organization knew the Cavs were in trouble. Durant was the reason why.

"You take one of the best teams that we had ever assembled last year, that we saw in the regular season and in the postseason, and then in the off-season you add a high-powered offensive talent like [Durant] and a great basketball IQ like that, that's what stands out," James said. "It's no if, ands, or buts. It is what it is. We got to figure out how to combat that, which is going to be a tough challenge for us. But that's what stands out."

Cleveland returned home down 0-2 in the series, which forced Lue to make some changes. He was frustrated with the lack of focus he was seeing defensively. Guys were turning their heads and getting beaten on backdoor cuts. The defense would stay locked in for twenty seconds, then break down at the end of shot clocks. Lue had been hesitant to use some of the blitz schemes that were so effective against East teams because of how powerful the Warriors were. They simply deployed too much shooting, and double-teaming guys was viewed as too risky, particularly against the starters. But nothing else was working and Lue was running out of options.

As we walked toward the Cavs locker room prior to Game 3, Lue told me he was going to run two defenders at Steph Curry and Durant and force the ball out of their hands.

"We've got to try something," Lue said. "We aren't just going to roll over and die."

The Cavs played one of their finest games of the season in Game 3. James scored thirty-nine points and Irving scored thirty-eight. A three-pointer from Smith, who struggled badly in the first two games, extended Cleveland's lead to 113–107 with 3:09 left. But it was the last basket of the night for the Cavs. Kerr, who returned for Game 2, kept reassuring his players that James and Irving were eventually going to wear down. James played forty-six minutes and Irving forty-four. Eventually, Kerr was right. James and Irving appeared exhausted by the end of the game. James's last field goal came with 6:55 left, Irving's with 5:29 to play. The Cavs missed their last seven shots and the Warriors escaped with a 118–113 victory. James and the Cavs threw their best punch and it still wasn't enough.

"Before the series even started we knew what we was dealing with. I said it after we won the Eastern Conference finals that we're getting ready for a juggernaut. It's probably the most firepower I've played in my career. I played against some great teams, but I don't think no team has had this type of firepower," James said after the Game 3 loss. "So even when you're playing well, you've got to play like A-plus-plus. We made enough plays tonight to still win the ball game, but they made a couple more."

The Warriors were one victory away from becoming the first team in history to go 16-0 in the postseason. They were also one win away from dousing the visiting locker room at Quicken Loans Arena again in champagne, the site of their first championship celebration in 2015. James spoke on the day before Game 4 like a man resigned to his fate, like a man who knew he was outmatched. When asked about whether what the Warriors did was fair by adding a superstar like Durant to an already established juggernaut, James never hesitated.

"Is it fair? I don't care. I mean, I think it's great. It's great for our league," he said. "Look at our TV ratings, look at the money our league is pouring in. I mean, guys are loving the game, our fans love the game. Who am I to say if it's fair or not? No matter who I'm going against, if I'm going against four Hall of Famers, like I said before the series started with Draymond, Klay, Steph, and KD, or if I'm going against two or whatever the case may be, I'm always excited to play the game. And I'm not one to judge and say if it's fair or not if guys are adding players to their team. Is it fair that the New York Yankees in the '90s was adding piece after piece after piece after piece? Is it fair that the Cowboys added Deion Sanders? I mean, listen. It happens. It's sports. You have an opportunity to sign one of the best players, and you can do it, go ahead and do it. Why not? If I become an owner, I'm going to try to sign everybody."

The Cavs avoided the sweep with a magnificent performance in Game 4. Forty-eight hours after that crushing Game 3 loss that left the locker room devastated, the Cavs found the strength to rally behind James's triple-double (thirty-one points, ten rebounds, eleven assists) and Irving's forty points. The Cavs smashed the Warriors 137–116, setting up another round of half-hearted "Warriors blew a 3–1 lead" jokes. Only these weren't the same Warriors. Not with Durant.

He scored thirty-nine points in Game 5, and the Warriors extracted their revenge with a 129–120 victory and their second championship in three seasons. Durant was named NBA Finals MVP and James went home a loser, despite becoming the first player in history to average a triple-double in the Finals. When the Cavs lost to the Warriors in 2015, James sat at his locker for nearly an hour wrapped in a towel with his face hidden in a second towel. This time, however, he was showered, dressed, and at the podium before the Warriors had all of the champagne bottles uncorked. Although he denied it on the podium following the Game 5 loss, it seemed throughout the series that James knew he didn't have enough to topple these revamped Warriors.

"I left everything on the floor every game, all five games. So for me personally, I have no reason to put my head down," James said. "I have no reason to look back at what I could have done or what I shouldn't have done or what I could have done better for the team. I left everything I had out on the floor every single game for five games in this Finals, and you come up short . . . it's just not my time."

The Finals loss thrust Griffin into the spotlight one more time. While Lue signed a rich five-year, $35 million contract after the season that made him one of the game's highest-paid coaches, and guys like J. R. Smith, Tristan Thompson, Kevin Love, and Iman Shumpert all got contract extensions, Griffin never got his rich extension. That he was working on the final year of his deal was one of the quiet mysteries of the season.

When Masai Ujiri had two years left on his contract in Toronto and the Warriors' Bob Myers had two years left on his deal, owners tore up their old deals and offered the executives new extensions to keep them in place. But that didn't happen here. And while Griffin and Gilbert chatted during the season, Gilbert never expressed a desire to bring Griffin back.

Gilbert went through a bit of an ownership shakeup following a dispute with his partners, Jeff Cohen and Nate Forbes. They had been friends since college, but Cohen and Gilbert had a falling out over a business deal outside of the Cavs. After he was such an important piece of reuniting James with Cleveland, Forbes also pulled back in his involvement with the team.

Griffin, meanwhile, had his own list of demands that included a significant raise and more power within the organization. He privately said on more than one occasion that he'd only come back if certain demands were met. The Cavs' season ended on Monday, June 12. Griffin and Gilbert met to discuss an extension on Friday, four days later. Gilbert was surprised by some of Griffin's requests. So surprised, in fact, that he canceled a second meeting set for Sunday. Griffin continued to work in the GM role, which meant working the phones for trades to upgrade the roster.

On Monday, Gilbert called Griffin down to the Q to meet again. On the one-year anniversary of the Cavs' championship parade, when more than one million people flooded into downtown Cleveland, Griffin drove to the arena expecting a contract extension. Instead, Gilbert told him they were done. He was essentially fired with eleven days left on his contract. Trent Redden, the Cavs' number two man in the front office, went with him.

Redden's contract also expired at the end of the year. He should've been next in line. When Danny Ferry walked off the job in 2010, Chris

Grant was promoted. When Grant was fired, Griffin was promoted. Redden spent eleven years in various roles with the Cavs after he was hired straight out of college by Grant to be an intern. But he was a bit of a prodigy. The Cavs were so impressed with his work that they sent him out to scout games, which is unheard of for an intern. He worked his way up to assistant GM, but at thirty-three, he was out, too. No one really knows what Redden did to get removed, other than the fact that he never really fostered much of a relationship with Gilbert.

Griffin's removal began a 2017 summer of upheaval. Irving went to Cavs ownership in early July and requested a trade. He can't become a free agent until 2019, but he has grown tired of living in LeBron's shadow. He wants the opportunity to guide his own franchise and enjoy the power that comes with it. Nothing lasts forever, particularly in the NBA. Grant, Griffin, and Irving all played various roles in guiding Cleveland to a championship. By the start of the 2017–18 season, all of them were gone.

Irving was traded to the Boston Celtics, while Koby Altman was promoted from third chair to GM, replacing Griffin. Now the focus will turn back to James, because the lens is never far from him anyway. James accomplished his goal of bringing a championship back to Cleveland. Now he can be a free agent again in the summer of 2018. Somewhere out there, another franchise is assembling another blueprint. . . .

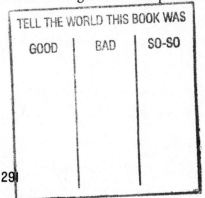

TELL THE WORLD THIS BOOK WAS

| GOOD | BAD | SO-SO |

ACKNOWLEDGMENTS

This book never would have been possible if LeBron James didn't return to Cleveland and bring the city a championship. Thanks first to him for being the most accessible superstar of this generation. Before and after games, in private moments in locker rooms and hallways across the country, LeBron always has time for those of us who travel everywhere the Cavs go. For that I am grateful.

Special thanks to Chris Grant for pulling back the curtain during his time as Cavs general manager and revealing enough of the breadcrumbs to lead me down this trail. To past and present team officials Danny Ferry, David Griffin, Trent Redden, Koby Altman, Zydrunas Ilgauskas, and Brock Aller. Coaches Tyronn Lue, David Blatt, Mike Brown, and Byron Scott. Cavs media relations officials Tad Carper, B. J. Evans, Jeff Schaefer, Sarah Jamieson, Cherome Owens, and Alyssa Dombrowski.

To past and present players Kevin Love, Kyrie Irving, Richard

Acknowledgments

Jefferson, Channing Frye, Matthew Dellavedova, J. R. Smith, Iman Shumpert, Anderson Varejao, Tristan Thompson, Tyler Zeller, Brendan Haywood, and Dion Waiters.

Thanks to my agent, Bridget Matzie, for bringing this project to me. I knew this book existed in my head, but Bridget brought it to life. Thanks to my Penguin Random House editor Jill Schwartzman and her staff for tolerating me when I went off the grid for stretches during the season and for poring over every syllable of this manuscript.

Thank you to fellow beat writers Joe Vardon, Dave McMenamin, and Joe Gabriele. Every night is a Saturday night with you. And to past and present colleagues Mary Schmitt-Boyer, Bob Finnan, Chris Haynes, Brian Windhorst, Rachel Nichols, and Lee Jenkins for providing a lifetime of laughs and memories. To Bruce Hooley for making me a better reporter.

To my children, Alex, AJ, and Ava, I'm so sorry I'm not home more. This job takes me to all corners of this earth and I miss you so much when I'm gone. One day I hope you'll forgive me for missing so many birthdays. To my wife, Alessia, thank you for wearing so many hats in my absence. I love you all.